£8

D1491545

MEDIEVAL MAN
AND HIS NOTIONS

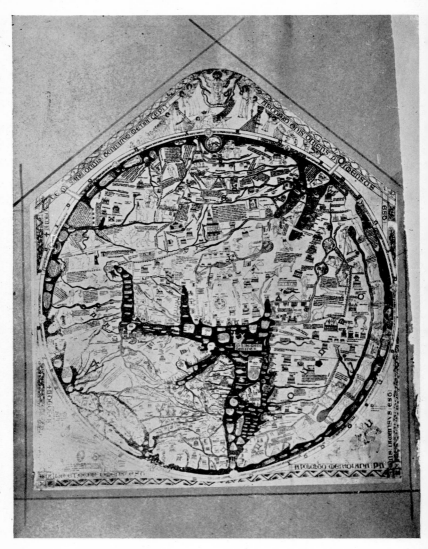

The Hereford Map

MEDIEVAL MAN
AND HIS NOTIONS

By

FREDERICK HARRISON

CANON, CHANCELLOR AND LIBRARIAN OF
YORK MINSTER

LONDON
JOHN MURRAY, ALBEMARLE STREET, W.

First Edition *1947*

Made and Printed in Great Britain by Butler & Tanner Ltd., Frome and London

CONTENTS

CONTENTS

ILLUSTRATIONS

PAGE

PROLOGUE

THE welcome that was accorded to *A Book About Books*, which was published in October, 1943, has encouraged the publisher and the author to issue the present book. The short study of the history of the Book which was contained in the previous book was based on the writer's almost daily acquaintance with medieval books in manuscript and with early printed books. For many years he has been interested in the byways, rather than the highways, of medieval life in this country. Not that the byways can be understood without an acquaintance with the highways—far from it. Of that interest this book is the outcome. No claim is made that it contains more than a brief survey of a few of the activities of the medieval man, or that any of the subjects of the chapters have been treated at all fully. The book is intended not for the specialist, but for those, older as well as younger, who, either not having access to the authorities on which the book is based or not feeling inclined to dig out the information for themselves, have an abiding interest in the medieval man, woman and child, that is to say, in themselves as they would have been had they lived in the middle ages.

Nearly everything in the book is derived from an original source. The number and the range of the authorities that have been used may be surprising to those who read the book. To those authorities which in places have been quoted word for word, the publisher and the author express their indebtedness. Most of these, having been published as parts of series of volumes, are less well known than they deserve to be. Being reprints of original documents, they are indispensable to those who like writing history from its sources better than trying to write it from second-hand information. Much new ground is waiting to be tilled by the student who is prepared to till it. The sources which have been used are :

(1) THE ROLLS SERIES.
 Saxon Leechdoms.   Volumes I to III, 1864–1866.
 Ralph Higden's Polychronicon.   Volumes I to IX, 1865–1886.

(2) THE EARLY ENGLISH TEXT SOCIETY.
 Early English Meals and Manners.   1868.
 Andrew Borde's Introduction of Knowledge, etc.   1870.
 The Book of Quinte Essence.   1866.
 The Earliest Arithmetics in English.   1922.
 Ludus Coventriae.   1922.
 The Towneley Plays.   1887.   (Also the Surtees Society's edition, 1836).
 The Macro Plays.   1904.
 The Non-Cycle Plays.   1909.

(3) GENERAL.
 Extracts from the Municipal Records of the City of York.   Robert Davies.   1843.
 The York Mystery Plays.   Lucy Toulmin Smith.   1885.
 The Digby Mysteries.   New Shakespeare Society.   1882.
 The Miracle Plays in England.   S. W. Clarke.   n.d.
 Schools of Medieval England.   A. F. Leach.   1915.
 Churchwardens' Accounts.   J. C. Cox.   1913.
 Life of Dean Colet.   G. H. Lupton.   1887.
 Bede : his Life, Times and Writings.   Ed. A. Hamilton Thompson.   1935.

(4) CAMDEN SOCIETY.
 Volumes for 1859, 1862 and 1875.

And many books, old as well as new, about Geography, Maps and the Middle Ages in general, with original medieval records in manuscript.

Here and there, the writer has drawn on his experience of and acquaintance with the medieval man who either built a great medieval church or served it in other ways after it had been built. This man was a simple soul. His life was a unity. What he was in any one of his activities he was in every other. The aspects of his life which have been chosen for the purpose of this book have almost chosen themselves. For, while those aspects have little claim over others which might have been chosen, they represent activities of life and thought all of which are simple and easily understood—the medieval man's ideas of the earth on which he lived, of the skies above his head, of the way in which his children ought to be brought up, of the past of his race and his country, of foreign countries which he had never seen and never would see, of the ills that afflict the bodies and minds of mankind everywhere and at all times, of the methods of combating those ills, of spending his spare time profitably, of travelling from one place to another, of the management of a large estate with manor-houses, and of that perennial source of interest and profit to the human race, play-acting. It is the hope of both publisher and author that the copious quotations that have been printed in the language in which they were written will, even if at a first reading their meaning here and there may not be obvious, convey to the reader a far clearer idea of the medieval man, whose language was part of himself, than if they had been dressed up in the hybrid English of the twentieth century. As well dress him up in a lounge suit and a felt hat, give him a collar and a tie and low shoes, and put a pipe into his mouth, as clothe his ideas in any tongue except the one which, because he had learnt it at his mother's knee, was as much part of himself as his eyes and ears and limbs.

Yet, apparently limited though the scope of this book may seem, it is surprising to realise the classes of people who are portrayed in it, and the relationships which they bear to one another. There are bishop and household, schoolmaster and pupil, monk and novice, actor and audience, doctor and patient. There are also the student in his study and the scientist in his laboratory. And, in addition, the " man-in-the-street ", the traveller, the map-maker, the astronomer, the great lord in his household, and the chorister in his role of boy-bishop. The reader is taken, in quick succession, from the inside of Bede's monastic home at Jarrow to the confines of the then-known world with all its wonders ; from more than one " grand tour " of Europe, in reality as well as in imagina-tion, back to the daily rounds of a busy medical man as he visits his patients ; from Alfred the Great to Edward III, a period of five centuries ; and from trade and commerce and the market-place to the travelling players and the gilds of actors, who did much to brighten the lives of people who had to make their own amuse-ments ; from school to the workaday world ; and from the home of the peasant to the castle home of the great lord. This is the pageant of human life that is spread before the eye of the reader. And, as the chief actor therein, the medieval man, woman and child, our own kith and kin.

Roughly speaking, our period is one of seven centuries, from c. 800 to c. 1500. This is a period almost twice as long as that which separates us from the middle of the sixteenth century. Yet the gulf that divides the ways of thought and life of the men of the twentieth century from those of the fifteenth is far wider and deeper than that which separated the early Tudor man from the man of the time of Alfred the Great. These two men had the same habits of thought. Their interpretation of the universe was the same ; their superstitions were the same ; their devotion to an ecclesiastical system was the same. Indeed, the later medieval man was probably even more devoted to that system than the earlier ; and both were unable to break away from it, even had they wished to do so. Intellectually, socially, ecclesiastically, politically and economically, they were bound in fetters. On the whole, what Bede thought about chronology, Higden thought ; the principles of cartography which Ptolemy expressed in his maps were even more scientific than those to be discovered in the making of the Hereford map a thousand years later ; under Alfred the Great, education was not behind that under William of Wykeham at Winchester ; and no more light is thrown on the knowledge of treating disease in the York medical book than in the Anglo-Saxon herbarium. There can be no doubt that, of the two periods, Anglo-Saxon England and the England of the Wars of the Roses, the former was the less enslaved to the dead hand of tradition. It is no figment of the imagination to regard the medieval man as having made little or no mental progress for seven or eight centuries. If justice has been done in the summaries and the extracts which form much of this book, the picture of the medieval man that the readers of the book will gain will, it is hoped, be clear-cut. The activities which have been chosen for illustration are familiar and easily understood. It is hoped that those who read the book will, when they put it down, have a definite idea of the kind of persons we ourselves should have been had we lived in the middle ages.

CHAPTER I

EDUCATION

(1) SCHOOLS

AS a rule, the word *education* is used to denote that formal preparation for adult life which is made in schools and colleges. In recent years, educational establishments have been either adapted or founded which give what is sometimes called " vocational " instruction in arts and crafts in order to prepare young people for the work by means of which they will have to earn their living. Strange as it may seem, this double preparation for the future began to be made as long ago as the middle ages, though it was not offered to every young person. Girls received little or no education unless they were the daughters of landed gentry ; and only certain boys, amongst them, however, sons of poor parents if they were promising, were fortunate enough to receive any kind of education whatsoever. But education in the middle ages was imparted in accordance with a system.

The revival of Christianity in this country at the end of the sixth century A.D. was the signal for the foundation of schools in connexion with the early religious foundations at such places as Canterbury, York and Winchester. The regular system of worship which Augustine introduced demanded a knowledge of Latin and music. With a rigid adherence to a practice which had been more or less natural amongst peoples whose languages were akin to Latin, Augustine failed to appreciate that the then universal language of worship and sacred study was not suited to British needs. Even Bede, an Englishman to the backbone, wrote almost exclusively in Latin ; and the library founded at York by Alcuin, also an English-man, who alone amongst Anglo-Saxon scholars is worthy to stand by the side of Bede, contained only books written in Latin. In the schools attached to these early religious foundations, the boys learned chiefly the art of singing the services in Latin ; but to sing in Latin they had to be taught the language. In the grammar schools which existed side by side with the song schools, the education of the boys, directed as it was to the end that they should embrace the religious life, consisted mainly of instruction in Latin as it was adapted for the study of the great Christian writers known as the Latin Fathers. It was in this way alone that boys could be prepared to occupy clerical and legal positions, and to receive that culture which was demanded from all who aspired to high posi-tions in the state. Rhetoric, that is, the art of speaking and debating in public, philosophy, mathematics and astronomy, all studied from books written in Latin, com-pleted the equipment without which no youth could enter one of the few learned professions. In such a simple study as arithmetic there survive no treatises in English that were written before the fourteenth century. It is easily realised that only a small minority of the boys of this country could hope to receive this kind of education. The remainder grew up in ignorance of what is sometimes called " book-learning ".

As the middle ages progressed, as the number of religious foundations grew, and as the universities, estab-lished in the early part of the thirteenth century, attracted more and more youths, the curriculum was extended. The mark of an educated man was that he had received instruction, and had satisfied the examiners, in subjects which composed what were known as the trivium, or group of three (grammar, rhetoric and logic) and the quadrivium (arithmetic, geometry, music and astronomy). These constituted the " seven liberal arts ".

Grammar, that is, Latin Grammar, included vocabulary, accidence and syntax. Nouns and adjectives were treated in *catholica* (sc. *verba*), or " words in common use ", compiled about the middle of the first century A.D. and adapted by later writers for use in schools and colleges. Dictionaries were to be found in the libraries of all educational foundations, some of them being etymological. The more difficult part of the study of Latin, namely, the writing of verse or prose, demanded a skill not only in the choice of words but also in syntax. By far the most popular book on these during the whole of the middle ages had been written by Aelius Donatus, a Roman of the fourth century, under whom Jerome, the translator of the medieval Bible known as the Vulgate, had studied. This book, however, was mainly used in an abbreviated form under the title of *ars minor*, which was so well known all over Europe that, just as in this country until fairly recently Geometry according to Euclid, and the subject itself, were known simply as " Euclid ", so *ars minor* was always called " Donatus ". Even after the invention of printing the book continued to be produced. The larger Donatus, *ars major*, was used at the universities. When, towards the end of the fourteenth century, William of Wykeham founded Winchester College, he ordained that the subjects for scholarship examinations should be reading, singing, and " old Donatus ", that is, *ars minor*. Other Latin grammars existed, such as that of Priscian of Constantina (c. 500 A.D.), of whose book, which is quoted by Aldhelm, Bede and Alcuin, more than one thousand copies still exist. Rhetoric was studied chiefly in Cicero's well-known treatise, a copy of which, with a companion book, the commentary, was found in nearly every medieval library in this country. From time to

A small class
Another lecture

A lecture to medical students
A monastic school

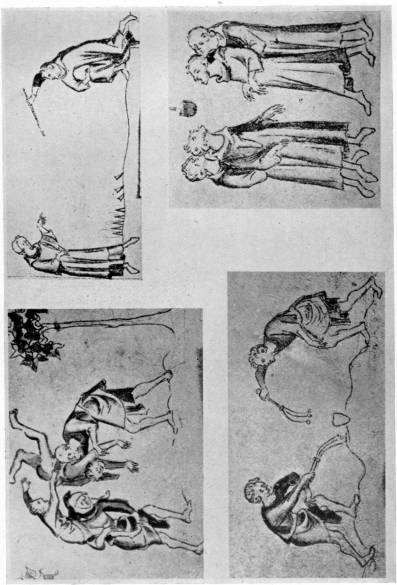

Skittles, and throwing a stick

Wrestling

time, in their lessons in rhetoric, the boys were required to give *impromptu* answers to questions put to them either by their masters or by their schoolfellows. Logic was studied in Aristotle's masterly treatise, the oldest of all text-books—for Aristotle lived from 384 to 322 B.C.—and in treatises by Cassiodorus, Isidore of Seville and Boethius. Treatises on all four of the subjects of the quadrivium abounded and were found in every medieval library. In astronomy, Ptolemy's system was taught as the only orthodox one. And, to crown this structure, came theology, the " queen of the sciences ", that is, the queen of knowledge.

In the year 1431, a century before the Reformation, the course of study, though still kept within the framework of the trivium and the quadrivium, was revised at Oxford. The work for each academic year of four terms, in each of which thirty days were set aside for lectures, was assigned by university regulation. The trivium of Grammar, Logic and Rhetoric was to be covered in $2\frac{1}{2}$ years. The aim of this portion of medieval study was to form the gateway to eloquence, so that the would-be scholar should be able to speak and to write fluently and intelligibly. The quadrivium, the gateway to wisdom, with the addition of philosophy (natural and moral) and metaphysics, was spread over $5\frac{1}{4}$ years. A student might obtain " inception " in arts, that is, the degree of bachelor, in $2\frac{1}{2}$ years for his knowledge of the trivium ; but a further course of $5\frac{1}{4}$ years was expected from him before he could claim the degree of master. The doctorate in divinity demanded a more advanced course of study. At the same time, books were prescribed, some of them by authors who had not before received recognition. In all the three branches of philosophy, however, Aristotle reigned alone and supreme. Less than a century later, however, Boethius lost his place as the arithmetician, for being concerned only with the properties of numbers in the old system of the abacus, in favour of writers of the new system of algorism, amongst whom was Cuthbert Tunstall, bishop successively of London and Durham. The position won and maintained by Priscian in Latin Grammar is reflected in the Aldine edition of his work produced in 1527.

The foundation of St. Paul's School by John Colet forms what may be called a conservative reform in education. The new school, which came into existence in 1509 or not long after, bears the impress of Colet's mind. Colet stood between two worlds, the old and the new. He was the friend of More and also of Erasmus, both of whom looked up to him with veneration. His liberal and progressive mind is revealed in his provision that the scholars of his school, 153 in number, the number of fish in St. John xxi. 11 (compared with 70 each at Winchester and Eton), should be instructed in " good litterature, both laten and greke " ; and his reverence for ecclesiastical tradition led him to qualify " good litterature " as

> very Romayne eloquence joynyd with wisdome, specially Cristyn auctours that wrote theyre wysdome with clene chast laten other [either] in verse or in prose.

Thus his aim was that his scholars should be able to read and to write pure classical Latin, not the ecclesiastical Latin of the Church. His models however were not Cicero and Vergil but writers such as Lactantius, the Christian apologist of the beginning of the fourth century, and Prudentius, the almost contemporary Christian poet. The boys were therefore brought up on the style, but not the subject-matter, of the classical writers, or, as Colet put it :

> those that hath with wisdome joyned the pure chaste eloquence.

As the man best qualified to attain the ends that he had in view, Colet chose as the first high master of his school William Lyly, who ruled the school for the first ten years of its existence and has the distinction of being the first schoolmaster in this country to teach Greek to his pupils. It was only a step from this to the study of what is now called " humane letters "—in Colet's own phrase, " litera- ture, not blotterature ".

Greek also began to be taught at Colet's school, held by Erasmus to be the best school of the time, towards the end of the fifteenth century. But English found no place in education for another half-century, the first school to adopt it as a school subject being Merchant Taylors under its first headmaster, Richard Mulcaster, from Eton and King's College, Cambridge. Of English, Mulcaster wrote :

> Our naturall tung being as beneficiall vnto vs for our nedefull deliuerie, as anie other is to the peple which vse it : & hauing as pretie and as fair obseruations in it as anie other hath : and being as readie to yield to anie rule of Art as anie other is : why should I not tak som payns to fynd out the right writing of ours, as other cuntrimen haue don to find the like in theirs ? & so much the rather bycause it is pretended that the writing thereof is meruellous vncertain and scant to be recouered from extreme confusion without som change of as great extremitie ?

Those were courageous words of a pioneer in educational reform. Where would have been the stylists to express in English the meaning of the Bible had English not become a literary tongue ?

Though nobody suspected it, at the time when the new school attached to St. Paul's Cathedral was coming into being, a youth was growing up on the Cotswold hills who was to form the ambition of translating into English, that English which was the foundation of the incompar- able English of the Authorised Version of the Bible, the

Bible so that the merest ploughboy would be able to read the Scriptures for himself. That youth's name was William Tyndale. A new age was dawning, and medieval England was becoming modern England.

In an early sixteenth-century book on philosophy written in Germany, there is an attractive illustration of the " tower of knowledge ". This shews a broad tower, the door of which is open to all who wish to enter in. In front of the door stands a woman, holding a board on which the alphabet is written and leading to the open door a young man who wishes to ascend the tower. The first two stages of the building are occupied by the two medieval masters of grammar, Donatus and Priscian, the third by Aristotle, the master of logic, Cicero, the master of rhetoric, and Boethius, the master of arithmetic, the fourth by Pythagoras, the master of music, Euclid, the master of geometry, and Ptolemy, the master of astronomy, and the fifth and highest by Peter Lombard, the master of theology or metaphysics. This is a graphic representation of the intellectual equipment and the ambition of the perfectly-educated medieval man, and of the stages through which he must ascend to the knowledge of God, the aim of all true education.

It was only a chosen few who could hope to ascend this tower. It would however be a mistake to conclude that only the sons of the privileged could receive this kind of education, the finest of the day. For careers in the Church, and nowhere else, were open to the sons of poor parents, and many a poor boy rose to a high position in the Church in spite of his lowly birth. All the grammar and song schools, besides the two foundations of Winchester and Eton colleges, were founded for poor boys of ability. Yet, in spite of good intentions, only a minority of such boys were able to find their careers through education at schools and colleges. A statute of Richard II

(1388) decreed that the children who worked at the plough or at any other kind of farm work until they were 12 years of age should not be apprenticed to any other trade or craft. Shortly afterwards, owing to the dearth of labourers on the land, it was decreed that nobody should be allowed to take a child from work unless the parents should own land to the value of twenty shillings a year. Other parents were allowed to send their children to school at the age of 12—an almost useless concession.

For the common academic studies and for ecclesiastical lore, the nobility had little inclination, except where young men were willing to give their lives to the Church as unmarried men or were anxious to learn music. Their sisters might learn to play musical instruments and to sing, but their lack of general education in most cases prevented them from acquiring much proficiency in these arts. The lore which all the high-born absorbed from their earliest years was that of the aristocratic world in which they lived, a world which demanded knowledge of men and affairs, skill in riding, hawking and hunting, ability to use bow and arrow, the rapier and the fencing-stick, familiarity with the etiquette of the court, the bishop's palace and the banqueting-hall, together with a mastery of the art of wooing and winning a high-born lady. In this world, the trivium and the quadrivium were likely to be more of a hindrance than a help.

As time went on, the number of grammar schools increased as more and more well-to-do people, wishing to perform some good act which would earn for them a reward in the next world, founded educational institutions. The monastic schools had a less wide appeal than the schools of the secular foundations, which included associations of clergy who were not monks but members of collegiate bodies, whether canons attached to cathedrals or clergy attached to non-cathedral churches. There was

room for both kinds of schools, but to enter a monastic
school meant almost inevitably embracing the monastic
life, a life for which by no means every young man was
fitted. In the later middle ages, probably one in every
ten adult males gave his life to the profession of religion.
At the Reformation, the monastic schools were abolished
with the monasteries to which they were attached. The
schools of the secular foundations such as York, and the
grammar schools not attached to such foundations, continued under the altered conditions, and thus have a long,
continuous and honourable history.

The vocational training given to boys during the middle
ages will be dealt with in the next chapter. A few
illustrations will now be given of specific cases of the
education of young men in various noble and other houses.
As early as the reign of Henry II, it was considered an
honour for even the sons of nobles to be received into
the house of an archbishop or a bishop, so that they
might learn, from him and his chaplains, not only those
things which a Christian boy ought to know to his soul's
health but also how to serve their elders and to comport
themselves with dignity and grace. Becket used to
receive such boys until they had won their knighthood,
when he would send them back to their homes. Even
Henry II sent his eldest son to the house of the very
archbishop whose death, later on, was precipitated by
his hasty words. In Becket's establishment, the youths
learned to mix with their equals as well as with their
superiors, to wrestle, to talk intelligently, to wait on their
master's bidding, and to hold their own in a changing
society. It was far different with the household of
William of Longchamp (bishop of Ely 1189–1198, and
chancellor of England). We are told by Roger of Hove-
den that the young noblemen in his household were not
allowed even to raise their eyes to him unless he first

spoke to them. If they displeased him, he was in the habit of pricking them with a goad.

In those days, parents were strict with their children. Lady Jane Grey told Roger Ascham, the schoolmaster, author of the famous book entitled *The Scholemaster*, that when she was with her parents :

> whether I speake, kepe silence, sit, stand, or go, eate, drinke, be merie or sad, be sewyng, plaiyng, dauncing, or doinge anie thinge els, I must do it, as it were, in soch weight, mesure and number, even so perfitelie as God made the world, or els I am so sharplie tauntid, so cruelly threatened, yea presentlie some tymes, with pinches, nippes, and bobbes and other waies I will not name for the honor I bear theym . . . that I thinke my self in hell till tyme cum when I must goe to Mr. Elmer, who teacheth me so jentlie, so pleasantlie, with soch faire allurementes to learning that I thinke all the tyme nothing whiles I am with him. And when I am called from him I fall on weeping.

Corporal punishment was both common and severe. Of the tyranny of one schoolmaster it was written :

> They holde up their hand at the bar
> For all their noble bloude
> He pluckes them by the hood
> And shakes them by the ear
> And bryngs them in such feare
> He bayteth them lyke a bear
> Like an ox or a bul.
> Their wittes, he sayth, are dul,
> He sayth they have no brayne
> Their estate to mayntayme,
> And makes them bowe the knee
> Before his Majestie.

One boy, an Eton scholar in the comparatively early days of that famous college, wrote this verse about the discipline there :

> From Paul's I went, to Eton sent
> To learn straightways the Latin phrase
> When fifty-three stripes given to me
> At once I had.

For fault but small or none at all
It came to pass ; thus beat I was.
See, Udall, see the mercy of thee
To me, poor lad !

Udall became headmaster of Eton.

John Lydgate, who became a monk of Bury St.
Edmunds in 1389, has left a poem in which he makes
confession of his boyish escapades.　He tells us that up
to the age of 15, " the sesoun of my yeerys greene ", being
" voyd of resoun " and given to wilfulness, he was " loth
to lerne " and " lovid no besynesse ", used to weep for
nothing but soon forgot his troubles.　Yet he stood in
awe of being punished.　But he " hadde in custom to
come to scole late, nat for to lerne but for a contenaunce
with my felawys redy to debate".　In school he talked,
told lies to avoid punishment and made fun of his masters
behind their backs.　He " ran in to gardyns, and applys
ther I stol ", robbed vines, " scorned folk " and japed at
them, liked counting cherry-stones better than going to
church, rose late " with vnwassh handys reedy to dyneer ;
my pater noster my Crede or my beleeve cast atte the
cok ", snubbed his friends, shammed illness when he was
well, and " to folowe my lust for no man wold I spare ".

Yet Lydgate became the most famous poet in this
country in the fifteenth century, owing to his translation,
into English verse, of *Bochas upon the Fall of Princes*, a very
long poem, and his equally well-known poem, *The Story
of Thebes*.　Though he was born too soon to have been
educated at Winchester College, the motto of which is
Manners makyth man, at his monastery he taught rhetoric
and poetry to young noblemen.

As early as the end of the twelfth century, when two
parish churches in London, " Bow " church and St.
Martin-le-Grand, besides St. Paul's cathedral, had schools
attached to them, the festivals of their patron saints were

observed by a meeting-together of all the pupils, who, according to one record, were encouraged to try their oratorical powers in sophistry, with " a vast heap and flow of words " in attempting to draw false conclusions from their arguments in order to provoke others to discover their fallacies. Boys would wrangle in verse about the principles and rules of grammar ; others would lead attacks on their masters without mentioning their names, and would give point to their criticisms " with true Socratic wit ".

Sports were permitted which would now be condemned. On Shrove Tuesdays, as if to work off his animal spirits before Lent, each boy brought to school his own fighting-cock, and the morning was spent in sanguinary cock-fights, the whole school looking on. In the afternoon, the boys played football. On each Sunday during Lent, mock battles between teams of boys, on horseback as well as on foot, were staged before distinguished visitors, who might include the king and his retinue. Running races, archery, wrestling and jumping were common exercises. In winter, boys were encouraged to attend boar-fights and bear-baitings, and they skated on home-made skates of bones. Yet they worked as hard as they played, for Roger Bacon, a sound judge of learning, testifies that, at schools in every town, city and castle, the love of learning had never reached so high a level in so many different subjects as in his day.

CHAPTER II

EDUCATION

(2) OUT OF SCHOOL

THE remainder of this chapter will be occupied with accounts, from contemporary literature, of the training of the young at their own homes and in great houses. It would be a mistake to think of these great houses, however, as always and everywhere clean and wholesome. The extracts which will be quoted, and the accounts which will be given, of the good manners which it was necessary to instil into even well-bred youths will be regarded as evidence of a lack of training at home in the decencies of social behaviour. Even Edward IV was no model of personal cleanliness. His personal attendant, who groomed him, cut his hair and tried to turn him out looking as royal as a king should look, wrote thus :

> This barbour shall haue every satyrday at night if it please the Kinge to cleanse his head, legges or feet, and for his shaving, two loves, one picher wine. And the ussher of chambre ought to testyfye if this is necessaryly dispended or not.

There seems some doubt whether it would be the royal pleasure to be cleansed royally. Soap was used only for washing clothes. But, as a writer of seventy years ago observed :

> The temptation to value manners above morals, and pleasantness above honesty, is one that all of us have to guard against.

But, if rich men might be lacking in cleanliness, those less able to afford the luxury of soap were even more so. William Langland wrote :

As a bondman of his bacon his berd was bi-dravelled,
With his hood on his heed, a lousy hat above,
And in a tawny tabard of twelf winter age
Al so torn and baudy and ful of lys crepyng
But if that a lous couthe han lopen the bettre,
She sholde noght han walked on that welthe so it was thred-bare

The son of a king could thus address his father :

Nay, first, good fellowe, tell me true,
Hast thou noe creepers in thy gay hose ?
Art thou not troubled with the scabbado ?

There is evidence that, in Henry VIII's kitchen, scullions lay about naked, or tattered and filthy. The scandal became so great that the king issued orders that

the three master cookes shall have everie of them by way of reward yearly twenty marks, to the intent they shall prouide and sufficiently furnish the said kitchens of such scolyons as shall not goe naked or in garments of suche vilenesse as they now doe, and have been accustomed to doe, nor lie in the nights and dayes in the kitchens or ground by the fireside ; but that they of the said money may be found with honest and whole course garments, without such uncleannesse as may be the annoyance of those by whom they shall passe.

And it is well known that the streets of the towns were so full of garbage and other decayed matter that epidemics and plagues could not but descend on the people, as a judgment on them for their unclean habits. Erasmus gave it as his opinion that the plague, from which the country was scarcely ever completely free, was caused partly by the insanitary houses and partly by

the filthiness of the streets and the sluttishness within doors. The floors are commonly of clay, strewed with rushes, under which lies unmolested an ancient collection of beer, grease, bones, spittle, excrements of dogs and cats, and everything that is nasty.

When we read this, it is not hard to believe that cleanliness may be next to godliness.

We now turn to the interesting treatises which form the chief subject of this chapter.

Here we are introduced to

The Babees Book,

or, a " lytyl reporte " of how young people should behave.

> In this tretys the whiche I thenke to wryte
> Out of latyn in-to my comvne langage,
> He me supporte (sen I kan nat endyte)
> The whiche only after his owne ymage
> Fourmyd man-kynde. For alle of tendre age
> In curtesye Resseyve shulle document
> And vertues knowe, by this lytil coment.

In this poem of the late fifteenth century, babees, that is, young persons " of tendre age ", are taught the principles of virtuous conduct. For

> Vertues to knowe, thaym forto haue and vse
> Is thing moste helpfulle in this worlde trevly.

The writer looks for no reward save that

> This Book myghte yche man plese.

On entering, at " an esy pace ", the room in which the lord is, say " god spede ", salute all who are present and then kneel on one knee before the lord. Should anybody speak to you, look at them " with stable eye ", not letting your eyes rove but giving your full mind to what is said to you. Answers must be " on esy wyse ",

> In wordes gentylle and also compendious
> For many wordes ben rihte tedious.

Stand still till you are bidden to sit, keeping your head, hands and feet still, not " clowyng youre flessh " or leaning " to no poste " or touching anything at all. If the lord should speak to you, " looke withe oon accorde ", backing out of the room should anybody " better thaune yee " enter.   If the lord is drinking,

> be in righte stable sylence
> Withe-oute lowde lauhtere or Iangelynge,
> Rovnynge, Iapynge or other Insolence,

sitting if the lord should bid you sit.
Your conversation must be " lowly, blythe and hale ", without " vnhoneste tale " or scorn.   Should anybody praise you,

> Rise vp anoone and thanke him withe herte free.

Take no part in conversation between the lord and his lady about household affairs, and be ready to serve drinks or to hold a light when such service is needed.

> So shalle yee gete anoone a name of price.

For the best reward which you can ask of God is to be " nurtred ", that is, well bred.

Should the lord offer you his cup to drink, rise when you take it, take it with both hands, do not offer it to anybody else, and immediately you have drunk give it back.   When, at noon, he is ready for dinner, take water to him, some holding the water, others the towel.   Do not move till grace is said and you are bidden to sit,

> Withe clene handes ay Redy him to serve.

Keep your knife clean and sharp, ready to carve the lord's bread and meat.   Have a clean trencher for your own use, eat your soup with a spoon and without noise, do not leave your spoon in the dish, do not lean on the table, and " from embrowyng the clothe yee kepe clene ".   Do not drink while your mouth is full, or hang over your dish, or pick your nose, your teeth or your nails ; and do not fill your mouth so full that you cannot speak.   After you have drunk, dry your mouth and do not leave marks

on the cup. Avoid seasoning your food by dipping it
into the salt-cellar

> but lay it honestly
> On youre trencher, for that is curtesy.

Above all,

> Youre knife with mete to your mouthe nat bere.

For politeness' sake do not refuse to partake of any food
that is served ; and if your dish be taken away while it
still has food in it do not ask for it to be brought to you
again. If guests are present, see that they have a share
of all the food that is carried to the table. And

> Kutte nouhte youre mete eke as it were Felde men,

but take a delight in " curtesye and in verrey gentylnesse "
and " eschew boysterousnesse ".

For eating cheese you will need a clean trencher ; and

> in youre fedynge luke goodly yee be sene.

Do not jangle. At the end of the meal, cleanse your
knives and restore them to their places. After you have
washed your hands, leave the table and be ready to wait
on your lord. After grace, fetch water so that your lord
can wash his hands, others holding the towel.

> Other service thanne this I myhte comende
> To yow to done, but, for the tyme is shorte,
> I putte theym mouhte in this lytyl Reporte.
>
> And, swete children, for whos love now I write
> I yow beseche withe verrey lovande herte,
> To knowe this book that yee sette your delyte ;
> And myhtefulle God, that suffred peynes smerte,
> In curtesye he make yow so experte
> That thurhe your nurture and youre governaunce
> In lastynge blysse yee mowe your self auaunce.

The Lytylle Childrens Lytil Boke, or Edyllys be

As a change from the formal advice contained in the last poem, here is some charming advice charmingly given. The poem, which consists of 108 lines, is of the fifteenth century.

> Lytylle childrene, here ye may lere
> Moche curtesy that is wrytyn here ;
> For clerkis that the vij artez cunne
> Seyn that curtesy from hevyn come
> When Gabryelle oure Lady grette
> And Elizabeth with Mary mette.
> Alle vertues arne closide yn curtesye
> And alle vices ye vylonye.

Children must get up early in the morning and cross themselves on breast and forehead before they wash their hands and faces, comb their hair and ask God to help them in all they will do during the day. They ought to go to church and hear a Mass, at which they will ask forgiveness for their sins, wishing those whom they meet as they leave the church " good morne ". Before break-fast they must cross themselves on the mouth, the better to enjoy their food. They are warned not to cut their bread " to thynne ", or to break it " on twynne ", or to put their fingers into the dishes or their meat into the salt-cellar, or to drink with full mouths, or to pick their teeth with knives, or to sit with their elbows on the table. Before and after the meal, grace must be said, with a Paternoster (the Lord's Prayer) and an Ave (Hail ! Mary), for " the saulys that in peyne be " (that is, in purgatory).

The work of the day then begins. As Holy Scripture says :

> Yffe thot labour thou muste ete
> That with thi hondes thou doyste gete.

Therefore idleness is to be shunned. " Luke thou be trew in worde and dede ", the advice continues, for

> The weys to heuen thei bene thus tweyne,
> Mercy and treuthe, as clerkes seyne.

Promises must be fulfilled, because God and one's neighbour demand one's love ; and meddlesomeness must be avoided. The poor must not be despised, for courtesy and honour are due to everybody. At table, whispering, touching food with one's fingers, laughing, grinning and untidiness are grave faults. Meat must be cut, not bitten, and it is bad manners to eat with one's mouth wide open or to blow on one's food to cool it. Bones must not be thrown on the floor.

In addition, in demeanour to others be meek, do not always be the first to speak, look at the person to whom you are speaking, and be sparing of words. Tale-bearing is abominable, and so is swearing. There follows some sound advice about money, or, as it is called, " gowd " (gold) :

> Get the gowd with treweth and wynne
> And kepe the out of dette and synne ;
> Be lothe to greue, and leffe to ples ;
> Seke the pes, and lyf in es.
>
> When thou commys vn to a dore,
> Say, " God be here ", or thou go ferre.

As a guest, stand until you are invited to sit, especially at table, and remain in your seat until others move from theirs at the end of grace. When all have washed their hands,

> Aryse up soft and stylle,
> And iangylle nether with Iak or Iylle [Jack or Jill],
> But take thi leue of the lorde slowly
> And thank hym with thyne hert hyghly ;
> Than men wylle say therafter
> That a gentylleman was here.

¶To the honorable Sir William
Cecill Knight, principall Secretarie to the Quenes most excellent Maiestie.

Ondry & reasonable be the causes why learned men haue vsed to offer and dedicate such workes as they put abrode, to some such personage as they thinke fittest, either in respect of abilitie of defense, or skill for iugement, or priuate regard of kindenesse and dutie. Euery one of those considerations, Syr, moue me of right to offer this my late husbands M. Aschams worke vnto you. For well remembryng how much all good learnyng oweth vnto you for defense thereof, as the Vniuersitie of Cambrige, of which my said late husband was a member, haue in chosing you their worthy Chaunceller acknowledged, and how happily you haue spent your time in such studies & caried the vse thereof to the right ende, to the good seruice of the Quenes Maiestie and your contrey to all our benefites, thyrdly how much my sayd husband was many wayes bound vnto you, and how gladly and comfortably he vsed in hys lyfe to recognise and report your goodnesse toward hym, leauyng with me then hys poore widow and a great sort of orphanes a good comfort in the hope of your good

¶.ij.

Roger Ascham's " Scolemaster." Dedication page. (Printed in 1570.)

One version of the poem ends :

> Therfore, chyldren, for charyte,
> Louyth this boke though yt lytil be.
> And pray for hym that made it thus,
> That hym may helpe sweet Ihesus
> To lyve and dye among his frendes
> And neuer to be combred with no fendes [fiends].

Similar advice on behaviour at meals is given in the well-known poem attributed to John Lydgate, the monk of Kings Lynn, called *stans puer ad mensam* (the boy standing at the table).   The poem ends :

> Thus endith the book of curteisie that is clepid *stans puer ad mensam.*

There follow now two companion poems, *How the Good Wijf taughte Hir Doughtir*, and *How the Wise Man taught His Son*.   If they are full of worldly wisdom, they are no worse for that.

> The good wijf taughte hir doughtir
> Ful manye a tyme and ofte
> A ful good womman to be
> And seide, Doughtir to me dere
> Sum good thou must lere
> If euere thou wolt thee [thrive].

Love God and holy Church, she begins, and go to church when you can, in spite of the rain.   Tithes must be paid to the church, and alms given to the poor. Behaviour in church must be reverent, and courtesy must be shown to everybody.   Then comes the advice to the girl whom the mother wishes to see happily married.   No offer of matrimony must be despised, but there must be no unwisdom or folly in accepting it.   Once the betrothal has taken place,

That man that schal the wedde bifore God with a ryng
Loue thou hym and honoure moost of ertheli thing ;
Meekely thou him answere, and not as an attirling (shrew),
And so maist thou slake his mood and ben his dere derlynge ;
Dooth wraththe slake,
    Mi leue child.

Fair of speche schalt thou be, gladde & of mylde mood,
Trowe in worde & in dede, and in conscience good ;
Kepe thee from synne, fro vilonye & fro blame,
And loke that thou beere thee so that men seis thee no schame ;
For he that in good lijf renneth,
Ful ofte weel he wynneth,
    Mi leue child.

A good wife, the mother continues, must behave in a
seemly manner, not riotously or noisily ; she must walk
in a dignified way ; she must not " gad about " or go
from house to house ; nor must she drink ale immoder-
ately. Instead of going to wrestling-contests or to cock-
shootings, " as it were a strumpet or a giggelot ", she must
stay at home. It is folly to be over-free with men or to
accept presents from them. The house must be properly
kept, and all in it should do their share of the work, in
which the young wife will be wise to set an example to
her servants. Keys should not be entrusted to any but
trustworthy persons. Wages should be paid when they
are due. It is silly for a woman to be jealous because
her neighbour's wife has a more fashionable frock than
she has ; rather should she

thanke the God of heuen for that he hath geuene.

On Sundays and holy-days she ought to worship God, and
on all days to love her neighbour. Hospitality and alms
are expected from the rich, but even the rich wife must
not overspend :

Make not thin husbonde poore with spending
Ne with pride.

For disobedient children there is but one punishment :

> And yf thi chyldren ben rebel and wole nat hem bowe,
> Yf ony of hem mys dooth, noyther banne hem ne blowe,
> But take a smert rodde and bete hem on a rowe
> Till thei crie mercie and be of her gilt aknowe.

Birthdays of daughters are occasions for putting away for them those things that they will need when they marry.

A Saxon Couple

Finally, says the shrewd wife, in effect : " You have been taught as my mother taught me. Think about it night and day ; carry out my advice, and your husband will always be glad that he married you. And every blessing shall follow ".

> The blessynge of God mote thou haue, and of his modir bright,
> Of alle aungils & of alle archaungils and of alle holy wight,
> And that thou mowe haue grace to wende the wey full right,
> To the blis of heuene there sittith God Almyght. Amen.

The advice of the good wife to her daughter occupies 219 lines ; the wise man's teaching to his son is given in only 152 lines.

This poem has been attributed to a date early in the reign of Henry VI. First, the boy must say his prayers every morning lest during the day he should fall into sin. He must keep a firm hold on his tongue and must work hard. Strangely, he is warned " noon office to beere " apparently lest he offend his neighbours or fail to give satisfaction. What kind of office is referred to is not made clear ; but if what is called the public service is meant, either in his township or in his trade or craft gild, the advice seems churlish, disingenuous and un-worthy. It is better, the father continues, to be deaf and dumb than to go on " yuel questis ", whatever these may be. Drinking, gambling with dice, keeping late hours, marriage for money—these are to be shunned. Better a wife who is " meeks, curteis and wiis " than one who has nothing to commend her except money. A meek wife must not be overburdened,

> For it is betere with reste and pees
> A melis meete of hoomeli fare
> Than for to haue an hundrid mees [messes or dishes]
> With grucchinge & with myche care.

The writer of the book of the Proverbs seems to have inspired this advice. Perhaps the boy's father was speaking from experience.

Then comes advice about the soft answer that turneth away wrath. A man must not displease his wife wantonly or call her names, because

> Softe and faire a man may tame
> Bothe herte and hynde, bucke and do.

No man must believe every complaint that his wife makes to him. He must not be in a hurry to leave his neigh-

bour's house when he is comfortably seated amongst
friends, or men will say of him, " This foole can no where
abide." The more of this world's goods that a man has
the meeker he should be, for no man can take his money
with him when he dies—another echo of Holy Scripture.

> For deeth wole take bothe highe and lowe,
> And than fare-weel al that there is.

And often, when a woman inherits property from her
husband, another husband gets it :

> And therfore do thou bi my councelle
> And take ensaumple of othir men,
> How little her good dooth hem a-vaile
> Whanne thei be doluen [buried] in her den,
> And he that was not of hys kyn
> Hath his wijf and al that there is.
> Sonne, kepe thee out of deedly synne,
> And assaye to gete thee paradijs.

Finally, the chief thing in life is to save one's soul :

> And deeth is euere, as y trowe,
> The moost certeyn thing that is,
> And no thing is so vncerteyn to knowe
> As is the tyme of deeth, y-wis.
> Therfore, my sonne, thinke on this
> Of al that y haue seid bifore,
> And ihesu bringe us to his blis
> That for vs bare the crowne of thorn.

> Amen.

CHAPTER III

MEALS, STARS AND CHRONOLOGY

THIS chapter will contain an account of some aspects of the daily life of the medieval man. As a historian counts time, it is not very long since history used to consist of little more than a record of those events that were largely arranged by kings, soldiers and politicians. It is true that these events concerned the ordinary man and woman almost intimately, and that they were supposed to be arranged in the name of the whole people. But, being mainly wars, quarrels between monarchs and their nobles or between the nobles themselves, with, here and there, a pestilence or an epoch-making enactment such as the signing of the Great Charter, they did not include much that reflected the daily lives of the people of the country, their thoughts, their ambitions and their actions. During the past fifty years the scope of history has been greatly enlarged, and an enormous amount of research has gone to elucidate the social, economic, domestic, religious and private lives of the people of this country in all ages. It is something of that kind which will be attempted in this chapter, which is based mainly on the publications of the Early English Text Society, a society which, for nearly a century, has been enriching our knowledge of the literature of our country in Anglo-Saxon, Old and Middle English and thereby throwing light on the very things, formerly wrapped in obscurity, about our ancestors which we most want to know. It is a wholesome, if at times amusing, exercise, to look at ourselves as we should have been had we lived centuries ago.

We begin with the Anglo-Saxons, who were far less uncivilised than we imagine. The historian who remarked that Napoleon could move his armies across Europe hardly any more quickly and comfortably than Julius Cæsar could implied more than he stated. It is true to say that, on the whole, the gulf between the mode of life of the Anglo-Saxon and that of those who were alive when the battle of Waterloo was fought was much less than that between our mode of life and that of our forefathers of a century-and-a-half ago. To realise the truth of this, it is necessary only to think of the operations of cooking, heating, travelling, lighting, manufacturing, coal-mining and even ploughing in order to assess the extent to which we are dependent on stores of what is properly called " energy " ; for the storing of this energy has been possible only within the last-century-and-a-half.

In Anglo-Saxon England, time was reckoned in the Roman way, the hours being counted from 6 a.m. This method was adopted by the Christian Church from the earliest times ; and, when the " hour " offices or services were drawn up as the daily routine of the clergy, three of them, terce, sext and nones, were named after the third, sixth and ninth hours of the day because they were said or sung then. Later on, however, these times were not strictly adhered to, owing to the requirements of the monastic rules. From *none* was derived the Anglo-Saxon word *noon*, which, to the Anglo-Saxon, meant 3 p.m. ; and it was at that hour that he ate his midday meal or dinner. The word *noon* is not found in its sense of 12 midday until much later. An Anglo-Saxon saying ran : " As soon as they hear the none-bell they take to meat."

Food and drink in great quantity and variety were at the command of the Anglo-Saxon man, according to his means. The cow, the ox, the calf, the sheep and the pig were bred then as now, and in some parts of the country the hart and the reindeer. The common barnyard fowl, geese and ducks were in abundance, the fowler using the noose, the trap, the net and bird-lime to make his catches. Fish abounded in the rivers and in the coastal waters, and in great variety—salmon, herrings, fresh-water fish, oysters, crabs and lobsters. Fruit was plentiful, wild as well as cultivated, though not in such great variety as now, pears, plums, apples, peaches and cherries, with wild fruits, being as easily grown as in our day. But grapes and the much-advertised banana were unknown. The only sweetening material was honey. Of liquid refreshment there was a large variety, but all of it home-produced—beer, ale, mead, sweet wines and a kind of claret. Food was flavoured with salt made chiefly in salt-pans by the coast, and in Cheshire and Worcestershire.

The signs of the Zodiac
(from an early printed book)

Feasts were serious as well as social occasions. When a lord gave a feast, he had his table set with his finest silver and cutlery, he provided an abundance of food in great variety, and he hired musicians who played far into the night. As time went on, feasts became more and more sumptuous. An important event such as the marriage of the daughter of a great lord or the enthronement of a bishop or an archbishop was celebrated by a feast which might last for several days. Even the monks were allowed to indulge themselves when they got a new abbot. At one great feast to celebrate the enthronement of an archbishop, there were provided 300 quarters of wheat, 330 tuns of ale, 104 tuns of wine, 80 oxen, six wild bulls, more than one-thousand sheep, 300 pigs, 300 calves, more than 3,000 geese and capons, 100 peacocks, 200 cranes, 200 kids, 2,000 fowls, 4,000 pigeons, 4,000 rabbits, 4,000 ducks, 400 herons, 200 pheasants, 500 partridges, 4,000 woodcock, 400 plovers, 100 curlews, 100 quails, 400 stags, bucks and roebucks, 1,500 venison pasties, 5,000 dishes of jelly, 400 tarts, 6,000 custards, 300 pike, 300 bream, 8 porpoises, 4 seals, and a great variety of biscuits, bread and the like. Such a gargantuan feast, lasting for days, usually cost the host the whole of his first year's income in his new position.

When compared with this gluttony, the diet of a boy who was being educated in an Anglo-Saxon religious house was indeed plain fare—beef, mutton, fish, cheese, butter, beans, and light ale.

England was then chiefly an agricultural country. Settlements of groups of people were plentiful, but none of them was large. They grew up at the mouths, or at the limits of navigation, of rivers, or round monastic settlements. Names of cities and towns which have grown out of these early communities will at once spring to the mind. But their existence did not spoil the countryside. Agriculture was the chief industry. In one way or another, almost everybody earned his livelihood on the land. Gardening, as a means of obtaining fresh food and of growing flowers, was widespread ; it was the beginning of an Englishman's love of a cottage in the country with a garden attached to it. The countryside, however, was far more open than it now is. Hedges were less numerous ; so were roads, these being mainly those left by the Romans. Farming, which comprised arable and grazing, was made easier by the scarcity of hedges and trees and the consequent rarity of weeds. A large number of allotments comprised a large field, separated from one another much as modern allotments are. Trespassing was less common than it is now, but cattle strayed so easily that it had to be enacted that those who had lost cattle were empowered to demand evidence of ownership from those whom they suspected of harbouring their strayed beasts. The meadows, under grass and field crops, presented the appearance with which we are familiar. Mowing was done with sickle and hook ; the hay was tedded and cocked, and then stored in lofts. Roads were subject to toll-charges, due to local land-owners, whose duty it was to keep them in repair. Yet a clever man could avoid the payment of tolls if he knew how. One, an old miser, used to boast that he could use every road within 70 miles of London without paying.

Starcraft

Another treatise contains details of the lengths of the shadows cast by the sun at 9 a.m. and 3 p.m. on Christmas Day, January 6th and 21st, February 4th and 17th, March 6th and 21st, April 5th and 20th, May 6th and 23rd, June 1st, 13th and 24th, July 6th, 8th and 21st, August 21st, September 5th and 20th, October 6th and 21st, November 5th and 20th, and December 2nd and 14th. The lengths of time when the moon shines on each of the days of its course are here listed from 48 minutes to 12 hours. And two days in every month are given on which any task then begun will never be finished.

The most interesting of the contents of this treatise on starcraft contains the substance of the writings, on astronomy and cosmogony, of Bede, " the wise teacher ",

who " collected from books of many wise doctors learning
about the courses of the year from the beginning of the
world ". First, God created the world, with light and
darkness, heaven or the firmament. Heaven however
cannot be seen because of its height above the earth, the
clouds and the weakness of the human eye. The
firmament, solid and star-spangled, and as deep under the
earth as it is high above it, moves about the earth swifter
than any mill-wheel. There are more heavens than one,
for Solomon spoke of " the heaven of heavens ", and
St. Paul wrote of a man who was caught up to " the
third heaven ", where he heard words which no man
may utter.

For three days the world was dark. God then created
the sun, the moon, and the stars, beasts and cattle and,
before He rested on the seventh day, Adam and Eve.

Every day the sun lights up the world, moving between
the heaven and the earth, and shining by night on the
other and " under " side of the earth. The stars and
the moon are not seen by day because the sun outshines
them, for they have no light except from the sun. The
sun betokens Christ, the Healer, Who, the Sun of
Righteousness, arises with healing in His wings. The
moon, which waxes and wanes, betokens the church or
congregation ; it waxes because children are born, and
wanes because people die. The bright stars betoken the
faithful in the church, whose lives are a shining example
to others. Christ illuminated everything through His
grace, which " lighteth every man that cometh into the
world " (St. John i. 9).

The day of the vernal equinox was the fourth day of
creation, there being three days without the light of sun
and moon and stars. God set the sun in the east, where
the equator is. On the same day He made the moon and
placed it in the east with bright stars, and he determined

the time of Easter by means of the place where he first fixed the moon. The first day of the world was March 18th, and the day of the equinox March 21st.

Night was given to mankind as a time for rest. It is caused by the shadow of the earth between the sun and human beings. The moon receives its light from the rays of the sun. Even though the whole of the circle of the moon is not always seen, the moon is always whole. The night has seven divisions—gloaming, the time when the evening star appears, silent night, midnight, cock-crowing, dawn and the interval between dawn and sunrise. The date of Easter is fixed in accordance with the incidence of a full moon.

A lunar month lasts for 29 days and 12 hours. In some years the moon in renewed 12 times from Easter to Easter, and in other years 13 times. The year as it was recognised in Bede's time has 12 new moons ; in the year called *embolismus*, or leap-year, it has 13. The lunar month has in one month 30 nights, and in the next 29.

There are four seasons—*ver* (spring), *aestus* (summer), *autumnus* (autumn) and *hiems* (winter). The obliquity of the axis of the earth to the plane of the ecliptic causes the lenten equinox (on March 21st) and the harvest equinox (on September 21st).

In Egypt there is no rain in the winter. But the Nile overflows its banks after harvest-time, and as after that there is no rain for a year the Egyptians do not suffer from scarcity of corn.

The Universe

The firmament bounds the world. It turns about the earth, between the two being an incalculable space. Each revolution occupies 24 hours. All the stars revolve with the firmament. Through the power of God, the earth remains fast, so that it never moves.

The Equinoxes

The lenten equinox falls on the 12th day before the kalends of April, that is, on a day 11 days before April 1st. The date of Easter must be determined by the " true rule ", not by the previous method of reckoning abolished at the synod of Whitby. At the equinoxes, day and night are equal all the world over. In India the shadow turns south in summer and north in winter. At Alexandria the sun is vertical at the summer solstice at midday, without any shadow being cast. At Meroe Island, " where the Ethiopians live ", the longest day in the year lasts for about 12½ hours ; in Italy 15 hours ; and in England 17 hours. In the north, at Thule, six days' journey from England by sea, at the summer solstice there is no night for six days, the sun only just dipping under the horizon. There are five zones : (1) one tropical, " boiling hot and uninhabitable for the nearness of the sun " ; (2) two temperate, neither too hot nor too cold, the northern part being the home of " all mankind " ; and (3) two arctic, cold, uninhabitable and sunless.

With regard to the moon, " no Christian man shall do anything of witchery by the moon ; if he doth, his belief is naught ". The weather can be foretold by the colour of the moon, the sun and the sky. Trees should be felled at full moon, being then harder and less liable to attack by worms. The sea and the moon wax and wane at the same time, the former in the tides.

Stars

Stars do not fall from heaven. Meteors, which appear to do this, are made of fire from the sky, which springs from the heavenly bodies as sparks from fire. Many stars are still in the positions in which, when God created the

world, He fixed them. They will not move as long as
the world lasts. There are also seven planets. One
constellation, Arctos, has seven stars ; it is called
septentrio, or north, or " the churl's wain " (the Great
Bear), and never goes under the earth. In the south
there is another such constellation, which we cannot see.
Two stars never move—the north, or " ship ", star (so
called because ships can be steered by it on clear nights),
and the south star. They form the ends of the axis of the
universe. *Pleiades* is the name given to seven stars which
in the time of harvest " go up ", in winter shine eastwards,
in summer go " under the earth " at night, " come up "
above it by day, and in winter go " under the earth " by
day and " above it " by night. Comets, seen only
occasionally and without warning, emit rays like sun-
beams. They appear as portents of something new, but
not of necessity evil.

The Elements

The word *element* then had a meaning different from
its modern meaning ; it signified one of a number of four
to six substances of which all material substances are
composed. These elements are four in number—air, fire,
earth and water. The air which supplies the breath of
man which is not his soul, and which enables birds to
fly as water enables fish to swim, " mounteth up pretty
near the moon ". Everything is composed of these four
elements. Because a stick will catch fire owing to
friction, the stick must contain fire ; and because, as it
burns, the moisture is driven out without smoke, it contains also water. Apparently what is left of the stick in
the form of ash is earth ; apparently, too, the stick holds
air in its pores, some of which are invisible. So the
reasoning is complete.

The Winds

Air in motion is called wind. Winds are named from the four quarters from which they blow. The four chief winds are : (1) east or *subsolanus*, because it blows from the quarter in which the sun rises ; (2) south or *auster*, which is the origin of lightning, cloud and plagues ; (3) west or *zephuros* (Greek) or *favonius* (Latin), which brings and gives life to herbs and disperses and thaws the frost of winter ; and (4) north or *aquilo* (Latin) or *boreas* (Latin) or *septentrio* (Latin), which heralds snow and forms dry clouds. In between each adjacent pair of these winds is another pair of winds. From the north-east came *aquilo* or *boreas* (the latter term being also used for the north wind), a wind that is high and dry and cold and that disperses the mortality brought by *auster*, the south wind. The other six " intermediate " winds are not named. " To us ", adds the writer, " it seemeth too complex to speak further about this ".

Rain

Through the power of God, the air draws up moisture from the earth and the sea, conserves it and releases it in the form of showers, which in their turn are dissipated by winds and the heat of the sun. Through the heat of the sun and the " broadness of the air ", the salt water from the sea is turned, in the process of being drawn up, into fresh water. The weather is ordered by God, who " would not be almighty if any arranging were a difficulty to him. His name is the Omnipotent, that is, Almighty, because he is able to do all that he willeth, and his power nowhere is put to effort." When drops of rain are frozen, they fall to the earth as hailstones, while snow is " thin moisture ", which freezes before it has been separated into drops and therefore falls continuously.

Thunder

Thunder is caused by heat and moisture. The struggle between these produces a terrifying noise, and the fire bursts out in the form of lightning, and damages crops if it is more powerful than the moisture. The hotter the summer, the more thunder there is. The thunder which was heard by St. John in the Apocalypse was not natural but spiritual. " Let this narrative be here ended. May God help my hands ! " So the writer brings his story to an end.

Many things which are explained in this treatise will be recognised in the chapter on geography and maps. Amongst them are the solidarity of the firmament ; the view that the universe is grouped round the earth as its centre, the sun revolving round the earth ; the impossibility of getting to know much about the universe ; the impossibility that there should be inhabited regions beyond the regions then known ; the apparent size of the envelope of air surrounding the earth, reaching almost to the moon ; the recognition of the signs of the Zodiac, sketches of which appear at the heads of the months in medieval calendars ; the inclination of the axis of the earth to the plane of the ecliptic or the path of the sun, and its effect on the climate of the zones of the earth ; the northern limit of the then-known world in the fabled island of Thule ; the authority of Holy Scripture in cosmic matters ; the four elements ; and the rule of the world by God.

But much knowledge is shewn (1) about the influence of the moon on the date of Easter, which recalls the controversy at the synod of Whitby in the year 664 between the two rival schools of reckoning (the Northumbrian or Irish, and the Roman), and (2) about the phases of the moon, the signs of the Zodiac, the number of moons from

Easter to Easter, the zones of climate and the cause of them, leap years, the discountenancing of the common idea of the " witchery " of the moon, and the kinds of heavenly bodies—fixed stars, meteors, planets, constellations, the pole stars, comets and epacts. Limited as was Bede's knowledge by his loyalty to an interpretation of Holy Scripture which has now almost everywhere been superseded, he was a careful observer of more things than is generally realised, and for his time he was more than ordinarily enlightened. For a theologian he had a vast range of interests. This Anglo-Saxon summary of the scientific work of Bede has to be set against the background of the life of study as it was lived in the century between the coming of the mission of Augustine in the year 597 and the time of Bede's early work as student and author. In that time the Christian Church had gained a firm foothold in Kent, Northumbria, Mercia, and Wessex. Scholars from England such as Chad, Egbert, Willibrord and Witbert had also settled for a time in Ireland. During this century, something approaching thirty famous scholars had been produced by the newly-founded church in this country ; and here and there a woman had found her place in this distinguished group. Much teaching, too, had been imparted by word of mouth. Those who have tried to assess the scholarship of this first century of the life of the English Church have found much to interest them in the subjects of study as well as in the scholars themselves. Holy Scripture naturally takes first place, as might be expected, seeing that the clergy, whether regular or secular, alone amongst their fellows received any education. Commentaries were written in large numbers ; pupils were taught ; meditation was enjoined ; the writings of the Fathers were studied ; and there was some reading of the classics in Aristotle, Cicero, Vergil, Terence, Juvenal and a few

others. But of scientific studies there are few records.
Astronomy was studied in Kent ; Aldhelm, first bishop
of Sherborne, refers to astrology ; and geometry and
physics were taught by those few English students
who went to Ireland. But these references are so
scarce amongst the copious records of theological and
ecclesiastical study that they cannot be regarded as
other than merely incidental if not accidental. It
may be said with fairness and truth that in his scientific
studies Bede broke fresh ground for an Englishman.
His background is represented by the opening words of
the nineteenth psalm : " The heavens declare the glory
of God : and the firmament sheweth His handiwork."

When Bede had reached that maturity of mind and
knowledge that are essential to the claim of a writer
and teacher to be heard and heeded, the Easter controversy had not yet run its course. The visits to Rome
of Benedict Biscop and Wilfrid had reminded English
Churchmen of the debt which they owed to Rome. In
the south there was no risk that this debt would be forgotten. In the north and in Scotland, however, the
connexion with Rome was much more remote. Lindisfarne had received its foundation from a king and a saint
who had looked to Iona and, beyond that, to Ireland
as the rock from which their religion had been hewn.
When Roman customs of, for example, the tonsure and
the date of Easter reached this country through Benedict
Biscop and Wilfrid, a sharp controversy was provoked,
to settle which a synod was summoned to meet at Whitby.
These questions were settled by the victory of the Roman
party. Bede was born only nine years after this. Iona
and the north of Scotland had refused to accept the
Roman method of reckoning for each year the date of
Easter. There was even more in the question than that,
for the date of Easter determines the dates of all the

greater festivals of the Church from then to (but not including) Christmas, the dates of Ash Wednesday, Good Friday and Lent, and the incidence of the number of Sundays after the Epiphany and after Trinity Sunday.

As the data for settling the question were astronomical, Bede was more than ordinarily interested in the controversy. The evidence produced on both sides is fairly stated by Bede in his *Ecclesiastical History of the English Nation*. The details on which each side had built its case cannot be noticed here ; it is enough to say that the case of each depended on apostolic authority, for St. John had kept Easter between the 14th and 20th days of the moon, and St. Peter between the 15th and 21st days. The views of the Roman party prevailed, and the question was answered once and for all. But it was not accepted everywhere with a good grace. Bede knew of the controversy not only from hearsay but also because he knew those who, while having accepted the ruling of the synod, had not accepted it willingly. It may have been this controversy and the grounds on which it was based that led him to the study of astronomy and chronology. As might have been expected, seeing that he had been the pupil of Benedict Biscop, Bede justified in his writings the wisdom of the settlement that had been made. When the saying was quoted : " Rome is in error ; Jerusalem is in error ; Antioch is in error ; only the Scots and the Britons are right ", who, being a faithful son of the Holy Father, could accept it?

Let us glance now at Bede's work on chronology. Beginning with the smaller units of time, the day, the hour, the week, the month and the year, he arrived at the longest unit of all, the age. He had studied Pliny and, to a greater extent, Isidore of Seville. Following Augustine in *de civitate Dei*, Bede adopted the division of the ages of man from Creation, through the Flood, Abraham, David, the Babylonish Captivity, and the Incarnation, the first five bounded by these events. The sixth began with the Incarnation and ended with the end of the world. The seventh consisted of the " age " of the souls in the intermediate state, from the deaths of the first human beings to the Last Judgment ; and the eighth was Eternity, stretching from the Last Judgment for ever. Some of these divisions will be recognised as those adopted by Ralph Higden in *Polychronicon*. So far, Bede had followed Isidore and Augustine. But he went his own way in matters of chronology. He proved to his own satisfaction that none of the first six ages had lasted for exactly one thousand years, and that this was likely to be true in that the length of the seventh and last earthly age, from the Incarnation to the Last Judgment, was known to none but God. Those—and they were many—who expected the world to come to an end with the year 1000 A.D. would have been reproved by Bede had he then been alive. Events proved him to have been right. For his Old Testament dates, Bede relied not on the Septuagint but on the Vulgate. For his refusal to accept the established dates he was accused of heresy, though not formally tried for it.

Bede's study of history, chronology and astronomy go together. As the starting-point of his conclusions on the length of each of the commonly-accepted " ages " of the world was the creation of the world, it was necessary for him to calculate not only the year but also the date of the first day of creation. This, as was pointed out in the summary of his views given above, was March 18th, three days before the summer solstice. From this he was naturally led to a study of the position of the earth in the universe, the apparent movements of the sun, the moon and the stars, and the other kindred matters referred to in the summary already given. He did not shirk difficulties. Those caused by the differences in the lengths of the months, by leap years and by the differences between the solar and lunar years, he faced and tried to resolve. The exact study of the apparent motions of the heavenly bodies in relation to the motions of the earth, only one of which he recognised, namely, that round its own axis, demands a knowledge of mathematics such as few possess. Yet, with the help of his own books, those in the library of his abbey, and others which doubtless he borrowed, he tackled every problem. He knew about the " epact ", that is, the excess, in number of days, of the solar year over the lunar year, which gave the number of days in the age of the moon on the first day of each " calendar " year, in Bede's time March 1st. He dealt with the difference in length between the calendar months and the lunar month, the latter being the time—about twenty-nine days—which the moon took from one full moon to the next. He visualised that the path of the sun in its apparent—though to him real—movement round the earth, a journey completed in a solar year, formed the limit of an imaginary plane surface called the ecliptic, that the axis of the earth was inclined at an angle of about twenty-three degrees to this imaginary plane, and that this ecliptic formed the limit within which eclipses could take place. The " signs " of the Zodiac were constellations which were seen within a belt of eight or nine degrees on each side of the ecliptic, and it was within these limits that the apparent motions of the sun, the moon and the chief planets took place. Bede knew this ; and he knew also that during each month of the year the sun appeared to pass through one of these signs, each consisting of a group of stars the names of which were well known. The lunar cycle of eighteen years especially interested him, as it was the basis of the computation of the date of Easter every year. The solar cycle was twenty-eight years, which, in the Julian calendar, resulted in the days of the week falling on the same dates once every twenty-eight years. This too was well known from the works of the early astronomers. When Bede drew up his table of the dates of Easter from the year 532 to 1063, he performed as great service to the Church and to the whole of Christendom, which celebrates Easter in one way or another, as those who, in the Book of Common Prayer of the Church of England, drew up hundreds of years afterwards the tables " by means of which to find the date of Easter Day " till the year 2299 inclusive.

In these complicated reckonings, Bede was no mere copyist, for he used his authorities as far as his theological beliefs could accept their conclusions. His industry was remarkable even in days when monks worked as hard as anybody else. He wrote at least forty treatises, his history being the best-known of them and the only reliable authority for the history of this country and people from the time of the Britons to within a few years of his death in the year 735. In addition, he wrote on theological subjects of many kinds, and on astronomy, chronology, arithmetic, medicine, philosophy, grammar (following Donatus), rhetoric, poetry and music. And part of each day was spent in teaching and in the daily religious observances required from every monk. He is said to have refused the office of abbot so that he might be free to write and to teach, to the number of 600 at a time, students who flocked to sit at his feet. The judgment has been passed on him that he was not distinguished by originality, except in history, and that he shared the credulity of his age. It is true that he was a theologian first of all. But he was the finest scholar, the holiest man and the greatest ornament of his time.

A circular calendar

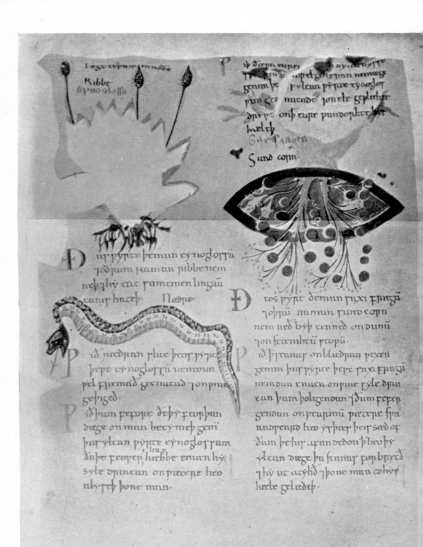

A page from an Anglo-Saxon Herbarium

CHAPTER IV

STRANGE IDEAS

Superstitions

MORE is known than is commonly realised about the manner of life and the hopes and fears of our Anglo-Saxon progenitors. It may or may not be true that, as time goes on, the human race becomes more enlightened. Be that as it may, every age brings to those who live in it its own crop of hopes and fears. In spite of the growing realisation of the connexion between cause and effect, there are still those who believe in the superstitions attached to Fridays, the number 13, walking under a ladder, spilling salt, and the like. A thousand years ago, while there is much evidence of other kinds of ignorance, no trace is evident of the superstitions which haunt thousands in our day. The Anglo-Saxons had their own hopes and fears.

We begin with a list of days on which it was regarded as very dangerous to drink medicine or to be blooded, for fear of either a long illness or even death. Further, those warnings were based on the authority of Latin writers, and could not be ignored. There were 24 such days in the year, the first being what was then New Year's Day, March 1st, because it was the common belief that the world was created in March. The full list of these days was March 1st and 27th, April 10th and 19th, May 3rd and 24th, June 10th and 15th, July 12th and 21st, August 1st and 29th, September 3rd and 20th, October 3rd and 21st, November 5th and 17th, December 7th and 21st, January 1st and 24th, and February 4th and 25th (or 26th). It is solemnly added, in proof of

the truth of this, that a leech had experimented on his
horse in the light of this list and that the horse had died.

In addition, the influence of the moon had to be
reckoned with, for blood-letting was discouraged on the
fourth and fifth nights of the age of a moon, and on All
Hallows' Day (November 1st).

Another superstition was that no female child could be
born at the end of December and on certain days at the
beginning of February, and another that the body of any
boy born on any of these days would not putrefy after
death. The writer adds—very truly, had he only
known—that few understand these mysterious things.

Dream-lore has always had an attraction for many
people, amongst whom we may name the Anglo-Saxon
man. A pre-Conquest manuscript at the British Museum
has the title :

de somnuim diuersitate secundum ordinem abecedarii danielis prophete.
(Of the variety of dreams according to the order of the A B C of
Daniel the prophet.)

Happiness and prosperity followed if a person should
dream about catching fowls, receiving a ring, wearing
a beard, being white-haired, seeing wax tapers, receiving
or reading books, talking with the dead, being robed
like a bishop, having a well sunk in the house, having
a child born, seeing a hen with chickens, seeing bucks,
goats, a bright sun or moon, stars, rain, a lion running,
a smooth sea or snow, hearing music on the pipe, accepting a loaf of barley, hearing thunder, being flogged,
seeing a lock of hair or a flying dragon, seeing oneself
as a judge, bathing in cold water, seeing one's house on
fire, and building a house. On the other hand, it
portended evil to dream about bees flying into one's
house, snakes, being in exile, onions, being with one's
superior, a savage bear, darkness, fat, brimstone, lead,

sheep being sheared, fish throwing stones, waiting in an amphitheatre, being a gladiator, seeing emmets or a flood, having one's face unwashed, trying to run and not succeeding, using bow and arrow, and giving a ring.

To what extent dream-lore was familiar to the average man or woman it is impossible to estimate. It is, however, safe to believe that dreams were a common subject of conversation amongst those who knew the stories of the dreams of Jacob, Joseph and Daniel in the Old Testament, and of Joseph, the Magi and the wife of Pilate in the New Testament. And the belief in the influence of the moon over the destinies and on the minds of human beings is very ancient. The combined effect of this belief about the moon and in the prophetic nature of dreams was enough to form the basis of a dream-table which is found in a manuscript of the pre-Conquest period. The table is summarised as follows, the numbers of the days signifying the days in each period of the progress of the moon from " new " to " full " :

1, 2, 3, 10, 14. No harm can follow.
4, 5, 11, 17, 18, 19, 24, 27, 28, 29. Good will follow.
7, 12, 13, 15, 30. The dream will come true.
6. The dream must not be forgotten.
8, 9. The subject of the dream will become public property. If it is an unpleasant subject, turn your face to the east and pray for mercy.
16. The dream will not be fulfilled for some time.
25, 26. Trouble will follow. Turn your face to the east and pray for mercy.
22, 23. A bad dream, full of gambling and trouble.
20, 21. A dream about trade and barter.

Fortunately, on only four nights is trouble prophesied. And, as probably only a small proportion of people dream every night, the Anglo-Saxon could go to bed on most nights with a mind free from anxiety about the subject of his dreams.

The moon was held to have an influence on the male children born on any of the thirty days of its period :

1. Long life and wealth.
2. Sickness.
3. Long life.
4. False in words.
5, 8, 15, 17, 20.   Early death.
6. Long life and happiness.
7. Long life and honour.
9. Perilous birth.
10. Suffering.
11. Travel abroad.
12. Honour.
13 and 14.   Piety and goodness.
16. Usefulness.
18 and 19.   Happiness.
21. Esteem.
22. Stout championship.
23. Thieving and roguery.
24. Hard work.
25. Abstemiousness.
26. Greedy of work.
27. Born to mischief.
28. Neither poor nor rich.
29 and 30.   Goodness and hospitality.

These prophecies might however be complicated by others that were made about children born on the days of the week :

Sunday.   Handsome ; no anxiety.
Monday.   To be killed by men (*laie or cleric be he*).
Tuesday.   Corrupt, sinful and perverse.
Wednesday.   Sharp, bitter and cautious in word.
Thursday.   Peaceable, easy, good, and averse to women.
Friday.   Silly, crafty, evil, dishonest and cowardly.   Death in middle age.
Saturday.   Renowned and long-lived.   The child will become an ealdorman.

For each of the days of the age of the moon there was an activity which would be crowned with success if undertaken on it. These include petitions to the king if made at the third hour of the day, i.e., 9 a.m., or at high tide ; the purchase of land ; travel or marriage ; management of an estate in land and the good company of friends ; fishing ; reconciliation with enemies ; the settling of disputes ; ploughing, grinding or selling ; the advice of a counsellor ; providing fresh hay for one's bed ; building a church or a ship ; requests to a lord ; fishing, or taking blood-money from a nobleman ; choosing a bishop, an ealdorman or a king ; moving into a new house, taking to it oil and milk, or milking cattle ; dyeing, ordaining a priest or admitting a nun ; hunting harts or wild swine with hounds ; travelling abroad ; and entering or founding a " minster " (that is, a large church). Only the first seventeen days of the age of the moon are so dealt with.

A similar table, but much longer, contains a list of objects that would be attained on each of the thirty days of the period of a moon. These include the promise that a male child will be clever, scholarly, wise and famous ; that a female child would be good-tempered, good-looking, pure, sagacious and marriageable ; letting blood ; refraining from letting blood ; taming cattle or castrating boars ; the birth of children who will not prove to be amiable ; the progress, long or short, of illness ; the fulfilment or the non-fulfilment of dreams ; felling trees ; sowing seed or changing the homes of bees ; commending sick people to God ; sending children to school ; sowing, marrying or travelling ; buying serfs ; death to a thief ; taking a bride to her new home ; the birth of a child who will become a leech ; and hunting. Chiefly, however, the promises concern the characteristics of children born on each day of the age of the moon, the fulfilment or the non-fulfilment of dreams, and the progress of sick people towards recovery.

Finally, the weather, perennially a source of specu-
lation. The mass-days of mid-winter are the days chosen.
If this mass-day falls on a Sunday, the winter will be
mild, the spring boisterous, and the summer dry, and
vineyards, sheep and bees will be profitable. If on
a Monday, there will be a hard winter, a tempestuous
spring, mortality amongst women and kings, and a wet
summer. If on a Tuesday, the winter will be variable,
the spring pleasant and the summer windy. If on
a Wednesday, a hard and fierce winter, an unsatisfactory
spring and a warm summer, with a poor yield from
vineyards and bees. If on a Thursday, each season will
be true to type, and there will be a prosperous yield
from everything. If on a Friday, the winter will be
changeable, the summer good and the yield rich. If on
a Saturday, the winter will be good and abundant, the
spring tempestuous and fruit scarce ; sheep will die, and
the innocent will be found guilty.

Similar prophecies are made in connexion with the
twelve days from Christmas Day to the Epiphany on
January 6th. Priests, ealdormen, sheep and cattle are
likely to die, fruit to perish, high winds to spoil the
prospects of the harvest, and fire to destroy property ;
trees will come into leaf late, and battles will be fought.
Sunshine on the same twelve days may betoken, according to the day of the week on which these dates fall,
prosperity, quarrels, peace amongst kings, a good fruit-
harvest, abundance of milk, fruit and fish, and, on one
day in the week, bloodshed.

Thunder is also the subject of prophecy, according as
it is heard on each day of the week. It may betoken
bloodshed, the deaths of princes, judges, husbands and
women, and poor crops.

Alchemy

The so-called chemists of the middle ages spent much time in the search for the universal solvent (*alkahest*), the universal remedy (*panacea*) and the universal transmutation of the baser metals into gold (alchemy). Those of them who were interested also in remedies for the diseases which have always attacked human beings and in the prolongation of human life, if possible for ever, pursued the will-o'-the-wisp of the quintessence, the fifth essence of the ancient medical lore which was the substance of which the heavenly bodies—the sun and the stars—were made. This essence was regarded as having been hidden from human knowledge and yet as existing in a hidden form somewhere on earth. It was confidently believed that it could be obtained by distillation, and in consequence the search for it became one of the chief preoccupations of medical chemists. To the Hindu mind there were five " elements ", these being earth, air, water, fire and ether. As long as forty centuries ago, the Chinese five were earth, water, fire, metals and wood. What was meant by *element* was never settled. Even the Greeks, pioneers of the sciences, believed that gold and silver could be manufactured. Those who believed in Hermes, the god of reproduction, had him as their sun-god, who, they believed, hid himself among the souls of the dead. It was on such unpromising material that the Isaac Newtons of the future had to build the sciences of chemistry and physics. The wonder is that they were ever able to build anything at all.

The Book of the Quintessence

In the same class as the books of cures for the diseases that afflicted mankind may be placed :

The Book of Quinte Essence or the Fifth Being ; that is to say, Man's Heaven. A tretise in englisch breuely drawe out of the book of quintis essencijs in latyn that hermys the prophete and kyng of Egipt, after the flood of Noe, fadir of philosophris, hadde by revelacioun of an aungil of god to him sende.

It is one thing for the elderly to wish that they might regain their youth : it is another thing for them to believe that anything under the sun can give it back to them. The medieval man not only entertained this high hope, but also had faith that it could be realised. He was encouraged in this faith by this remarkable book, a copy of which, written during the reign of Edward IV, is amongst the Sloane collection in the British Museum. The bearer of this exclusive revelation of the one and only method of regaining lost youth is stated to be Hermes, king of Egypt and " father of philosophers " :

that the wijsdom and the science of this book schulde not perische but be kept and preserued, vnto the eende of the world, of alle holy men from al wickid peple and tyrauntis for greet perilis that myghte falle therof.

This astonishing treatise of about 9,000 words begins with the confident statement that " olde euangelik men and feble in kynde " can be restored to their first youth only if they have not suffered from " thunder blast " or violent injuries, and have not wasted their vigour by overmuch fasting. The miraculous remedy went by the names of " burning water ", " the soul in the spirit of wine ", " the water of life ", or, more generally, " quinte essence ", believed to be the substance of which the heavenly bodies were composed, and to be latent in everything. Further, it could be obtained by means of distillation. The belief in such a substance was widespread, the ancient Hindus and Chinese believing that it existed or could be made. By preserving from corruption " what pece of fleisch, fisch or dead bird " might be immersed in it, this heaven-sent remedy was indeed worthy to be called " man's heaven ". The divine secret, however, must be kept from wicked men. In the most serious and sober way the writer of the treatise describes five ways of making it.

(1) Distil the best wine, or any wine that is not sour, to obtain the dregs, which are composed of the "four elements". When these have been distilled seven times, "burning water" will be obtained. This in its turn must be distilled until it is converted into "Quinte Essence" and separated from the four elements. After one-thousand more distillations :

> by the which it is sublymed to so myche highnes of glorificatioun it schal come that it schal be a medicyn incorruptible almoost as heuene aboue and be of the nature of heuene.

Let many days elapse before the vessel is unstopped, when,

> if ther come out a passynge heuenly swete flauour that alle men that come yn naturely drawe therto, thanne ye haue oure *quinta essencia*, and ellis sele the vessel and putte it to the fier agen till ye haue it.

(2) Pour the "burning water" into an amphora, seal it securely, and bury it, neck downwards, in horse-dung. When the impurities have settled in the neck of the amphora, puncture the seal and release the "erthey water". What is left is "oure quinte essence".

(3) As in (2), but, instead of burying the amphora in horse-dung,

> birie it well in the wombe of an horse.

(4) Use a strong glass vessel, or one of "erthe strongly glasie", with a tube of glass one foot long which hangs downwards from the top of the vessel so that the vapour, as it condenses in the process of distillation, can be collected from the glass tube. It is comforting to learn that

> this instrument may ye do make without great cost.

(5) Distil the "burning water" ten times in "hors dounge contynuely digest".

Lest it be thought that the credulity of the medieval man was without foundation in a belief more secure than that in the virtues of ordinary wine, the treatise makes it plain that the properties of "quinte essence" are conferred on it by

serene mineralle, fynyd [refined], schynynge, incorruptible,

which is "very gold of the myn", the power of which is derived from "sol the planet". On this remarkable process of reasoning is based also the method :

how pore euangelik men may haue withoute cost and almoost for noughte the gracious influence of gold.

All that these men have to do is :

to preie a riche man that is youre freend to leene you a good floreyn of Florence,

to heat it on an iron plate, to throw it into "burning water" or white wine, quenching the fire quickly, and to repeat this process 49 more times, using a fresh supply of water each time so as to obtain a good deal of the "burning water" so treated. This curious mixture must then be added to "quinte essence" :

Thus ye haue oure heuene, and the summe in him fixed, to the conseruation of mannys nature and fixacioun of oure heuene, that is, oure quinte essence.

Medieval inventiveness knew no bounds. The writer of this treatise knew how to produce fire :

withoute cole, withoute lyme.

Declaring that :

the priuytee is so vertuous that the vertu herof may not all be declarid, he lets out the secret. Mercury that is sublimated with vitriol and common salt and " sal armoniac " seven times must be mixed in equal portions, ground small, spread on a marble stone and left at night :

> in a soft cleer eir or ellis in a coold seler,

when it will turn into water. This liquid is so strong that :

> if a little drope herof falle opon youre hond anoon it wole perce it thorough out and in the same maner it wole do if it falle vpon a plate of venus or Iubiter into this water, it turneth hem into lijknes of peerl. Who so coude reperale and preparate kyndely this fier, withoute doute it wolde quanche anoon a brennynge sijknes clepid the fier of helle . . . And this is a greete priuytee.

The substance was called " sal amarus ".
Quinte Essence could also be made out of antimony :

> The science to drawe out of antymony . . . is a souereyn maistre and a priuytee of alle priuytees.

The antimony must be powdered and put into the best distilled vinegar, and the mixture heated in a glass " vpon a litit fier " until the vinegar turns red. The vinegar must then be poured out and fresh vinegar poured on the remains of the antimony. When this has been repeated several times, all the vinegar must be put into a " distillatorie " :

> First the vynegre wole ascande. Thanne after ye schal se merueilis, for ye schal as it were se a thousand dropis of blessid wiyn discende doun in maner of reed drops, as it were blood, by the pipe of the lymbike [alembic]. The which licour gadere togidere in a torumbe [vessel] and thanne ye haue a thing that al the tresour of the world may not be in comparisoun of worthines therto aristotle seith that it is his lede in the boke of secretis although he telle not the name of the antymonye aforseide. Forsothe this doith awey ache of alle woundis and wondirfully heelith. The vertu therof is incorruptible and merueilous profit-

able it needit to be putrefied in a rotumbe and seelid in fyme
and thanne it worchip greet priuytees. Forsothe the quinta
essencia of this antymony that is reed, in the which is the secreet
of alle secretis, is sweetere than ony hony or sugre or ony othir
thing.

To obtain the quintessence from blood, obtain some

reserued of Barbouris whanne thei lete blood, also fro fleisch of
all brute beestis, and fro alle eggis and othere suche thingis.
For als myche as mannes blood be the perfitist werk of kynde in
us as to be encrees of that that is lost, it is certeyn that nature
they 5 essence maad so perfight that withoute ony othir greet
preparacioun withoute the veynes it berith forth that blood anoon
aftir into fleisch, and this essence is so nygh kynde that it is moost
to haue. Forwhy, in it is merueylous vertu of oure heuene sterris,
and to the cure of nature of man worchith moost deuyn myraclis,
as withinne I schal teche you. Therefore resceyue of Barbouris
of yong sangueyn men, or colerik men, whanne thei be late blood,
the which vse good wynes. Take that blood aftir that it hath
reste, and caste awey the watir fro it, and braie it with the 10 part
of comen salt preparate to medicyns of men, and putte it into a
uessel of glas clepid amphora, the which, sotely seele, and putte
it withinne the wombe of an hors, preparate as tofore, and nenewe
the fyme oonys in the wike, or more, and lete it purifie til al the
blood be turned into watir and it schal be doon at the mooste in xxx
or xl dayes, or aftir, more or lasse. Thanne putte it in a lembike
and distille it on a good fier what so euere may ascande, putte that
watir vpon the fecis brayed, meyngynge vpon a marbil stoon,
putte it aghen manye tymes rehersynge. And whanne ye haue
this noble thing of blood, therof the 5 beynge drawe out putte
aghen the watir in the stillatorie of circulacioun till ye brynge it
to so myche swetnes and an heuenly sauour as ye dide the
brennynge watir. And this is the 5 beyngs of blood deuyn, and
miraclis more than man mai bileue but if he se it.

If :

capouns, hennes and al maner of fleisch of brut beestis and al
maner eggis of foulis that ben holsum and medicynable to ete
for mankinds be

ground up in a mortar, with one-tenth part of common

salt added, and the whole be put into the womb of a horse
and distilled :

> til it be brought to the swete heuenly sauour and small aforseid,

more quintessence is at your command.

This portion of the treatise ends with a long and tedious
and almost incomprehensible account of how to draw the
" fifth being " out of all the four elements—earth, air,
fire and water—and then to separate them from each
other.

The " book of medicyns " follows, in which the various
doses of the quintessence are prescribed.

> An oold feble euangelik man can be made to fele him self of the
> statt and the strengthe of xl yeer withinne a fewe dayes, and he
> schal haue grete joie that he is come to the statt of yongthe.

But he must continue to take small doses of the medicine
and to :

> vse ofte good wiyn at his mete and at the soper, in the whiche be
> fixed the 5 essence of gold as I taughte you before.

The miraculous medicine could also be used to restore to
health a man :

> so mygh deed that he is forsake of lechis . . . for right few lechis
> now lyuynge knowe this priuytee.

Leprosy caused by :

> corrupcioun and putrefaccioun of any of the principal humouris
> but not the lepre that cometh to man of kynde of the fadir or of
> the modir ne the lepre that is sent of God by his plage,

also yielded to treatment if the leper could be washed in
water made of the juice of the strawberry or the mulberry.
Palsy, frenzy and gout were easily cured in similar ways,
it being pointed out that " colerik ", " sangueyn " and
" flewmatik " men, and men " that habounde in blak

coler, that is, malencoly " men, need no longer despair of recovery.

These medicines, however, can do more than heal bodily disorders, for mental troubles melt away before them :

Forsothe these medicyns puttith awey wickid thoughtis and an heuy herte malencolious, thei gladith and clense the brayn and alle hise myghtis, and brynge yn egalnes and merye thoughtis thei putte awey also the craft of the feeindis temptaciouns and ymagynaciouns of despeir thei destroie, and make a man to forgete almaner of yueles and naturaly bryngith him aghen to resonable wit. And for as myche as saturne the planete naturaly ys coold and drye, and is enemye to al kynde, forwhy, euery snow, euery hayl, euery tempest, and also the humour of malencoly cometh of him, and he hath his influence vpon derk leed and vpon derk placis vnder the erth, foule and stynkynge, and derke wodis, and vpon foule, horrible, solitarie placis, as it is preyed in *vitas patrum*, that is to seye, in lyues and colaciouns of fadris. And also the moone, naturely coold and moist, hath his influence vpon the nyght and vpon myche moisture and vpon the placis whanne 4 weyes metith togidere, forsothe in alle siche placis thei wole abide and schewe hem to her foloweris, but forsothe tho thingis that ben of the nature of Iupiter and of sol, goode planetis, are displesynge to him, and contrarie and naturaly deuiles fle awei from hem for thei haue greet abhominacioun of ther vertuous influence, therfor it schewith weel that tho thingis that ben in this world, summe thei ben that bitokene the glorious yoie of heuene, and summe thing that figure the derknesse of euerlasting peynes of helle. Forsothe the sunne and iupiter, goode planetis, and gold, pure metal and alle pure thingis that gladen a man, figurynge by resoun the ioie of heuene and blak Saturne, and the spotty moone, figure and bitokene the condicioun of helle. Therfore thei hate the clennesse and ioie of oure lord god and of his seyntis, also thei haten the sunne and his cleernes, and pure thingis that maken a man glad, and naturaly it plesith hem to dwelle in derk and in blak, horrible, stynkynge placis, in heuynesse, wreche and malencoly, and in tho thingis that pretende the condicioun of helle. And sith oure 5 essence aforseid is to heuenly a thing, and by sotil craft brought to so myche swetnes, it is so soueryn a medicyn that it may weel be lijkned to the ioie of paradise. For-

whi, it makith a man light, iocunde, glad, and merie, and puttith
away heuynesse, angre, malencopy, and wraththe, the whiche
that deuilis loue and *ideo nostra essencia digne vocatur celum humanum*
(on that account our essence is deservedly called the human
heaven). Also if a man be trauelyid with a feend and may not
be deliuerid fro him, let him drinke a litil quantite of oure
5 essence, with 5 essence of gold and peerl, and with an eerbe
called ypericon, i.e., *fuga demonum*, and the seed therof be grounden
and aftirward distillid, and the watir therof a litil quantite medlid
[mixed] with the othere *quintis essenciis*, and anoon the deuel wole
fle awey fro him and fro his hous.

It seemed good to quote in full this long statement of
promises. Prescriptions follow which are guaranteed
" for to hele yche and for to distrie lies " (destroy lice),
to cure " quarteyn fever " (a fever of which one symptom
was a seizure or paroxysm every fourth day, or, as it
would now be calculated, every third day), persistent
fever, and tertian fever (in which the seizures recur every
second, not every third, day), and " to make a man that
is a coward hardy and strong ".

Finally, pestilential fever, which cannot be cured if it is
sent by God " to ponysche synne ", a man would be
a " gret fool " if he presumed to try to cure, though all
such other fevers that :

come to mankynde by perilous influence of yuele planetis, by the
grace of God and good governaunce, may be cured partially,

with the essence that was guaranteed to cure :

a man that is almost consumed and waaisted in al his body and
right leene.

But, in addition, those afflicted with this fever must take
every morning :

a eye-schelle ful of good brennynge watir and also vse in the dayes
two or thre smal *pelotes pestilenciales*

[i.e., pills to cure the pestilence], and also fumigate his house

> with frank-encense, mirie and rosyn, terbentyn [and rewe,
> a perfight cure for the feuere pestilence.

But—and here the writer breaks into Latin—should these secrets become known by worldly, tyrannical and reprobate persons, with the result that their lives be prolonged only so that they may continue in their evil courses, dire calamities will ensue. Therefore only good and holy men must know of them. The treatise ends :

> Ego autem quantum in me est propter solos sanctos librum hunc
> constituo et ipsum custodiae Ihesu Christi commendo nunc et in
> eternum.

Which, being translated into English, means :

> And, so far as in me lies, for the sake of these good people alone,
> I commend this my work to the keeping of Jesus Christ, now
> and for ever.

CHAPTER V

MEDICINE—I

THE invention of the Greek legend that Asklepios
(Latin, Aesculapius), son of Apollo, learned the
art of healing from Cheiron the centaur, and that, in
fear lest men should be rendered immortal through his
aid, Zeus slew him with one of his thunderbolts—the
invention of this legend—is the beginning of the history,
in the written records of mankind, of the art of healing.
Temples were erected in honour of Asklepios near
medicinal springs much as, in modern times, spas have
grown up round such springs ; and, by the end of the
third century B.C., the study of the art of healing was
introduced into Rome. As Asklepios was probably
a real man, mixed up with much that is legendary about
him was something that was true. Solid ground is
touched for the first time, however, with Hippocrates,
who, not long after the middle of the fifth century B.C.,
was born at Cos and became a follower of Asklepios.
Like all the greatest of the Greeks, he pursued his aims
intelligently and scientifically. If indeed they can all
be attributed to him, he left behind him not far short
of one-hundred treatises, which reveal his greatness as
a pioneer. He was no specialist, being both physician
and surgeon. Of the operating theatre he wrote that the
qualities to be aimed at were skill, grace, speed, painless-
ness, elegance and alertness. As every newly-qualified
medical man takes the Hippocratic oath, he must realise
his debt to his great forerunner.

The next famous student of medicine and surgery in
the classical world was Galen, who died at the beginning

of the second century B.C. After studying in Asia Minor and at Alexandria, he settled at Rome. His chief contribution to the study of medicine and surgery lies in his skilful dissection of the bodies of apes and other animals and his research in physiology. These two, Hippocrates and Galen, laid a sure foundation of which, for many centuries, those who came after them were not worthy.

Anglo-Saxon Medicine

Pliny the Elder, who lost his life in the eruption of Vesuvius in 79 A.D., tells us a good deal about the superstitious attitude of the " wise men " of the East, in his time, towards disease. The plant known as feverfue (*pyrethrum parthenium*), a remedy reputed to put fevers to flight, must be plucked with the left hand, the name of the patient must be spoken as the plant is being gathered, and in no circumstances must the person who gathers the plant look behind him as he goes on his way. This and other plants were regarded as cures for a variety of diseases, such as headache, poor eyesight, rheumatism, gout, lumbago, toothache, " phrensy " or delirium, epilepsy, snake-bite and dysentery, and even as a protection against ghosts, mad dogs and family quarrels. Anybody who swallowed the live heart of a mole would be endowed with gifts of divination ; and the blood of a mole, if sprinkled on the head of a maniac, would cure him. Needless to say, primitive people also believed in the power of amulets and charms ; indeed, all through the history of the human race the " mascot " has had, and still has, its devotees. But, side by side with these beliefs of the childhood of the human race, the properties of certain herbs were known and applied. There existed, therefore, the glimmerings of scientific knowledge of the healing properties of those natural products which form the bases of many drugs which are still in daily use,

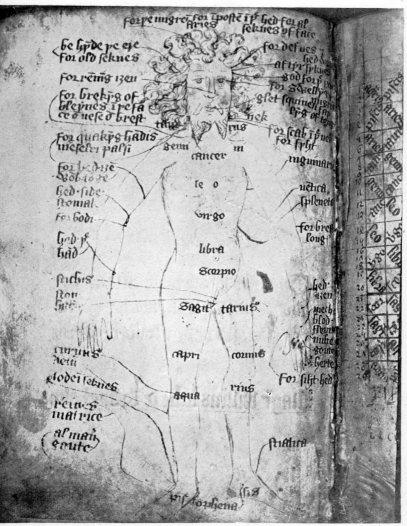

The Human Body and the Signs of the Zodiac

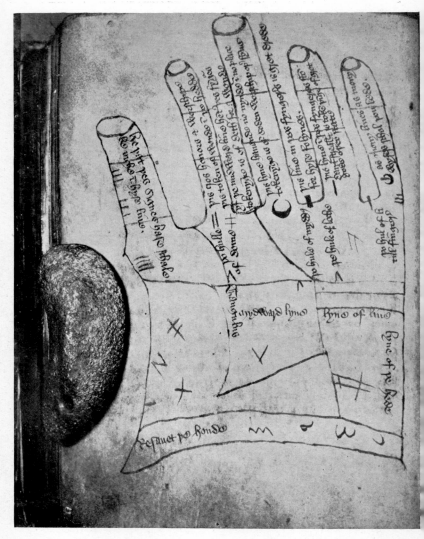

Medieval Palmistry

though now applied by those who have been trained in their use.

As time went on, the early physicians and surgeons regarded the head as being the seat of the " humours ", the chest (because it contained the heart) of the blood, the abdomen (because it contained the organs of digestion) of the " raw bile ", and the bladder of the " swart bile ". Each of these was thought to be peculiarly liable to attacks of disease at certain seasons of the year, a delusion which even the Greeks entertained. An Anglo-Saxon manuscript in the British Museum attributes to Plato and Aristotle the belief that, beginning with Christmas Day, the " humour " in the head increased for three months, and so on with the " humours " in the other parts of the body. There were also forty-five days in the year during which nobody ought to be bled. Then follow remedies against almost every conceivable form of disease, a few of which may be given. Sleeplessness could be cured by drinking a mixture of wormwood and either wine or warm water ; nasal obstruction (caused by a cold in the head) or difficult breathing, by sniffing powdered hellebore into the nostrils ; and loose teeth could be tightened by holding in the mouth the " ooze " from a pounded leek, mixed with vinegar and honey and thrice boiled, and taken into the mouth " as hot as a man can bear it ". According to the Greeks, " man's dignity and all necessity is on the teeth . . . and the tongue is companion to the teeth in speech ". Teeth are of three classes, (1) the first teeth, " which in a manner receive wisdom ", (2) those that break the meat, and (3) the grinders, " for they grind all that man liveth on ". Teeth, however, are not made of bone, because they have no marrow and because, unlike bones, when they break they cannot be " set " and made to knit together. But when the moisture from the head, falling upon the teeth, loosens them, they can again be made firm by holding in the mouth water which has been boiled in a new pot with a piece of the hide of a hart. If this remedy is used as often as necessary, the teeth " will soon be mended ".

These remedies, which are typical of those found earlier in this treatise, could be paralleled by scores of others which were in common use against diseases of the head such as sores, ulcers, giddiness, diseases of the ears, blindness, dimness of sight, a stye on the eye, sores on the tongue, loss of voice, chilblains, scurfy nails, loss of skin, asthma, heart disease and acidity of the stomach, and also diseases of the abdomen. The treatise ends with the views of Hippocrates that in some bodies there are more veins than there are in others, the bodies of people who have more veins being warmer than those who have fewer veins. And another treatise, of which only a fragment is left, explains how the sex of a child can be foretold before it is born.

Those who have read Bede's well-known History will remember that he has two references to the work of surgeons. When Ethelfryth, wife of King Egfrid, who had left her husband for the nunnery of Coldingham, suffered from a swelling, she was treated by a surgeon but died soon afterwards. The second is the well-known story of Herebald, the favourite pupil of St. John of Beverley, who, against the wishes of his master, joined his fellow-pupils in horse-races and was thrown from his horse, fracturing his skull. A leech set the broken bone and bound up the young man's head so skilfully that, aided by the prayers of his master, Herebald recovered. The Anglo-Saxons produced kings such as Alfred the Great, ecclesiastics such as Dunstan and Ethelwold, and scholars such as Aldhelm, Alcuin and Bede, but few, if any, men of science. Only Bede wrote about such subjects as astronomy and geography ; and his knowledge of these was conditioned by the teaching of the Church. As time went on, as much reliance was placed on charms as on prayer and the skill of the leech. The need was met by the creation of the order of exorcists, which, in the third century A.D., was added to the other orders conferred by the Church. At certain periods of the year, evil spirits that were regarded as the cause of bodily or mental disorders were exorcised by the appointed ministers of the Church. The ministry was no sinecure, for the demand for it was great. Using his book of exorcisms, the exorcist would bid the evil spirit depart by invoking the Name of the Trinity.

Side by side with the exorcist there lived and worked in Anglo-Saxon England the wizard, the witch and the " medicine man ", all of whom were ready to sell their skill even in such obscure and troublesome problems as unrequited love, to which end drugged beer and ale could work wonders.

The leech had to undergo training before he was allowed to practise his art. " As leeches know how " is a phrase that is met in Anglo-Saxon writings, though few leeches knew how to use surgical instruments, relying solely on blood-letting, whatever disease they were pretending to cure. The names of very few leeches have survived from these early times.

With the belief in witchcraft went a belief in elves, who were supposed to live on high land, in woods or near water. Anyone who suffered from the disease of the water-elf, one symptom of which was manifested by livid finger-nails and watery eyes, could be cured only by the use of certain herbs and incantations. There was a kind of hiccup known as elf-hiccup. Dwarfs were shunned as workers of evil and as being in league with the devil. Their fabled power to make themselves invisible by wearing the " hell-cap " or " hell-clothing " made them specially fearsome. Storms and tempests and even death were caused by witches and wizards. An attempt was made by king Cnut to put a stop to these superstitious practices ; his actual words are worth quoting as revealing his enlightened nature :

And we forbid earnestly every heathenship, that a man reverence idols, that is, that a man reverence heathen gods, the sun or the moon, fire or flood, waterwylls or stones, trees of the wood of any sort, or love witchcraft, or perform underhand work in any wise, either by way of sacrifice or divining, or perform any act of such delusions.

Yet even Bede believed that storms could be raised by witches. He records that the ship in which Germanus, bishop of Auxerre, and Lupus, bishop of Troyes, were voyaging home was driven out of its course by demons, who, however, dispersed when the two holy men bade them, in the Name of the Trinity, depart. Then the storm ceased.

But the supernatural was not always resorted to. In our far-away ancestors there was a strong strain of common sense ; and from early times the medicinal use of herbs and other natural products was studied and applied. One record of this study, a *herbarium*, is to be seen in a beautifully-written book containing drawings of the plants so that they could be identified. They include waybread, cinquefoil (five-leaf), henbane, adderwort, beewort, lions'-foot, calvewort, mugwort, dock, field-wort, cress, great wort, hart clover, woodruff, beet, strawberry plant, marshmallow, hock leaves, horehound, madder, white poppy, verbena, clover, celandine, fern, bramble, yarrow, rue, salvia, basil, mint, dill, parsley, mandrake, gorse, foxglove, liquorice, elder, cummin, larkspur and nettle. Hydele was prescribed for application to the gums if the teeth were sore or " if they wag " ; horehound was efficacious in many cases, such as cold in the head, catarrh (" in case a man hreaks heavily "), stiffness of the joints and lung-trouble. A fractured skull, called " a broken head ", was treated with the application of foxes' foot ; falling hair with water-wort ; sleeplessness with a mixture made of the poppy-flower ; bad eyesight, headache and burns with celandine ; gout and wounds, especially those caused with iron, with groundsel. Yarrow (*Achilles millefolium*), said to have been used by Achilles, cured toothache, hiccup, snake-bite or bites from mad dogs, wounds and hardness of the veins ; an unconscious person could be restored with rue, which was recommended also for nose-bleeding and eye-trouble ; spearwort had to be eaten when the patient with loose teeth was undergoing a fast, the claim being made for it that " it steadies the teeth " ; and adder-wort, when hung on a line in front of a hive, besides being a remedy against the bite of an adder kept the bees inside the hive.

Examples may be given of the directions contained in the herbarium :

If a man become tired in mickle riding or in mickle walking let him take of betony the wort one full drachm ; seethe it in sweetened wine ; let him then drink at night fasting three cups full ; then will he be soon unweary.

If any man swallow poison let him take of betony wort three drachms by weight and four cups of wine ; let him boil them together and drink. Then he will spew up the poison.

For the bite of a mad hound, take betony wort, knock it very small, and lay it on the wound.

For sore of loins and if a man's thighs ache, take of the same wort by weight of two drachms ; boil it in beer and give him to drink.

If any propose to make a journey let him take in hand mugwort, and let him have it with him. Then he will not feel much toil in his journey.

For sore of feet, take the same wort and pound it with lard lay it to the feet ; it removes the soreness.

For swollen glands, which wax on the groin, take dock, pound it with old grease without salt, three parts of grease to one of dock. Mix it into a ball, fold it in the leaf of a cabbage, make it smoke on hot ashes, and lay it on the glands, bandaging it to them.

For lunacy, lay peony on the lunatic as he lies down ; when he gets up he will be cured, and the lunacy will not attack him again.

To stop nose-bleeding, apply rue to the nostrils ; it stanches the blood wonderfully.

To avert evil, take wood thistle at sunrise when the moon is in Capricorn. No evil can then approach.

Some remedies were connected with outside things or occurrences :

To avoid inflamed eyes, when you see a star fall or cross the heavens count quickly, for you will be free from the trouble for as many years as you count numbers.

For the same, write on a clean sheet of paper, οὐβαίχ, and hang this round the sufferer's neck with a thread from a loom.

For pain in the eyes, tie in unwrought flax as many knots as there are letters in the patient's name, pronouncing each as you tie a knot, and tie it round his neck.

For cataract or white spots, catch a fox alive, cut his tongue out, let him go, dry the tongue, tie it in a red bag, and hang it round the neck.

If a bone be stuck in your throat, say thrice nine times : " I buss the Gorgon's mouth."

When you have toothache, say *argidam margidam sturgidam*, spit in the mouth of a frog and ask the frog to make off with the toothache.

For a sore eyelid, poke the sore with nine grains of barley and say : Flee, flee ; barley thee chaseth.

For quinsy, take hold of the throat with the thumb, the ring finger and the middle finger, cocking up the other two fingers, and the quinsy will disappear.

The use of herbs, however, did not exhaust the ingenuity or the credulity of early man, for animals such as the badger, the fox, the wolf, the hare, the goat, the ram, the

boar, the lion, the bull and the dog were pressed into
service when he was ill :

> Catch a badger, draw his teeth while he is alive, and say :
> " I thee slay and draw thy teeth." Then tie them in a garment
> and they will protect thee from hail, storm, wicked men and
> pestilence. Take his right forefoot " for a leechdom ". With
> its aid thou shalt be victorious in any fight. With the suet from
> the badger thou shalt smear an horse that is in a fever and it shall
> recover.
>
> For difficult breathing, put the lung of a fox into sweetened
> wine and drink the mixture.
>
> For sore ears, mix a fox's gall with oil and smear the ears with it.
>
> To avoid oversleeping, drink a hare's brain in wine ; " wonder-
> fully it amendeth ".
>
> For dimness of eyes, mix a hare's gall with honey and smear
> the eyes with it. It " brighteneth the eyes ".
>
> For sore feet, beat a boar's lung small, and mix it with honey.
> " Quickly this salve healeth the sore ".
>
> For sleep, lay a wolf's head under the pillow. " The unhealthy
> shall sleep ".
>
> If, while you are on a journey, you see a wolf, he will not
> attack you if you have with you a wolf's back hair and tail-hair,
> the extremest part thereof. You shall journey without fear, and
> " the wolf shall sorrow about his journey ".
>
> Let those who suffer apparitions eat lion's flesh ; they will not
> again see apparitions.
>
> To remove ugly marks from the face, smear the face with the
> blood of a bull. " It taketh away all the marks."
>
> For a bad spasm, drink in heated wine a bull's marrow. " That
> amendeth."
>
> For pain and pricking sensation in the eyes, break to pieces
> the head of a hound. If the right eye ache, take the right eye,
> if the left eye ache, take the left eye, and bind it on the affected
> eye. " It healeth well."
>
> For toothache, burn to ashes the tusks or the canine teeth of a
> hound, heat a cupful of wine, put the dust in, and drink. " So
> do frequently, and the teeth shall be whole."

The more serious maladies which attack human beings
are not, however, regarded as being beyond the skill of

the Anglo-Saxon leech, as the following remedies will shew :

> For hare-lip, pound mastic very small, add the white of an egg, and mix well. Then cut with a knife the false edges of the lip, sew the wound fast with silk, and smear the wound within and without with this salve. Continue the use of the salve until the wound be healed.

> In cases of leprosy, the fat of a horse mixed with salt was regarded as efficacious. Directions are also given for the making of a bath for a leprous person, the water used being boiled with rind of various kinds.

> To relieve attacks of lumbago, two pennyweights of betony and two bowlfuls of sweet wine were mixed with hot water and given to a patient to drink while he was fasting. Groundsel was also used for this purpose, the juice being squeezed out of it.

The remedy for palsy was somewhat grim :

> Take a cupful of boiling water, another of oil, and a little salt, and shake thoroughly. This must be drunk " by drops ". After a short time, " poke thy finger into the gullet, spew up again all and more if thou may ". The next morning, let blood from the arm, scarify the patient, smear him with hot oil and give him a pinch of salt. Then cover up the wounds and let them heal.

A somewhat revolting description is given of a man who has " lung disease " :

> Hereinafter are set forth the loathly tokens of lung disease, whence it cometh and how one must work leechdoms against it. The breast is upblown, and the thigh muscle is sore, and the man's maw distendeth much, and his legs and feet swell much with evil unfeeling swellings, and a drier cough vexes him, and in the cough at whiles his voice is gone. Smear the man with oil and warm the sides and the ribs with new wool, and between the shoulders, a little before evening. Then let the oil remain on him. After that, let him blood from the sound elbow in an oven where the fire cannot harm him. If thou lettest him too much blood there will be no hope of his life.

Typhus was treated with prayer as well as medicine. The patient was given a hot drink of rams' gall, fennel

" *Put out your tongue* "

Leech and patient

Mumps   *Cataract*

Inhaling fumes   *A skin disease*

Two operations of trepanning

and waybread, over which, before the mixture was made, many masses were sung. Holy water was then added, the mixture was brought to the boil, and the patient drank " a great cup full, as hot as he may ". The names of the four evangelists were then said over him, and a prayer, with the words : " Thine hand vexeth ; thine hand vexeth ". The patient then wrote down the words of the prayer on his left breast, and someone put on his breast the words : " Emmanuel ; Veronica ".

Dropsy was treated by rubbing the patient with betony soaked in warm water, which the patient also drank for three days. He also drank a mixture of the juice of the root of the ashthroat or dwarf elder and wine. Another remedy was to give a patient to drink a mixture of wine and the juice of either the roots of the ashthroat or those of the dwarf elder—four spoonfuls to a bowlful of wine. Much space is given to the treatment of patients who have taken poison and even to protect people from the effects of poison :

> Against any poison. Eat ere the danger cometh radish and clote ; no man may then do thee mischief with poison.
> In case a man swallow poison, take horehound, work up a mickle deal of it, and adderwort, pound them together and wring the juice, pour thereon three measures of wine and give this to the poisoned man to drink. . . . For stroke of a viper, take a certain remedy, and say thrice the prayer of St. John.

One disease which is described is the " half-dead " disease, which attacks either side of the body ; the sinews are powerless and are affected with

> a slippery and thick humour, evil, thick and mickle.

The treatment consisted of blood-letting, medicine and leechdoms. The patient's mouth must be examined, when his tongue will be found to be whiter " on that side on which the disease is about to be ". He must be kept

warm and quiet, and of course in bed. If his hands are
cold, " on that cold vein let him blood ", using a cupping-
glass if necessary. Other remedies for this disease, which
appears to have been paralysis, are given. The disease,
the writer continues :

> cometh on a man after 40 or 50 winters. If he be of a cold nature
> then it cometh after 40 ; otherwise it cometh after 50 winters of
> his tale of years. If it happen to a younger man it is easier to
> cure, and it is not the same disease, though unclever leeches ween
> that it is the same half-dead disease. How can a like disease
> come on a man in youth in one limb, as the half-dead disease
> doth in old age ? It is not the half-dead disease, but some mis-
> chievous humour is effused on the limb on which the harm settles.
> But it is easier of cure, and the true half-dead disease cometh
> after 50 years.

Amputation finds a place. Here are directions how to
proceed :

> If thou wilt carve off or cut off a limb from a body, then view
> thou of what sort the place be, and the strength of the place,
> since some or one of the places readily rotteth if one carelessly
> tend it. Some feel the leechdoms later, some earlier. If thou
> must carve off or cut off an unhealthy limb off from a healthy
> body, then carve thou not it on the limit of the healthy body,
> but much more cut or carve it on the hole and quick body.

For *angina pectoris*, the following :

> Mix a cup of marred honey with half-a-cup of melted lard,
> boil it till it be " as thick as pottage ", and let beans be dried
> and ground afterwards and added thereto. Pepper it, then drink
> it as required.

As for blood-letting :

there are three days in the year which be dangerous days, in
which by no means for no occasion neither man's nor beast's
blood must be diminished. These are the last Monday in April,
the first Monday in August, and the first Monday in February.
He who on these three days shall diminish the volume of his
blood, be it man, be it beast, shall forthwith on the first day or

on the fourth day end his life. Or if his life be longer he will not reach the seventh day. Also if he drink any medicinal drink on those three days, he will end his life within fifteen days. And whosoever on these three days tastes flesh of goose will end his life within forty days' time. If any one be born on these three days, he will end his life by an evil death.

This account of the leechdoms of our early forefathers may end with instructions for finding cattle that are lost :

When first thou art told that thy cattle are lost, then say thou before thou say anything else :

> Bethlehem hight the borough
> On which kindled was Christ.
> It is far famed
> Throughout all the earth.
> So may this deed among men
> Become patent and public
> Through the holy rood of Christ. Amen.

Then say thy prayers thrice to the east, and say thrice, May the cross of Christ bring me back my beasts from the east (or the west or the south or the north), facing in the direction mentioned in the prayer. Then add, It was lost and is found. The Jews hung up Christ ; they did of all deeds the worst ; they hid that they could not hide. So may this deed be in no wise hidden, through the holy rood of Christ. Amen.

Blood-letting

While the practice of the art of healing in the middle ages was surrounded with ignorance of the rules of health, with faith in remedies that were no remedies and with treatment at the hands of those whose ignorance was less only than that of their patients, there was one place where, at any rate till it fell on evil days, a high standard of intellectual and artistic culture demanded, and was supplied with, the best that was known about the treatment of disease. This place was the religious house. The intercourse between the monastic foundations of this country and their parent houses abroad benefited the English houses to no small extent in the treatment of disease and, better still, in the maintenance of good health. While, even in the ancient universities until much later, this country could not boast a reputable medical school, both Salerno and Montpellier had their schools of medicine, in which, thanks to the intimate connexion between English and continental religious houses, far more English monks must have been trained to practise as physicians than the surviving records reveal. Further, the practice of blood-letting (*minutio*, the classical Latin word for the practice) was for centuries a regular part not only of the treatment of disease but also of the preservation of health.

While only the physician is qualified to pass an opinion on this common medieval practice, which in recent years has been resorted to in the interests of those who need a fresh supply of blood, there can be no doubt that the most skilled physicians of the middle ages must have had reason to believe strongly in the practice of blood-letting not only in cases of serious illness but also as a regular precaution. Even before the advent of the Norman religious houses in this country, as is proved by those Anglo-Saxon records which have been quoted, blood-letting cannot but have been resorted to in the case of the monk as well as in those of the secular clergy and the laity. No specific provision was made for it, however, until after the Norman Conquest. The terms *leech*, commonly applied to a physician, and *leechdom*, used to denote a remedy which did not necessarily imply the loss of blood, shew to what an extent, in the popular mind, the healing of disease and the drawing of blood were connected. Real leeches were used, with expert precautions. Doubtless both dry and wet cupping were used in addition ; and anything from two to twenty, or even more, ounces of blood, as the need seemed to demand, were withdrawn at one blood-letting. Lanfranc, who as archbishop of Canterbury was abbot of the great Benedictine house of Christ Church, Canterbury, made rules for the regulation of the practice. His example was followed by other Norman abbots, some of whom had received the best medical training of the day. Amongst early monks who were expert physicians may be reckoned Baldwin (abbot of Bury St. Edmunds), who was physician to Edward the Confessor ; Lanfranc ; Arfast (bishop of Thetford) ; Faricius (abbot of Abingdon), physician to Henry I and Queen Matilda ; Warin and John (abbots of St. Albans) ; Gregory (monk of Malmesbury) ; Thomas of Northwick (monk of Evesham) ; and Walter (almoner of Bury St. Edmunds). If the records were more complete than they are, this list could probably be added to. No list of lay leeches could be compiled that would be much longer than this.

The regulations which all the monastic houses observed in the matter of blood-letting provide for a varying time of absence from the services in the monastic church, generally for one to three days, during which an invalid diet was prescribed, and, if carried on in the guests' quarters, a relaxation of the rule which forbade conversation at certain times. On the occasions set aside for the practice, once in each quarter or slightly oftener, it was convenient for the whole of the monks in an establishment to be bled in turns, in groups of six to twelve, according to the size of the foundation.

The skill of the monks as physicians could not be altogether denied to sick people outside the monasteries, and not only to kings, bishops and nobles, but also to the poor at the very gates of the religious houses. In order to discourage the adoption of the profession of leech by monks whose vows, strictly speaking, forbade them to be anything but monks, Pope Alexander III forbade the monks to practise outside their own houses. In this country, at any rate, this injunction was freely disobeyed. The monasteries gained much from this touch with the outside world, limited though it must have been. In addition, gifts made in return for the help given to sick people, while not the property of the physicians themselves, benefited their houses in many ways. The almonry at Bury St. Edmunds and the tower of the church at Evesham were built, in whole or in part, out of such gifts. In the absence of schools of medicine at the universities of this country, the monasteries were the only places at which a tradition of medical study, through the medical books in the monastic libraries, many of which have survived to this day, and of the regular and systematic treatment of diseases, could be formed. It could not be expected that this tradition would influence the great medical schools abroad, but so far as this country was concerned the art of healing, however unscientific our own age would judge it to have been, reached its highest point in the great monastic houses. But when Andrew Borde wished to learn the art he had to travel abroad.

THE OATH OF HIPPOCRATES

I will follow the system of regimen which, according to my ability and judgment, I consider to be for the benefit of my patients, and abstain from whatever is deleterious and mischievous.

CHAPTER VI

MEDICINE—II

A Medicine-book at York

AMONGST the books in a monastic library there was always at least one on medicine. Sickness of one kind or another was inevitable in a community of men or women living together year after year ; and many of, if not all, the greater houses had their own medical man amongst their members. The most recently published list of medieval books that have been traced back to their original homes, monastic or secular, records eighteen such books on medicine ; and in addition there exist probably a few scores of other copies which either have not come to light or cannot be connected with any religious foundation or any individual owner. Amongst these is a copy in the York Minster Library which bears the title :

Medicine, by Will : de Killingholme. A.D. MCCCCXII.

As will be seen, this book consists of a compilation in several different hands and without doubt by as many separate individuals. William was responsible for 28½ folios or 57 pages, all written in a beautiful hand. At the end of this portion of the book are the words :

Magister Willelmus leche de Kylingholme.

Killingholme is near the mouth of the Humber, about ten miles north-west of Grimsby.

This interesting book contains eleven portions, each in a different hand, some of them hardly good enough to have been written by professional scribes. It is the kind

of book that might easily have belonged to a leech or
medicus in daily practice, perhaps even to William of
Killingholme himself. The extraneous matter, of which
there is a good deal, includes a list of kings of England
from Alfred the Great to Henry IV, with the number of
years during which each reigned. This, the first, portion
must therefore have been written during the reign of
Henry IV, a probable date for the whole of the writing.
A footnote is added to the effect that pestilences swept over
the land in 1328, 1361 and from 1367 to 1371, and that
in the middle of the night of January 14th, 1364, there
was a storm in which houses and trees were uprooted.
It is interesting to record here that the dates throughout
the book, and the numbers which are used in other
connexions, are written in Arabic, not Roman, numerals.

At the beginning there is a form of adjuration to be
used in cases of what are called " fevers ". The formula,
which is interspersed with signs of the Cross, may be
freely translated :

> I adjure you, ye fevers, by the Father, the Son and the Holy
> Ghost, by Emmanuel, Sabaoth, Adonai and the Mediator, by
> prophet and priest, by the signs of the Zodiac, by life and wisdom,
> by the Trinity and the Unity, by Almighty God, King of all, by
> Jesus Christ and in virtue of His blood, by the purity of the angels
> and archangels, by patriarchs, prophets, apostles, matrons, con-
> fessors and virgins, and because you have no power to hurt. For
> Christ was made obedient unto death, even the death of the
> Cross. In the Name of the Father, and of the Son and of the
> Holy Ghost.

And, below, written in red ink :

> A charme for the feueris.

There follows a prayer to be used when the fever shews
no signs of abating, but rather increases in intensity.

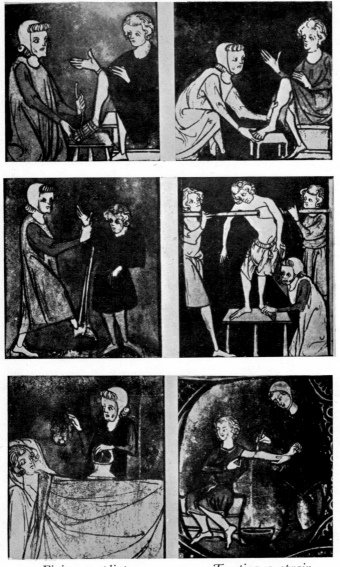

Fixing a splint
Replacing a dislocated elbow
A nurse ready to wash a patient

Treating a sprain
Replacing a dislocated shoulder
Blood-letting

An operation on a skull
Instruments being heated
An abdominal operation

Treatment for an ear
A wound being stitched
An arrow being extracted

Directions follow :

to hele the fallyng euyl.

Seye thes werdes in his right ere, agodes · platino · placete, and take hym be the ryght hond & he schal arise and yf ye wilt take hym swinegreue & the rede of henbane & gif hym to drinke fastynge durynge xl dayes & he schal be hole for euer more. Item write thes names & lete hym bere aboute his necke.

Then follow various names, with a direction that a reading to the patient of part of the first chapter of St. John shall be made. The patient shall hear the Mass of the Holy Spirit, after which he shall break a wafer into five parts and give one part to each of five poor people, and shall not cease to say, as long as he shall live, the Lord's Prayer and the Creed.

Item yf it be newe i-come to a man or a child seye in his ryght ere anamgapta iij & make a rynge and write thes wordis therinne & let hym bere hit upon hym & he schal neuer haue it whyles hit is abowte hym.

Then :

For sore tethe to take them out w^{t}out any instrument.

Take gum of yny and agryve euete & brenne the euete to pouder in anewe potte of erthe and medle the poudr with the gume w^t mele of spurge & put this poudr so medled under aston of arynge & than take the poudr and touche the sore tothe and it schal falle out in thi honde. To knowe the gums of yui (?) take in this monthe of januarii and bore a hole in ayny tre to this mydil of the tre and stoppe the hole fuste w^{t}apyn that no licony^d come out & let it be so in iij wykys and at the iij wykys ende ye schale fynd the hole fule of gume.

Miscellaneous information in the book includes diagrams and tables of the eclipses of the sun and the moon in the first half of the fifteenth century and the signs of the Zodiac, all of which were of importance to the leech. The most interesting of the diagrams is one of the body

of a man, drawn in outline, on the page opposite to which
is a complicated table of small squares, across which are
written, time and again, the names of these signs.   On
the sketch of the man's body are, in red ink, " legends "
which elucidate the meaning of the sketch.   From the
head to the feet, the names of the signs of the Zodiac
are written ;   Aries (head), Taurus (neck), Gemini
(shoulders), Cancer, Leo, Virgo, Libra, and Scorpio
(chest and abdomen), Sagittarius (groin), Capricornus
(upper legs), Aquarius (knees) and Pisces (feet).   Each
of these is connected with another legend or legends,
amongst which are :

for the migrein ; for imposter in the hed ; for al seknes of the
face ; for defnes and hed wert after syknes ; good for the ighen ;
for swellyng and migrein ;   behynde the ere for old seknes ;   for
scab in the nek ; for renning ighen ; for brekyng of bleynes in
the face or nose or brest ; for quakyng handis ; for bodi ; stichis ;
ston ;   soden seknes ;   reines ;   al maner goute ;   spleneta ;   for
brest and longs ;   hed aghen ;   meche blode ;   herte ;   and
sciatica.

The legends about the sketch of the human body are
explained :

Aries.   be war of cuttyng in the hed or in the face and theryn
cutte noght the hed veyne.

Taurus.   be war of cuttyng in the nekke or in the throte &
that yu cutte no veyne in tho placys.

Gemini.   be war cuttyng in the chulderys or in the armes or
in the handys & open no veyne in tho placys.

Cancer.   be war cuttyngs in the brest, of the rybbys, & of
hurtyng of the stomak & of the lyghtys cutte no veyne in tho
placys that longyth to the mylte.

Leo.   be war of cuttyng of sennys [sinews] & of hurtyng of
the sydes & of bonys cut noght in the bak nether with openyng
ne ventosyng.

Libra.   be war cut no wounde on the navel ne in the lower
parts of the wombe ne open no veyne in the bak ne ventose it
noght.

Scorpio. be war of cuttyng of the buttocks & of the ars and of the bledder & of hyrtyng of the marth, and cut no veyne ne the pruyte ne in man ne in woman.

Sagittarius. be war of cuttyng on the theyes & on fyngerys cut no bleynes ne non superfluyte of growyngys.

Capricorn. be war of cuttyng in kneis & cut no senue ne veyne in that place.

Aquarius. be war of cuttyng in the theyes ne the senues of hem to the lower parts of the knettyngths of the kne.

Pisces. be war of cuttyng in the feet in ony maner.

As with the Anglo-Saxons, so with the medievals, a good deal of superstitious matter is found in the medicine-books. The book at York is no exception to this, as the next few pages will shew.

Dreams and Palmistry

Then comes another heading in red :

Here be gynnyth the ex posyssyun of dremys that danyel the profete saw & dysposyd in babyloyne that tyme he wrot here & be took hem to the pepyl to rede & seyde I haue nout lernyd this of my self but of God the fadyr almyty for be hym thei ben made opyn to me as it tellyth here.

A man yf he dreme that he se bryddes fytyn ageyn hym it be tokenyth wratthe.

foulys gader to geder, wynnyng . . . to bere armor, worschepe.

And so on—a very long list of dreams and their meanings.

One of the most interesting excursions which are made in the book is in the realm of palmistry. It consists only of a rude sketch of a hand (a left hand, the hand which is the less marked with creases due to constant use of the hand for grasping things), on which certain legends are written, in reference to lines made on the hand :

(1) on the little finger : As mony lines as mony wyfes schal you lede.

(2) on the next : this lyne in these fyngeres stondant strength is token thinge of gret gode other state.

(3) on the next : this lyne hauende no nynde in no place token-
      ynge is of soden worship other sygne.

(4) on the next : this cros honore & worschipe this token of
      wonde in the hedde.

(5) He that thes signes hase schale be riche in hyse liue.

Between (2) and (3) :

this line in thes fyngeres is gret drede for hyse folynes.

Between (3) and (4) :

yf the midward line het thes fyngeres tokenynge is of deth for a
wonde.

Lines marked on the palm of the hand are :

mydward lyne ; lyne of liue ; lyne of the hede.

Immediately following the sketch of the hand comes
a short account of the meaning of the various types and
shapes of the features of the face and what they betoken.
Here are a few examples :

He that has a hey nase is a ryth abele man of wyt.

Whan the nase is brod and bowande in the myddys he is woordy
& a lyer.

Of the face.   He that hath a ful face makyth ofte debat & stryf.

He that hath a smal face is a spyer a boute in al doyng sotyl
& understdyng.

He that has . . . gret chekys is ful wrathful.

He that has gret erys sal be of good mynde & intencion.

Of ye nek.   He that has a long nekke & sinal is trowe & sotyl.

He that has a long nek & gret is leyrand & a gret marchaunt.

He that is large of body & armys (arms) be tokenes heynesse
& understandyng of counsel.

He that has long fyngers be tokenes hys lord potyng to many
crafts.

He that has short fyngers be tokenes wyt.

Of legges.   Gret be tokenes stalworthynesse gret knees be
tokenes feblenes.

In the monyth of genuer [January] whyht wyn is good fastyng
to drynke & blodlatyng forbere for viij dayes ben in that mone

[moon] or gret perel. (The days of the moon's age are the 1st, 2nd, 4th, 5th, 10th, 15th, 19th and 21st.)

In may erly ryse & erly ete & drynk & hote metys use & ete noght the hed ne the feet of no beste. [Then follow the days of " perel "] . . . and lete ne blod in the ende of may the v or the iiii day on whedyr arm so you wylt & you schal be sef fro alle maner euelys [evils].

In octobyr must that is newe wyn is good for to drynke & blod for nede to late & i day ther is of gret perel that is the vij day.

Andrew Borde

Our last example of a physician and his outlook on his calling takes us to the very end of the middle ages. His name was Andrew Borde (c. 1490–1549). Into the last twenty years of life he packed a good deal. At an early age he was admitted, probably at the Charterhouse, London, a Carthusian monk, and for more than twenty years he lived in this strictest of all the religious orders. But at the age of nearly 40 he grew tired of the religious life, and wrote for his release in these words :

I am nott able to byd the rigorosite off your relygyon.

After contemplating the possibility of his becoming bishop-suffragan in the diocese of Chichester, he decided to go abroad to study medicine. On his return he was able to treat one or two noblemen with such success that he was recommended to wait on " his pre-potent Mageste ", Henry VIII. He left England once again to obtain, in various medical schools abroad, " a trewe cognysyon of the practis of Physycke ", visiting and studying at Orleans, Poictiers, Toulouse, Montpelier, Wittenberg and probably other places. Back in England, he came into contact with Thomas Cromwell, who sent him abroad once again, to " Normandy, Fraunce, Gascony, Bayonne, Castyle, Biscay, Spain, Portugal and Aragon ", places which very few Englishmen of his day had ever seen. In 1536 he wrote to Cromwell :

> I am now in Skotland, in a lytle vnyuersyte or study named Glasco, where I study the practyce of Physyk for the sustentacyon of my lyuyng.

Back in London for a short time, he went on his travels again, this time going as far afield as Venice, Rhodes and the Holy Land. He is next found at the university of Montpellier, which he called

> the most nobilis vniuersite of al Europe for the practis of physyke.

For a time he lived in London, where he had many patients, but later on he settled at Winchester, where, sad to say, he was found guilty of loose living and was sentenced to be imprisoned in the Fleet prison, London. This is all that is known of this extraordinary man, who, in succession, was monk, bishop-designate, traveller, writer, physician and surgeon.

His interests may be appreciated by a consideration of the books that he wrote. These are :

(1) *The Fyrst Boke of the Introduction of Knowledge*, a book of his travels, the first of its kind. To the short title he added a longer one :
> The whych doth teache a man to speake parte of all maner of languages and to know the vsage and fashion of all maner of countreys. And for to know the moste parte of all maner of coynes of money, the which is currant in euery region. Made by Andrew Borde, of Physycke Doctor. Dedycated to the right honorable & gracious lady Mary, doughter of our souerayne Lorde Kyng Henry the eyght.

(2) *A Compendyous Regyment or a Dietary of Helth*, made in Mountpyllier, compyled by Andrew Boorde of Physycke doctour, dedycated to the armypotent Prynce and valyaunt Lorde Thomas Duke of Northfolche.

(3) *The Breuyary of Helth*.

(4) *The Boke of Berdes* [beards], which is known only through the answer made to it.

(5) *The Princyples of Astronamye.*

(6) *Itinerary of England.*

(7) *Itinerary of Europe*, which Thomas Cromwell borrowed but which is now lost.

(8) *A Book of Sermons.*

(9) *The Pronostycacyon for 1545*, based on astronomy.

Several other works, mainly autobiographical, have been attributed to him, but it is doubtful whether they came from his pen. Our concern is chiefly with his *Compendyous Regyment or a Dietary of Helth*, which was printed with two title-pages, on one of which there is a woodcut of the sign of the printer, William Copland, and on the other a woodcut of " Gaylen, prynce of Physycke ". The Duke of Norfolk (Thomas, eighth duke), to whom it was inscribed, had been a patient of Boorde, and had evidently gained his affection. In his *Breuyary of Helth*, |he translated into English many difficult words,

> some and mooste of all beynge Greeke wordes, some and fuer (fewer) beynge Araby words, some beynge Latin wordes and some beyngye Barbarus wordes ;

including in his second edition a list, in alphabetical order, of diseases and their treatment. In it he wrote :

> I do nat wryte these bokes for lerned men, but for symple and vnlerned men, that they may have some knowledge to ease them selfe in their dyseyses and infirmities. And bycause that I dyd omit and leaue out many thynges in the fyrste boke named the Breuyary of Helthe in this boke named the Extrauagantes I haue supplied those matters the whiche shulde be rehersed in the fyrst boke.

He also expressed the hope that those who should buy copies of this shorter book would also buy copies of his *Dyetary*,

> consyderyng that the one is concurrent with the other.

For his day, Borde was an enlightened man. His principles appear to have been :

(1) to warn his potential patients that if they would keep clear of " doctors of physycke " they must be careful about their diet ;

(2) to emphasise the virtues of quietness of mind and regularity of life in the interests of good health ; and

(3) to advise those who would build houses how they ought to build them so that they might avoid those things which would do harm to their health.

A Compendyous Regyment or a Dietary of Helth

Borde begins this with advice to those who are about to build houses to live in. He then passes to the management of income, and the care of body and soul. Water and wood, he points out, are essential to the well-being of the house and its inhabitants, with the right kind of soil, a good view, a supply of fresh air to " comfort the brayne " and make " good blode ", the avoidance of stagnant water, " stynkyng mistes " and marshes, an ample supply of nails, pins, laths, tiles, slates, straw, timber, lime, sand, stones, bricks, and labour, a foundation of gravel and clay, or of rock, or on a hill, a south-east or south-west prospect, the most convenient arrangement of the rooms, an orchard, a park for deer and rabbits, and a moat. So this is a big house that he has in view, not an artisan's dwelling. To secure peace of mind in money matters, the head of the house ought to divide his income into three parts : (1) for food and housekeeping, (2) for dress, liveries, alms, etc., and (3) for sickness, dilapidations and the " charges of a mans last ende ". He advises that no man should contemplate setting-up house until he has " ij or iij yeres rent in his

GALIEN PRYNCE OF PHISYCKE.

(*From Andrew Borde's Treatise.*)

Doctor Boorde.

cofer ". True to his opinion that exercise is necessary if good health be desired, he writes :

> And amonge other thynges, a payre of buttes is a decent thynge aboute a mansyon-place ; and other whyle for a great man, necessary is it for to passe his tyme with bowles in an aly ; when all this is fynysshed and the mansyon replenyshed with Implementes there must be a fyre kept contynually for a space to drye vp the contagyous moystnes of the walles, and the sauour of the lyme and sande. And after that a man may ly and dewll in the sayd mansyon without takynge any inconuenyence of syckness.

Spiritual was of even greater importance than physical health.

> For there is no catholycke or chrysten man lyuyng but he is bounde in conscyence to be more circumspecter aboute the welth of his soule than the helth of his body. Our Savyour Iesus Chryst saith, What shall it profyte vnto man yf he get all the worlde and lese hym selfe and bryng hym selfe to a detryment ?

A man therefore should so live that he can say with St. Ambrose, " I feare not to die bycause we haue a good God." Further, no man should be idle, but should train himself and his household to be industrious, for did not Henry VIII say, when he was young, " Ydlenes is chefe maistres of vyces all " ? He should see to it that the members of his household keep the commandments, and :

> specyally to punysshe swearers, for in all the worlde there is not suche odyble swearyng as is vsed in Englande, specyally amonge youth and chyldren, which is a detestable thyng to here it, and no man doth go aboute to punysshe it.

Moderate, but not excessive, sleep is necessary to all, for Christ said, " I say not onely to you, watche, but to all men I say, watche." For " sanguyne and colerycke " men, seven hours' sleep each night might suffice ; for the " flematycke " (phlegmatic), nine hours ; but the melancholy :

> may take theyr pleasure, for they be the receptacle and the dragges of all the other humoures.

Advice is given about having a fire in one's bedroom, wearing a scarlet nightcap, lying on the right side when going to sleep, exercise before breakfast, having a light supper, not standing in the sun and not sleeping in the daytime unless it is necessary, in which case one should sleep in a chair or standing against a cupboard.

The learned doctor then turns to the vital question of diet. He begins :

> Galen, declaryng Hypocrates sentence vpon eatynge to moche meat saith, " more meate than accordeth with nature is named replecyon or a surfete ".

The liver he likens to " the fyer under the potte ", which, when congested, cannot perform its function of helping the digestion. Over-feeding

> doth ingender infyrmytes, throwe the whiche breuite and shortnes of lyfe doth flowe.

Abstinence, he concludes, is

> the moste best and the perfytest medysone that can be.

For a " rest man ", that is, a man who does not lead an active life, two meals a day are enough :

> a laborer maye eate thre tymes a daye, and he that doth eate ofter lyueth a beestly lyfe.

There follows a survey of the various forms of drink— water, wine, ale, beer, mead, metheglyn (honey, water and herbs), whey, posset ale, and coyte (thin or " small " beer—a Dutch drink) ; and of food—bread, stews, broths, eggs, butter, cheese, milk, cream, fish, flesh meat, roots, herbs, fruits and spices. The judgments passed by this sixteenth-century expert in diet on these articles of food and drink are penetrating. About the brawn of a wild boar and that of a tame boar the wise medico writes :

> Brawne is an vsual meate in wynter amongset Englysshe men : it is harde of dygestyon. The brawne of a wylde boore is moche better than the brawne of a tame boore. Yf a man eate nother of them bothe it shall neuer do hym harme.

Other remarks are worthy of record here :

Of wylde beestes flesshe.

I haue gone rownde aboute Crystendome and ouerthwarte Crystendom, and a thousande or two and more myles oute of Crystendom, yet there is not so moche pleasure for harte and hynde, bucke and doo, and for roo bucke and doo, as is in England ; and although the flesshe be dispraysed in physycke I pray God to sende me parte of the flesshe to eat, physycke not-withstanding.

And of venison :

> The opynyon of all olde physycons was and is, that venyson is not good to eate, pryncypally for two causes : the first cause is that the beest doth lyue in fere ; for yf he be a good wood-man he shall neuer se no kynde of deere but on the grasse or brosynge on the tree, but he wyll lyfte vp his hed and loke aboute hym, the whiche commeth of tymorosnes ; and tymorosyte doth brynge in melancoly humours. Wherfore all Physycons sayth that venyson . . . doth ingender coloryke humours ; and of trueth it doth so. Wherfore let them take the skyn and let me haue the flesshe. I am sure it is a lords dysshe, and I am sure it is good for an Englysshe man, for it doth anymate hym to be as he is, whiche is, stronge and hardy. But I do aduertyse euery man, for all my wordes, not to kyll, and so not to eate of it, excepte it be lefully, for it is a meate for great men. And great men do not set so moch by the meate as they do by the pastime of kyllyng of it.

Of butter and cream, he writes :

> Butter is made of creyme, and is moyste of operacioun ; it is good to eate in the mornynge before other meates. Frenche men wyll eate it after meate. But, eaten with other meates, it doth

not onely nowrysshe, but it is good for the breste and lunges, and also it doth relaxe and mollifye the bely. Douche men doth eate it at all tymes in the daye, the whiche I dyd not prayse when I dyd dwell amonge them consyderyng that butter is vnctyous, and euery thynge that is vnctyous is noysome to the stomacke, for as moche as it maketh lubryfactyon. And also euery thyng that is vnctyous that is to say butterysshe, oyle, grese or fat, doth swymme aboute in the brynkes of the stomacke . . . and doth make eructasyons ; wherfore eatynge of moche butter at one refection is not commendable . . . A lytell porcyon is good for euery man in the mornynge yf it be newe made.

Charles Lamb would not have agreed with the doctor's opinion of pork :

Where-as Galen, with other auncyent and approbet doctours, doth prayse porke, I dare not say the contrary agaynst them. But this I am sure of, I dyd neuer loue it. And in holy scrypture it is not praysed, for a swyne is an vnclene beest, and doth lye vpon fylthy and stynkynge soyles, and with stercorus matter dyvers tymes doth fede in Englande. Yet in Hyghalmen and other hygh countres . . . men doth kepe theyr swyne clene and dothe cause them ones or twyse a day to swymme in great ryuers, lyke the water of Ryne, which is aboue Coleyne ; but Spaynyerdes, with the other regiouns anexed to them, kepe the swyne more fylthyre than Englysshe persouns doth . . . The Ieue, the Sarason and the Turkes . . . lovyth not porke nor swynes flesshe . . . yet for all this they wyll eate adders, which is a kynde of serpents. . . . This notwithstandynge, physycke doth approbate adders flesshe good to be eaten, sayinge it doth make an olde man yonge, as it apperyth by a harte eatyng an adder maketh hym yong agayne. But porke doth not so, for yf it be of an olde hogge not clene kept it doth ingender grose blode and doth humect to moche the stomacke ; yet yf the porke be yonge it is nutrytus. . . . Bacon is good for carters and plowmen, the whiche be euer labourynge in the earth or dunge.

Roots, herbs, fruits and spices complete the list of foods. Amongst them are onions, leeks, garlick, turnips, artichokes, endive, beet, thyme, parsley and lettuce, with figs, raisins, currants, grapes, peaches, strawberries, cherries, nuts, pears, apples, pomegranates, quinces, dates, melons, almonds, prunes, damsons, oranges, olives, pepper, cloves, mace, nutmeg, cinnamon and liquorice. The names themselves suggest much trade with other countries, one result of the voyages of exploration which have been mentioned in a previous chapter.

About herbs in general, the doctor writes :

> There is no Herbe nor weede but God haue gyuen vertue to them, to helpe man.

Of fruits :

> Strawburyes be praysed aboue al buryes, for they do qualifye the heate of the lyuer and dothe engender good blode, eaten with suger. Cherys doth mollyfye the bely, and be colde.
>
> Apples be good after a frost haue taken them, or whan they be olde, specyally yf red apples, and they whiche be of good odor and melow. . . . They doth comforte the stomacke and doth make good dygestyon, specyally yf they be rostyd or baken.
>
> Orenges doth make a man to haue a good appetyde, and so doth the ryndes, yf they be in succade, & they doth comforte the stomacke, and dothe prouoke an appetyde.

There follow recommendations of different kinds of diet for different kinds of men—sanguine, " flematycke ", choleric and melancholic—and to relieve sufferers from fever, colic, gout and leprosy, with the " falling sickness " (epilepsy), diseases of the head, consumption, short-windedness, palsy, insanity and dropsy. The thirty-ninth chapter is devoted to " a generall dyete for all manner of men and women, beynge sycke or hole ", and the fortieth to " an order or a fasshyon how a sycke man shulde be ordered, And how a sycke man shuld be vsyd that is lykely to dye."

The sick man must have " two or iii good kepers ", or nurses, of whom diligence is expected ; they must not be :

slepysshe, sloudgysshe, sluttysshe.

Nor must anybody :

> wepe and wayle aboute a sycke man, nor to vse many wordes
> nor that there be no greate resort to common and talke, For it
> is a busynes for a whole man to answere many men, specyally
> women, that shall come to hym.

The sick man ought to make a will, receive the rites of
the Church, and follow the counsel of his priest and
his doctor.

> For saynt Augustyn saith, " he that doth not the commaunde-
> ment of his physycyon doth kyll hym self."

Further, the sick-room must be full of " redolent odours "
and the room should be :

> replenysshed with herbes and flowers of odoryferouse sauour.

And :

> in any wyse lette not many men, and specyally women, be
> togyther at one tyme in the chamber, not onely for bablynge, but
> specially for theyr brethes.
>
> Yf the sycke man was sycker and sycker, that there is lytle hope
> of amendment, but sygnes of deth, that no man oughte to moue
> hym any wordly matters or busynes, but to speke of ghostly and
> godly matters, and to rede the passyon of Cryste and to say the
> paslmes of the passyon and to holde a crosse of a pyctour of the
> passyon of Cryste before the eyes of the sycke person. . . . And
> than lette euery man do indeuer hym selfe to prayer, that the
> sycke person may fynysshe his lyfe Catholyckely in the fayth of
> Iesu Cryste, And so departe out of this myserable world. I do
> beseche the Father, and the sone, and the holy ghost, thorow
> the meryte of Iesu Crystes passyon, that I and all Creatures
> lyuynge may do so. A M E N.

Andrew Borde on Sleep, Rising and Dress
Probably from the 1557 print of his *Regyment*

Men of any age who are in good health should take
their natural sleep at night and should avoid sleeping in
the middle of the day. But if sleep after a meal should

be a necessity let a man stand and lean and sleep against a cupboard, or let him sit upright in a chair and sleep. Sleeping after a full meal causes infirmities : it hurts the spleen, it relapses the sinews, it induces dropsy and gout, and it makes a man look evil-coloured. Be merry before you go to bed, or have merry company about you, so that as you go to sleep no anger, heaviness, sorrow or pensiveness (" pensyfulnes ") trouble or disquiet you. Have a fire in your bedroom night and morning to waste and consume the evil vapours, for the human breath may putrify the air in your room. Do not, however, stand or sit by the fire, but a good way off, taking the flavour of it, for fire arifies and dries up the blood and makes the sinews and the joints stiff. At night, let the windows of your house, especially of your own chamber, be closed. Lie at first on your left side, but sleep on your right. If you wake during the night, turn over and sleep always on the other side. To sleep face downwards is not good unless the digestion be slow ; but it is better to lay your hands on those of your bedfellow or on your stomach than to lie grovelling. Sleeping on the back is to be utterly abhorred. As you sleep, let no part of your body be uncovered except your head. Do not sleep on an empty stomach, or until about two hours after you have had a meal. Lie with your head high, lest the food in your stomach ascend to the " oryfe " (opening ?) of your stomach. Wear a scarlet nightcap. Let your quilt be of thick cotton, pure flocks or clean wool, and lay it on the feather-bed on which you lie. Be not too hot or too cold as you sleep. Old, ancient doctors of " physicke " say that eight hours' sleep in summer and nine in winter is sufficient for any man ; but sleep should be taken according to your " complexion ", that is, nature. When you rise in the morning, rise with mirth, and remember God. Brush your hose inside and out-

side, and air the inside at the fire. Wear linen socks or
linen hose. Stretch your legs and arms and body as you
rise ; then cough and spit. Truss your points (i.e.,
fasten your hose to your doublet) and comb your hair
several times a day. Wash your hands and wrists and
face in cold water, and brush your teeth. Walk in your
garden or park a thousand paces or two. Great and
noble men now hear Mass. Those what cannot do this,
owing to their business, should say some prayers, thanking
God for His mercies and asking mercy for their offences.
Before your refection, take exercise such as playing
tennis, casting a bowl, heavy weights or plummets of lead
in your hands to open your pores and to augment the
natural heat. At dinner and supper, do not drink many
drinks or eat divers meats, but partake of two or three
dishes at the most. After dinner or supper, do not work
at once, but spend an hour sitting or standing upright
with some pastime. Do not drink much after dinner.
Eat only light food for supper, and do not go to bed
with a full or an empty stomach.

As to apparel, in winter, next to your shirt wear a petticoat of scarlet. Wear your doublet at pleasure. Line
your jacket in this way : buy fine skins of white or black
lamb, let your skinner cut them triangle-wise, like half-
a-quarry of glass, and let him sew them together to make
a lining for your jacket. This fur, for wholesomeness, is
praised above sable or any other kind of fur. For
external wear, use your own discretion. In summer,
wear a scarlet petticoat of stamell or lynse wolse (a coarse
linen-cloth). In winter or in summer, let not your bed
be too hot, nor bind it too strait. Keep your neck warm.
In summer, keep your neck and face from the sun. Wear
gloves of goat-skin, perfumed with " amber-degrece ".
Do not stand or sit on stones, or barehead under a vault
of stone. Do not lie in old rooms which are not occupied,

especially those which have neither sun nor fresh air, or in a low room, except it be " boorded ". Do not catch cold in your feet or legs, and do not rise or go " in great and impytuos windes ".

Thus the attractive, alert, industrious, versatile and doubtless much-sought-after medical man of four centuries ago, a man in advance of his time. If we agree that when he decided to become a monk he made a mistake, we must give him credit for finding out his mistake before it was too late for him to make his mark in another kind of life. His peccadilloes do not concern us here. At a time when the theory of medicine was hide-bound by restrictions and superstitions he exhibited his independence by following his reasoning where it led him. For his time he was a pioneer of the scientific method, and he was interested not only in the cure but also in the prevention of disease. There can be no doubt that he enjoyed his work and his writing far more than he ever enjoyed being a monk or a would-be bishop. A century earlier, his career would have been ruined by his renunciation of his vows. But by the end of the fifteenth century ecclesiastical discipline was becoming, in fact if not in theory, far less strict ; and in consequence he was able to follow his own bent. Yet his simple piety never left him, and he was no less proficient in his new calling because of his piety. He was an ornament to his profession, and as a friend he must have been worth having. He is one of our lesser worthies, but still a worthy.

CHAPTER VII

GREAT HOUSEHOLDS

The Economy of a Bishop's Household

From the roll of Richard of Swinfield, bishop of Hereford
1282–1316, from Michaelmas, 1289, to Michaelmas, 1290

IT will readily be realised that a medieval archbishop
or bishop kept up the state of a duke or an earl.
This was a natural consequence of the position of the
archbishops and the bishops of the Church, who, from
the first, in this country at any rate, were the most highly-
educated of the people and therefore the natural leaders
of men in days when education was the privilege of the
very few. So it happened that they occupied positions
as lords-spiritual in distinction to noblemen, who were
lords-temporal. Like the lords-temporal, and indeed
everybody who held property in those days, before joint-
stock companies and government loans were thought of,
the lords-spiritual owed their incomes to the proceeds of
the land from rents and the yield of natural produce.
Like the lords-temporal, too, they naturally held property
in many estates. For example, the archbishops of York
held not only a palace near the cathedral of York but
also manors in several places, such as Bishopthorpe, Bishop
Monkton, Cawood and Scrooby. These manor-houses,
it must be remembered, were essential to every archbishop
and bishop. The diocese of York, for example, stretched
from the Trent to the Tees, and from Spurn Point to the
heads of the Yorkshire dales. In days when the average
number of miles that could comfortably be covered on
horseback in one day was not many more than 20 to
25, no prelate, least of all one who had passed middle

age, could travel more than a dozen miles from home
without staying somewhere overnight. It became the
rule for all archbishops and bishops to plan their visits
to parishes in their dioceses, and their journeys further
afield to London, in advance and in easy stages. The
procession of manors in various places in their dioceses
was a convenience to them in carrying out their formal
visitations or their less formal visits to parishes. Amongst
their hosts we frequently find abbots and priors, but, as
relations between monastic houses and episcopal authority
were often strained, this was not always possible. But
local clergy and squires could sometimes be found who
could entertain the archbishop or bishop. Of few if any
bishops could it be said that they had " not where to
lay " their heads. The picture we have before us, then,
is of the bishop, in one capacity, as independent trustee,
though not the owner, of large landed estates and therefore, in accordance with the custom of the times, a feudal
lord who inherited, and was responsible for preserving
and handing unimpaired to his successor in his office,
a great patrimony. Fortunately, owing to the survival of
account-rolls of lords, both spiritual and temporal, there
exist many authorities for exact information of the kind
of " establishment " that these men had to maintain.
The account-roll which lends itself to examination here
is that of Richard of Swinfield, bishop of Hereford 1282–
1316. It was printed, word for word, and elaborately
commented on, in two volumes of the Camden Society
nearly ninety years ago. This is an opportunity, taken
more than once in this book, for rescuing for a time from
its comparative obscurity an absorbingly interesting
document which, like scores of its kind, is studied at the
time of its publication and then, except for a chance
reference to it by an occasional student, is once more
allowed to return to its little-frequented corner.

This roll is a long one, 25 feet long, written on pieces of parchment a foot or 14 inches long and fastened together end on end to make a long roll which is preserved by being rolled up and kept in a cylindrical case. It is not quite complete, but it is complete enough to give us far more information than can be digested even after many readings of it. Naturally for its period, it is written in ecclesiastical Latin full of those abbreviations which puzzle the beginner but hardly ever the " old hand ". It covers the period from Michaelmas, 1289, to Michaelmas, 1290, when Edward I had been on the throne for seventeen or eighteen years and was interesting himself in Scotland after his recent adventures in Wales. It is necessary to rid our minds of the idea that, because the more populous areas are sometimes regarded as being of more importance than the less populous, the diocese of Hereford was of little importance to the country compared with, for example, that of York. For it included the counties of Gloucester, Hereford and Shropshire, all of them border counties, and it occupied a large part of rural England, then the only England that there was. In the diocese, many prominent noblemen even held lands of the bishop, including the families of Bohun (one of the historic families of England, with a pedigree from the Norman Conquest), the Cliffords, the Mortimers and the Valences. The bishop had twenty manors in the diocese, and two outside, with a house in Worcester and another in London. He possessed a dozen or more mills, at which the grain from his estates was ground and milled into flour. The food served at his table was varied in the extreme—bread and everything else that could be made from grain ; the flesh of all animals and birds that can live or be reared on the English countryside, including a large variety of game which was preserved for the benefit of the bishop ; and fish of all varieties found in this country in the rivers and lakes and in salt-water. For fuel there was abundance of wood and charcoal. Wine and beer flowed freely, as in all such establishments ; and eggs were plentiful.

A little more precise information may be given which is gleaned from the roll.   As throughout the middle ages, the tendency was for prices to rise and thus for the cost of living to rise in proportion.   During the period covered by the roll, according to the supply the price of wheat varied from 2s. 6d. to 5s. a quarter, and more than 6s. in London, where, however, a London quarter contained eight bushels, as in our day. Barley is hardly ever mentioned in the roll, though at York not many years afterwards it was in constant and generous supply for the making of beer and ale. Rye does not find a place at all. Bran was grown for horse-food, and oats for the meal on which hounds were fed. Poultry were fed on wheat and oats when they were being fattened.

The things that would strike us now if we could put the clock back and, with a knowledge of our age and customs, have free access to one of the hundreds of manors in this country, would be the enormous amount of food prepared and consumed daily. Beef, mutton, pork and veal were stored, not in joints but in whole or half-carcases. When we add to this profusion of meat food the flesh of the wild boar, venison and all kinds of game, it is natural to ask whether any of this was wasted. It will be remembered that, in the house of a lord, after every meal a basket filled with fragments of food not eaten was taken to the poor at his gate. There can be no doubt that, however great the obligation to feed the poor might lie on the conscience of a layman, it would lie more heavily on that of a prelate. For centuries, the deans of York were bound by statute to feed every day forty poor people and to wash their feet. Indeed, one of the reasons most often given to justify the wealth of a medieval bishop was that he was obliged to feed the poor. But it is impossible to avoid harbouring the suspicion, first, that overeating was common in a period when men worked and played and drank hard, and then that much food was wasted. When on a single manor we read that as many as forty poultry were killed at Christmas, and the same number a week afterwards— a number that on one occasion was more than fifty—it is impossible to imagine that every particle of their flesh that was edible was actually eaten.

As to fish and eggs, the story is the same. Both were needed, as matters of ecclesiastical obligation, on numerous days of abstinence and on the eves of certain feast-days—the whole of Lent (except the Sundays), every Wednesday, Friday and Saturday (unless any of these were saints' days), and so on. On Easter Day, 1290, 1,400 eggs were consumed by the bishop and his household, and on the next day more arrived. Fish was the most varied food of all—salmon, herrings, cod, haddock, hake, ling, plaice, mackerel, shad, pike, bream, tench and trout, with oysters and whelks. A bishop who had fishing rights in the Wye and in other rivers would have at his table every kind of fish that were caught in them.

The abundance of wine and beer or ale—but not, in what we now know as the cider country, cider—is an eloquent commentary on the absence in the middle ages of any ideal of total abstinence as a virtue. Foreign trade being restricted, and intercourse with continental countries for purposes of trade being exceptional, the varieties of wines familiar to us in our day were never so much as imagined by the medieval man. Red wine was imported, but all the white wine was made at home. Most of all, the monasteries had vineries of their own for the purpose of stocking their cellars with wine. For imported wines, the west country was well placed, for Bristol was the chief port in the country for the importation of wine from abroad. On two occasions, the bishop of Hereford purchased twelve pipes of wine, each pipe containing 126 gallons. It was not bottled, but drawn " from the wood " as it was needed.

The usual word, *cervisia*, is used in this roll for either beer or ale. The bishop had three *brasia* (Latin *brasium*, brewery), but we do not hear that, as was the custom at a college of priests attached to York Minster, he had an official in charge of the brewing of malt and barley and of the alehouse, called the *brasiator*. The three breweries were at Prestbury, two miles north-east of Cheltenham, Bosbury, four miles north-north-west of Ledbury, and Sugwas, four or five miles west of Hereford.

Here, therefore, even though from many parts of this roll, we have a description of the food consumed in the bishop's household. It is impossible to guess the size of this household. The roll however tells us a good deal about the officials without whose aid the bishop would have been unable to perform those higher duties which were of the very essence of his office. Like most modern archbishops and bishops, the bishop of Hereford had a chaplain who accompanied the bishop wherever he went. The particular duty of one of these chaplains was to take charge of the money and to disburse it in accordance with the wishes of the bishop. In accordance with the custom in monasteries and in large secular foundations, the official whose name is on a roll of accounts was the person responsible for the accuracy of the statements contained in it. The seneschal or steward collected the rents and the other sums due to the bishop, including the fines levied at the court of the bishop. Under him were several other officials—squires (generally young men who were being educated for higher posts or for the Church), valets (in personal attendance on the bishop and his chaplains), inferior servants and pages (the latter of whom might become squires). And, below all these, a small army of farmers, grooms, carters, larderers, falconers, porters, farriers, butlers, huntsmen and the like. And, in addition, members of the kitchen staff—cooks, bakers and kitchen-boys. Attached to the bishop's movable household staff there might be as many as a dozen servants, and, at each manor, another dozen or more, according to the size of the house and the estate attached to it. The bishop's chief falconer, Harpin by name, had a house at Ross high above the river. When the bishop wished to send him a message, he did so through his official messenger or courier.

The wage-bill of this army of servants was, even in the money of those days, a heavy burden on the official income of the bishop. The annual sums which they received in cash ranged from £1 a year down to 2s. In addition, everybody was kept and clothed, and many of them wore the bishop's livery. These were dressed in tunics made of striped cloth. The chapel clerks, whose chief duty was to sing the offices and to keep the chapel clean and tidy, the squires, the bailiffs and the lawyers had to wear the livery of the bishop, as had the pages, the waiters and the footmen. To clothe all these people, the bishop had cloth sent to him every year from London. One family, consisting of a widowed mother and her daughters, the bishop clothed for some years. But in his household, so far as can be gathered from the roll, there were no women servants. Yet it can hardly be expected that, like himself and his chaplains, all his domestic staff could be unmarried. Those who were married would live in cottages on the manors. Their wives could easily take in the washing of the bishop and his staff. From October 18th, 1289, to August 15th,

Turning the spit
Dishes being carried to the table

A royal banquet
Another banquet

A surreptitious drink

Scene in a courtyard

1290, the washing bill of the household amounted to £2 3s. 2¾d., which is at the rate of about one shilling a week, or, in the currency of to-day, 25s. to 30s. It must be remembered, however, that linen sheets were then unknown, and that before getting into bed all clothing was removed.

This list of servants does not exhaust the needs of the custodian for life of large landed property. Like his parallel in secular life, the bishop was constantly involved in litigation ; and as he could not plead his own causes he needed advocates and proctors in the civil as well as in the ecclesiastical courts, not only as far afield as London and Westminster but also at Rome. And, seeing that trial by combat was often resorted to, it was necessary for him to have his own champion, whom he inherited from his predecessor as bishop, and whose pay he raised from its original 6s. 8d. (a noble) a year. This champion was one Thomas of Bruges.

Like many other medieval prelates, Swinfield, not being able to enjoy the happiness of family life, undertook the guardianship of two boys, whom, doubtless out of regard for their parents, who by then may have been dead, he clothed and maintained and launched into careers. He also paid the expenses of one youth at the university of Oxford.

One feature of this roll is that, all the way through, it shews us the bishop and his travelling household " on the move ". In this it is typical of the records of the official acts of medieval archbishops and bishops which were written on sheets of parchment and afterwards bound to form registers. From these registers it is simple to compile the various itineraries undertaken by the archbishops and bishops whose doings the registers chronicle. So with Bishop Swinfield.

When a medieval prelate moved about the countryside, it was necessary for him to be accompanied by a retinue of attendants, some of whom were there to protect their master and his property from molestation and attack. While the bishop kept a large number of horses—it is impossible to say how many—and needed some of them for hunting, his chief need was for transport for himself and his attendants as they moved about. For an ordinary visitation of parishes in his diocese, the bishop had a train of between thirty and forty horses and their riders, and on one occasion, at Ross, seventy were counted. For a journey to London he took, as a rule, about fifty. His mounts included palfreys and sumpters, and, for his baggage, nags and even draught-horses. With him travelled grooms, drivers and farriers. Carts were needed for carrying the luggage. The bishop himself rode on horseback. He seems to have bought a new horse just about the time when the roll begins. His esquires and chaplains, too, were mounted, riding as his immediate bodyguard. The whole train, as it passed through the lanes and the villages at a dignified trot, must have been extremely picturesque. On such a tour, the bishop could spend nights at his own manors ; and in many records of similar tours it is plain that the route has been mapped out with the positions of these houses in mind.

We will now follow the bishop on his rounds in the year covered by the roll.

The itinerary began at Sugwas, the bishop's manor four or five miles west of Hereford, which he left on October 21st, 1289, after a stay there of three weeks. This may well have been his favourite residence. The house stood on the north or left bank of the river Wye. It possessed a mill, a dovecote, a fishing-ground and a private ferry across the river, with a fine park. From here the bishop could easily visit his cathedral ; and at least once in these three weeks he conferred with the dean and chapter in the chapter-house of the cathedral. The time spent at Sugwas was however mainly a period of rest. He left here, on October 21st as has just been said, for Bosbury, a distance, as the crow flies, of sixteen miles. The route lies through Hereford, along the Ledbury road for a few miles, and then almost due north-east for the last five miles. Here, at another of his manors, the bishop made a long stay of eight weeks, which the staff spent in hunting. Here, the bishop remembered, with gifts of venison and beef, at least three of his neighbours, one of whom was the vicar of Bishop's Frome, four miles north-north-west of Bosbury on the road to Bromyard. So many deer and cattle were killed that many hides were sold, while others were made into leather. The supply of candles was getting low, so the chandler was sent for, and he made 80 lbs. of candles, his charge for his work being 2s. 3d., probably for a week's work, and his travelling expenses 2½d. At the same time, Ralph of Marines and John of Baseville, two of the bishop's scribes, were sent to Bristol to buy wines, for which they paid £10 7s. 3d. in addition to the cost of carriage by water to Upton-on-Severn, ten miles from Bosbury, though the southern slopes of the Malvern hills had to be crossed on the way. The remainder was landed at a wharf on the Severn between Gloucester and Tewkesbury belonging to the prior and convent of Deerhurst, and conveyed to the bishop's manor at Prestbury. There is little doubt that Bosbury was the chief storehouse for the bishop's wine. While he was at Bosbury, the bishop instituted several clergy to benefices in the district. At Bosbury, too, he had a visit from a nephew of his, Walter of Scorene, whom he sent away with a gift.

On December 17th, the bishop left Bosbury for

Ledbury, where he stayed for only three nights. It was his most valuable manor, yielding to him a rent, in modern money, of more than £1,000 a year. While at Hereford and Ross he had had trouble with the lay-folk, his relations with the people of Ledbury were always pleasant. But he had arranged to spend Christmas at Prestbury, so on December 20th he set out once again, riding by way of Newent, where he had no property, to Highnam, less than three miles from Gloucester. At Highnam he received a welcome present of two palfreys from his friend the abbot of Gloucester, whom he had known for two years as prior of St. Guthlac, Hereford. Of the abbot, whose handsome face and snow-white hair attracted the attention of everybody, Edward I had remarked at the funeral at Amesbury of his mother, Eleanor of Provence, widow of Henry III, " There is not a prelate in my kingdom who appears to me so venerable as the abbot of Gloucester." Crossing the river, the procession entered Gloucester and rode by way of Cheltenham, or rather what is now Cheltenham, to the manor of Prestbury, where the bishop had decided to stay in his stone manor-house surrounded by a moat, until, after Christmas, he must make his way to London to attend a meeting of the Great Council of the nation, and another meeting of the bishops of the province of Canterbury, summoned by the archbishop of Canterbury, John Peckham. The date of his arrival at Prestbury was December 22nd.

Preparations were in full swing for the Christmas feast. The bishop's bailiff, Gerard of Eugina, had already carried out the needful repairs to the oven and the kitchen, and had bridged the gap between the kitchen and the larder with an awning. The usual fast was observed on Christmas Eve, but the company managed to keep body and soul together on as many herrings and codling and conger-eel as they could eat, and apparently the poor got nothing. An enormous salmon that had cost 5s. 8d. was also consumed. On this day, guests had arrived, for the number of horses had increased from forty-one to fifty-five. In this year, 1289, Christmas Day fell on a Sunday. At the Mass in the private chapel, the bishop contributed for himself and his family the large sum of 4s. 1d., and another 1s. for some of his workmen. For the Christmas feast the whole household appeared in clean linen. When all was ready, the boar's head was carried into the dining-hall amid scenes of acclamation and mirth. The roll tells us that, at the three meals on Christmas Day, two whole carcases and three-quarters of beef, two calves, four does, sixty fowls, eight partridges and two geese were consumed, and that the whole was helped on its way with ten sextaries (forty gallons) of red wine, one sextary of white wine and an amount of beer that was not measured. It may be concluded, with some certainty, that a large number of poor people were needed to consume the enormous amount of food that was left.

The journey to London was begun, on open roads, there not having been any frost, with fifty-one horses on December 28th, and Reading Abbey was reached, via Coln St. Aldwin's, where the abbot of Gloucester had a manor, at which the company was entertained, Farringdon, Lechlade ferry (where the Lech and the Thames were crossed at the junction of the two streams at a cost of 2d. paid to the ferryman) and Wantage. The date of their arrival at Reading was December 31st (not New Year's eve then, as the new year began on Lady Day, March 25th). For five nights they stayed at Reading Abbey, where they were entertained to music by Hugh, the abbot's harper, to whom the bishop gave a present. They set out for London on January 4th, and arrived at the bishop's London house in Old Fish Street, Queen-hithe, three days afterwards. This house, once the property (and probably also the town-house) of the well-known family of the Montalts, of Norfolk, had been bought from them by a bishop of Hereford fifty-five years earlier than this time, and had been bequeathed by him to his successors in the see. It was a roomy house, built of stone below and timber above; it had a dining-hall and several other large rooms, besides out-houses and stables. When the bishop needed the house, the tenant obligingly turned out for his lordship's convenience, being all the more ready to do this in virtue of a certain sum paid to him by way of compensation. Bedroom accommodation was, however, so limited that some of the party had to sleep on straw on the floor. As was usual, the bishop and his retinue fed well during their stay of almost six days. They took advantage of being near the river Thames to procure fish, such as gurnet and sturgeon, which they could not have from their own home streams. While they had brought their own game and venison with them, they were able to buy hares and rabbits, for in those days the solid mass of houses and other buildings that we know as London did not exist. Pastry is mentioned, and so is furmity or frumenty, which, then a delicacy, was made of wheat boiled in milk. But, though few details of the food are given in the roll, it is obvious that the visit to London was as costly then, in proportion, as such visits are now. The city and the surrounding villages and towns was full of nobles who had been called to Parliament, and their attendants. Wheat was double the price it was in the county of Hereford; and stabling was expensive because, at that time, the bishop had fifty horses in his train. One official was kept busy—Thomas de la Dane, who had to buy cloth for clothing for the next winter and to send it to the tailor to be made up ; wax and tapers, sugar and spices, had to be laid in ; and new boilers of brass had to be obtained in exchange for the old ones. And the bishop's favourite drinking-cup had to be repaired before the return journey could be begun.

The bishop himself had little time for anything but keeping his engagements. First, he had the duty of paying his court to the king and queen, then living at the magnificent new palace of Westminster, built by his father hard by the new abbey-church of Westminster, which also had been built by Henry III. To both, the bishop made a handsome gift—100 marks (£6 13s. 4d.) to the king, and 50 marks (£3 6s. 8d.) to the queen. Two days afterwards he was at Westminster again, and had to pay 12d. for breakfast for his valets at an eating-house, Westminster then being full of houses of entertainment and shops patronised by those who visited the court and Parliament. On another day some of the bishop's servants paid for their breakfast only five farthings. On yet another day, the bishop sent his attendants to and from Westminster by water. When the bishop arrived in London, he found that the bishops had already been in session for five days. Not being fond of meetings, however, he left London on January 13th, though the bishops continued sitting for another five weeks.

The first three days of the bishop's return journey were spent at Kensington, where, at the manor of the abbot of Abingdon, both he and his predecessor as bishop of Hereford had often stayed. The party left the manor on January 16th. Their next port of call was Bedfont, where they were fortunate enough to have a present from the rector of Stanwell, two miles from Staines, of hay sufficient for two days' supply for the horses. On the 18th they left Bedfont, and, avoiding Reading, went by way of the manor of Earley, three miles from Reading, where the bishop held ordinations in the chapel. Opportunity was taken to buy a supply of faggots at Reading to be taken home for the baking of bread. Horseshoes also had to be made. In consequence, the amount of food eaten was less than was usual, but on the evening of January 22nd they had beef, pork, fowls, venison and partridge to eat. The next day they arrived at Wantage, and the day after at Lechlade. Near there, the luggage-cart was upset, and a good deal of damage was done to the stock of dishes, cups and plates which the party carried with them. No fewer than 100 plates, 50 dishes, 50 saucers and 24 cups had to be bought to replace those that had been lost. Before the end of January the party were back at Prestbury, where at any rate they were at one of the bishop's homes. We need not follow the remainder of the tour in every detail. Between March 3rd, when Ledbury was left behind, and the end of September, when the roll ends, no fewer than twenty-five places were visited, some (e.g., Llandaff and Monmouth) being outside the bishop's diocese. At one place, the rector provided hay and corn as his contribution towards the stabling of the horses. At Llandaff, the great cathedral church had just been completed. On his way back from Llandaff the bishop called at Tintern, then in all its perfection. Ross was visited from March 14th to 18th. Here the bishops of Hereford had a prison, in accordance with directions given by Boniface, archbishop of Canterbury 1245–1273 :

> We enact that every bishop have in his episcopate one or two prisons for the confinement of wicked clerks, taken in crime or convicted according to ecclesiastical censure. And if any clerk shall have been so evil and incorrigible, and accustomed to the commission of the worst offences, for which even if he were a layman he ought, according to secular laws, to suffer extreme punishment, let such a clerk be sentenced to perpetual imprisonment.

All trace of this prison at Ross was lost until September, 1837, when, during excavations preparatory to the erection of a building on the site of the former episcopal manor-house, a vaulted room, with walls 5 feet 9 inches thick, and in length 16 feet and in breadth 12 feet, was discovered. Access to this room was not through a door but through an opening in the ceiling. One proof of the terrible fate of those who were confined in this prison was provided by the discovery, in one of the walls, of six enormous rings, each weighing 72 lbs. No man, however strong, could hope to escape, or even to move far, when fastened to such a cruel fetter. The presence of this kind of prison at Ross was enough to make the bishops unpopular there.

At Monkton, ten miles north of Monmouth, then the site of a priory, the prior entertained the bishop during a short visit by two country minstrels who had been specially hired, to each of whom the bishop gave 1*d*.— not a very generous acknowledgment of their services. At Colwall, at the foot of the western slopes of the Malvern hills, where the party stayed from March 31st to April 10th, and where the Easter feast, to which a large company had been invited, was celebrated, the food consumed on Easter Day was :

11 sectaries of Bosbury wine. Two carcases and a half of salt beef from the Bosbury larder. One bacon from the same. One boar from the household stock. One bacon from the same. One live ox from Ledbury, 16*s*. One carcase of fresh beef, by Baseville, 10*s*. 10*d*. Three pigs, 5*s*. 3*d*. Six calves, 9*s*. 2*d*. Nine kine, by Baseville, 3*s*. 2½*d*. Twelve kids, by the bailiff of Eastnor, 5*s*. Six capons, 12*d*. Eighty pigeons, by Baseville, 19*d*. 68 pigeons, from the Bosbury manor, 17*d*. Two pigs, one boar, six capons, six kids, presents. Out of these remain one carcase, one quarter of fresh beef, three pigs, one calf, five pigs, sixty pigeons. Three fat deer from the store. Four thousand eggs, 3*s*. 8*d*. Milk, by Baseville, 3*d*. Cheese, 12½*d*. Flour, 6*d*.

Suet, 2s. 6d.　Three bushels of salt, 16d.　Hay from the manor for 70 horses.　For their feed, four quarters seven bushels of oats, already accounted for.

The route that was then followed took the bishop to the northern part of his diocese, for during April he visited Cradley, Bromyard, Tenbury and Wenlock.　At Wenlock, on April 21st, he held a formal visitation. Beautiful Church Stretton had a visit from him on April 30th.　Another feast is chronicled at Bishops' Castle, where the bishop stayed from May 8th to 12th, this time the Ascension Day feast, the fast of the previous three (Rogation) days being over.　This is the entry :

Two quarters of flour baked from wheat bought from the manor, 6s. 8d.　Beer, 16d.　Half a carcase of beef, one roe, 11 kids, presents.　One carcase of beef, 6s. 0½d.　Two bacons from the manor, 3s.　Two calves, 12d.　19 geese, 4s.　28 fowls, 12d. 28 capons, 12 fowls, a present.　Out of these remain one bacon, 4 capons.　One side or flitch, 1 haunch, 1 rump of Bosbury venison.　2 sides, 1 haunch of hart, 1 side of doe, 1 fresh deer, 1 roe, a present.　There remain 1 side of hart, 1 side of doe, 1 lean deer.　Eggs, 10½d.　Milk, 3½d.　Bread or flour, 3d. Charcoal, by the bailiff, 7d.　Wheat for the kitchen, by the bailiff, 1½d.　Hay already reckoned for 34 horses ; their feed, 2 quarters 3 bushels of oats, accounted for.　2 bushels of bran, 2d.　The carriage of one horse-load of wheat from Ludlow, 3d. Horse-shoeing and other things, 3d.

The route then lay to the north-west, where the deanery of Leominster was situated.　On Sunday, May 15th, the bishop visited the parish church of Wigmore, where presumably he celebrated Mass ; and on the next day he presented himself at the abbey-church there.　He had not been there for three years, and meantime the injunctions then laid upon the canons had probably been forgotten by them.　Some of the brethren had then been engaged in secular trading ; the number of officers, some of them even the sons of the canons, had been excessive ; the sick brethren had not been cared for ; the usher, Jenkin Lightfoot, had been reported for gossiping ; and Richard, the sub-prior, has sown discord amongst the community. On this occasion the bishop contented himself with reproving the aged abbot, Adam, but three years later he was obliged to request him to resign in favour of a younger man.

The bishop next visited Leominster on May 20th, and lost no time in visiting the priory, then a cell or dependency of the abbey of Reading. This was his third visit since he had become bishop of Hereford, though the abbot of Reading had always exercised the power of sending to, or recalling from, the priory anybody whom he wished to move.

Sugwas, which stood in the same relation to the bishop's palace at Hereford as Bishopthorpe occupied in relation to the palace of the archbishops of York on the north of the Minster, was reached by the bishop on May 31st. He had now completed the most arduous of his tasks of visitation, that to the most remote part of his diocese.

The roll contains little more information about his travels, and ends with a call at his manor of Whithorne from June 17th to July 20th. There we leave him for his summer holiday, at home with his household.

This chapter may fitly end with a description of the household of a great lord, in which we see those whose education we have been studying actually at work. Our authority is *The Boke of Curtasye*, which, written not long before the middle of the fifteenth century, contains not only advice which has already been summarised, but also a good deal besides, expressed in iambic verse. The first book of the contents gives directions on the correct way to behave from the moment when a young man arrives at the gate of his lord. He leaves his weapon there with the porter, who gives him leave to enter the house. At the door of the hall, he doffs his hood and his gloves, greets the steward, the controller and the treasurer, bows to the gentlemen on each side of the hall, " takes heed " to the yeomen on his right hand, and waits to be conducted to the table. Bread is to be cut in two horizontally, the top half into four pieces and the bottom half into three. Bread must not be bitten, but broken. It is expected of those who sit at the lord's table that they will be agreeable, and that they will not fill their mouths like apes. They will not make noises when they drink their soup, nor will they scratch or stroke any of the dogs. Food must not be blown to cool it, knives must not be put into mouths, and mouths and eyes must not be wiped with the tablecloth. Those who drink when their mouths are full may choke and die. The first book ends :

Crist graunt vs alle his dere blessyng.

The second book is concerned with piety and conduct towards others. It is addressed to " young enfaunts " :

Yf that thou be a yong enfaunt
And thenke the scoles for to haunt,
This lessoun schalle thy maistur the marke
Croscrist the spede in alle the werke ;
Sytthen the pater noster he wille the teche,
As Cristes owne postles con preche
(Aftur thy Aue Maria and thi crede)
That shalle be saue as dome of drede ;
Than aftur to blesse the with the Trinite,
In nomine Patris teche he wille the ;
Then with Marke, Matthew, Luke and Ion,
With the per crucis and the hegh name ;
To schryue the in general thou schalle lere
By Confiteor and Misereatur in fere.

Then follow a list of Christian duties. Seek the king-dom of God and worship Him ; use holy water at the

door of the church ; kneel on both knees to pray, and
pray for all Christians, but to man kneel only on one
knee. Honour your parents ; do to others as you would
be done by ; do not be too meek ; seek peace, and be
ready to forgive ; be ready also to help others, with
good words if not with gifts ; be shrewd and cautious ;
speak the truth ; fulfil your promises ; and laugh spar-
ingly. The three enemies in this world are the devil, the
world and the flesh, which must be overcome by those
who would go to heaven. Do not gamble, even with
your lord. If anybody stumbles, help him to his feet
and do not laugh at him. Keep your secrets from
a shrew, and never speak " vnhonestly " of " woman
kinde . . . for alle we ben of wymmen born ". A wife
should " worschyp hyr husbonde bothe day and nyght,
to his byddyng be obediente, and hym to serue with-outen
offence ". Make peace in a quarrel. At a gate, allow
your equal and your superior to go in before you. If
you must share a bed with anybody else, let him choose
where he will lie and then lie as far away from him as
you can. And, strange to say,

> In no kyn house that rede non is
> Ne womon of the same colour y-wis,
> Take never they Innes for no kyn nede,
> For those be folke that are to drede.

Do not tell your enemy a lie, and always " onswere hym
mekely and make hym glose "; be still and quiet in the
presence of your lord and wash before eating ; at a feast,
sit not down in the highest place.

The third book treats of the duties of the various
officers in the service of a lord—the porter (who carries
the longest wand), the marshal, the usher (who carries
the shortest wand), the steward (whose wand is 18 inches
in length, and in breadth the thickness of a finger), the

squires, the butler and his staff, the grooms of the chamber, the controller, the surveyor, the clerk of the kitchen, the chancellor, the treasurer, the receiver of the rents, the avener (the deputy of the squire who is master of the horse), the baker, the huntsman, the water-carrier, the panter, the almoner, the sewer (the layer of the dishes) and the chandler. By itself, this list conveys an idea of the state in which a medieval noble lived, and to some extent explains the size and the disposition of those " stately homes of England " that have survived. Unfortunately, there is little clue to the amount of the payment which, in addition to board and lodging, this army of menials received, or to the full number of unskilled and untitled helpers at the disposal of most of them. It is difficult to resist the conclusion that the number of servants of one kind or another in the household of a medieval nobleman or bishop, even if he had only one large house or castle, can have been fewer than one hundred. An archbishop, who had manors in various parts of the country, as well as a palace not far from his cathedral, and a house in London, had to maintain the state of a duke.

The porter or janitor (Latin *janua*, gate) had charge of the small prison in which those who had committed offences against the lord's peace were confined until the lord could pass sentence on them. He had to exercise his discretion, often quickly, on the character of strangers who might present themselves at the gate. It was necessary for him to be a stout fellow, a match for any two ruffians who might have recourse to strength of arm or club. For his portion he seems to have received only his lord's livery and his " mete and drynke ". No doubt he had, in addition, those perquisites which depend largely on the ready way in which a man in that position, even to-day, tries to oblige those who need his help.

When his lord moved from one house to another, the porter was empowered to hire horses at

> foure pens a pece within the schyre.

The *marshal* of the hall was assisted by a *yoman-vsshere* and a groom, the groom having to provide the wood for the fires " in halle, chambre and kechyn ". It is interesting that the period for fires in the hall did not begin till " alhalawgh day " (November 1st) and came to an end at *cena domini*, that is, Maundy Thursday, the day next before Good Friday. The butler, the panter and the cooks also were placed under the marshal. The grooms of the chamber had the duty of making pallets of litter

> ix fote on lengthe withoute disware ;
> vij fote y-wis hit schal be brode.

Each lord was entitled to two of these beds, each hung with suitable curtains which

> reche shalle euen to grounde a-boute.

" Tapetis of spayne " was laid on the floor of the bedrooms, the fuel for which was carried by the grooms.

The usher of the chamber had to keep an eye on the tables and on the service as the meals proceeded. In addition, he was in charge of the lord's wardrobe and bedroom, the *wardroper* being under his orders. He provided the supplies for the buttery, candles, ale, wine ; and he even put the finishing touches on his lord at bedtime.

> Fro cupborde he brynges bothe brede and wyne,
> And fyrst assayes hit wele and fyne.
> But fyrst the lorde shalle vasshe I-wys,
> For the fyr hous when he comen is ;
> Then kneles the vssher and gyfes hym drynke,
> Brynges hym in bed where he shalle wynke ;

> In strong styd on palet he lay,
> At home tase lefe [takes leave] and gose his way ;
> Comon vssher be-fore the dore
> In vttur chambur lies on the flore.

The *steward* was not highly thought of, probably because the reputation of the only steward who is mentioned in the New Testament was poor.

> Now speke I wylle of the stuarde als,
> Few ar trew, but fele ar fals.

With the cooking of the food, the laying of the tables and the service in the hall, the steward had little to do. His was the responsibility for the accounts for the food and drink. This required a knowledge of arithmetic.

> At countyng stuarde schalle ben
> Tyl alle be beruet of wax so grene,
> Wrytten in-to bokes, with-out let,
> That be-fore in tabuls hase ben sett,
> Tyl countes also ther-on ben cast
> And somet vp holy at the last.

Household accounts which have survived from the middle ages have been printed in publications of antiquarian societies.

The *controller*, or, to give him his Latin title, *contra-rotulator*, was also regarded with suspicion. It was his duty to keep an eye on the accounts relating to the food and drink consumed every day, and of the stock that was left, and to revise the accounts of the clerk of the kitchen. The perspicacious writer ends his account of him with the words :

> Vncountabulle he is, as I you say.

The *clerk of the kitchen* had the difficult task of keeping stock of everything that was bought for use in the kitchen, paying the wages of the grooms and the yeomen, doling

out from the " dressour " the " mete dresset with honde ",
keeping the spices and the stores and being in charge
of the clothes of the officials of the kitchen. And, as
he appears to have been a convenient person on whom to
lay that responsibility which nobody else would accept,
the writer sums up his vague duties in this way :

> And mony thynges als, as I nought telle.

The *chancellor*—an official who is found in many medieval corporations, especially those of secular clergy,
though with different functions there—had charge of the
clothes of the yeomen and the *faukeners* and of the cover-
ings of the horses, and—it is interesting to note, was in
charge of the *cancella* or seal of the lord.

> If the lorde gyf oght to terme of lyf
> The chaunceler his seles withouten stryf
>
> .   .   .   .   .
>
> Ouerse hys londes that alle be ryght :
> On of the grete he is of myght.

The *treasurer*, " husbande and houswyf", received
everything due to the lord from the bailiff and the grieve
(A.S. *gerefa*, steward ; an official still found in Scotland),
and also from the lord's court. He also paid the wages
of the squires, yeomen, grooms, pages, receiver, treasurer,
clerk of the kitchen, chancellor, greeves, bailiffs and
parkers. For this he needed, above all, integrity and
ability. From his accounts the only appeal lay to
a " baron of chekker ", that is, a judge of the court of
exchequer, in which suits between the king and his
subjects relating to matters of revenue were heard.

The *receiver of the rents* was naturally in close touch with
the tenants of the estates ; he also had the duty of paying
the parkers (park-keepers) and of overseeing the " castles,
maners aboute ". For this, he received " sex pens ".

But for how long this had to last is not stated—probably only for a day.

> Nowe let we these officers be,
> And telle we wylle of smaller mene.

What follows refers to the less important officials—the avener, the baker and others. The *avener*, who, under a squire, was master of the horse, and, with the help of the farrier, who was paid $\frac{1}{4}d.$ for each horse that he shod, was responsible for feeding each horse in the stable with " two cast [armfuls] of hay and a pek of prouande [oats] " every day. About the stables, too, there were grooms, pages " mony one ", some at 2d. a day, others at $\frac{3}{4}d.$,

> Mony of hem fote-men ther ben,
> That rennen by the brydels of ladys shene.

The baker was expected to make out of " a lunden buschelle ", which was a little smaller in measure than the standard bushel, twenty loaves.

The *huntsman* had to feed the hounds for $\frac{1}{2}d.$ a day for every hound ; and greyhounds, in charge of the *feuterer*, were fed on bread. This was in addition to bones. Nothing is said about the wages of these men, but they received, for their " vantage ",

> Skynnes and other thynges with-alle
> That hunters can telle better than I
> Therefor I leue hit wytterly.

The water-carrier (*ewerer*) had the duty of providing all the water that was needed in the lord's portion of the house, and that of seeing that all were provided with towels. As no water-supply was " laid on ", his duty was no easy one.

The *almoner* said grace, and, this done, put on the table the alms-dish, into which the carver put a loaf and portions of two others.

While the administration of charity was probably

indiscriminate, and while no attempt was made, even on a small scale, to abolish poverty, at any rate everybody in the household of the great lord knew of the existence of poverty and want and had the opportunity of relieving them. The description of the work of the almoner is so graphic that it is worth quoting :

> The aumenere a rod schalle haue in honde,
> As office for almes, y vndurstonde.
> Alle the broken met he kepys y wate,
> To dele hit to pore men at the gate,
> And drynke that leues serued in halle,
> Of ryche and pore bothe grete and smalle.
> He is sworne to ouer-se the seruis wele,
> And dele hit to the pore euery dele ;
> Seluer he deles rydand by way,
> And his almys dysshe, as I you say,
> To the porest men that he can fynde,
> Other ellys I wot he is vhkynde.

The almoner therefore was, in the opinion of the writer of the poem, kind as an official but not as a man.

Even in a lord's kitchen no risk was taken with the food, all of which had to be tasted by the *sewer* before it was served.

> When the seuer comys vnto the borde,
> Alle the mete he sayes [assays] on bare worde,
> The potage fyrst with brede y-coruyn,
> Couerys hym agayn lest they ben storuyn [spoilt by being served cold] ;
> With fysshe or flesshe yf they be serued,
> A morselle therof shalle be keruyd [carved] ;
> And touche the messe ouer alle aboute,
> The sewer hit etis with-outen doute.
> With baken mete yf he seruyd be tho,
> The lydes [lids] vp-rered or he fyr go,
> The past or pye he sayes with-inne,
> Dippes bredde in graue no more ne mynne ;
> If the baken mete be colde as may byfalle,
> A goblet of tho self he sayes with-alle.

And the *butler's* duty was to assay or test all the wine. Any wine that was left over in the lord's cup was put into the alms-dish.

Finally, in this long list comes the chandler, who made and supplied the candles and the torches that were the only source of light. The lights had to be put out with scissors. Wax candles were used in the bedrooms, and in the hall " candles of Paris ", each mess having one from " alhalawghe day to candelmasse ", that is, from All Saints' Day (November 1st) to Candlemas (February 2nd). The long poem ends :

> Of alle oure synnes Cryst be oure leche,
> And bryng vs to his vonyng place [dwelling-place].
> Amen, saye ye, for hys grete grace,
>   Amen, par charite.

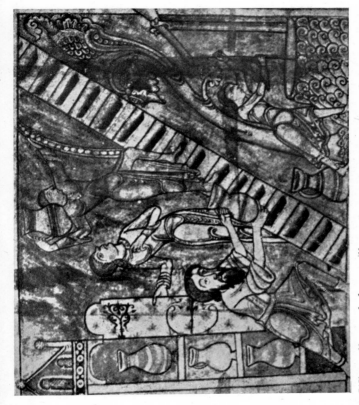

Wine-cellar and draw-well

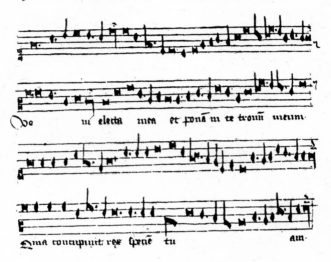

Music from the York Mystery Plays

CHAPTER VIII

PLAY-ACTING

(1) GENERAL

DRAMA, act and *play*, the three English words most used in connexion with the activity which forms the subject-matter of this chapter, are derived from different languages, but they have in common the same underlying meaning, that of action. The earliest occurrence of the word *drama* in English literature was in 1515 ; the word *plaie* is universally applied to a dramatic performance during nearly the whole of the middle ages.

The attraction of acting is universal and timeless. Children have always loved to " dress up " ; history is full of instances of acting a part in real life ; in ancient Greece there was no play so popular as that in honour of Bacchus, who became the god of drama ; and our passion for acting is shewn by our medieval forefathers and the crowded " houses " at the " cinema " and the real drama. These are examples of the love of acting amongst peoples who differed in age, in circumstance and in religious outlook. Much ancient drama was based on religion, and was presented only on religious festivals. At first, the Christians scorned the drama as a heathen custom and condemned it as undignified and immoral. The time was to come when the Church would use drama as a powerful aid in her work.

Medieval drama was almost exclusively religious in character. It centred round three kinds of plays— miracle, mystery and morality. None of these gained a firm hold on the people of this country till the thirteenth century. The medieval man loved plays about scriptural events and the teaching of the Church. When these were performed by members of trade and craft gilds, generally in groups called "cycles", they were called "mystery" plays, that is, plays performed by members of the "misteries" or trade and craft gilds; when they were performed by professional players, and sometimes by amateurs who were acting not as members of any trade or craft gild but as individuals, they were called "miracle" plays. The former date back in this country to the twelfth century, when, as a rule, they were written in Latin and performed by clerics, either regular or secular. Later, they were translated into, or written in, English, for performance by lay players, many of whom were members of strolling companies, the medieval predecessors of modern touring companies. A trilogy of plays in the Cornish dialect, about the Creation of the world, and the Passion and the Resurrection of Christ, is not merely the earliest surviving miracle play in one of our native tongues but also the unconscious prototype, in subject-matter, of the later mystery plays performed on the feast of Corpus Christi every year for more than two centuries. Many of the early miracle plays were based on French originals, and for many years some of them were rendered in the French tongue. These plays, as individual plays, were succeeded by others written all through the middle ages, and were supplanted by the cycles of mystery plays connected with Chester (first in the field at the end of the reign of Henry III), Wakefield (the Towneley plays), Coventry (*ludus Coventriae*), York, Newcastle-on-Tyne, Leeds, Lancaster, Preston, Kendal and, of course, London, where the acting was done by the parish clerks. Something more detailed will be said about some of these plays later in this chapter.

Morality plays never gained the popularity of the miracle and mystery plays. To begin with, they were too abstract and too allegorical to appeal to the popular taste. They were founded on the idea of the *Psychomachia*, or conflict of Virtues and Vices, of the thirteenth century. It was not hard for anyone with the dramatic instinct to represent these conflicts through stage characters carrying on imaginary conversations. To sustain the interest of the audience, the Devil was usually attended by one of the vices in the guise of a jester, who, if he were a born comedian, could make the audience laugh heartily at his quips and sallies at the expense of his diabolical chief. But the moralities came too late in the middle ages, and were too serious and abstract, to gain much support. They did, however, help to bridge the gap between the mystery plays and the very different kind of drama of the age of Shakespeare.

When the Normans came to this country, they brought with them the idea of religious drama. They knew how effective the presentation of religious plays in churches or churchyards could be ; they were alive to the necessity of putting into the mouths of the actors the very words of Scripture ; and they valued the use of action in helping to convey the atmosphere of New Testament times. The presentation of religious plays quickly became part of the attraction of local fairs held in scores of towns all over the country, a feature which until recently survived in the north of England in the form of " ghost-shows ". These itinerant shows sprang directly from the wandering minstrels and others who travelled from place to place over such roads as there were in the early middle ages. Much real talent for acting has found its opportunity in this nomadic life lived in caravans rather than in the theatre.

The wandering entertainers, whose greatest opportunity came on holidays—really holy-days, such as the Easter and Whitsuntide seasons—proved serious competitors to the Church. People were tempted to forsake the services of the Church for the attractions of the open air. The effect of this was to spur the Church to greater efforts to attract people to its own dramas. In fine and warm weather, religious plays were performed in the churchyards, where there was then much more free space than there now is, when graves occupy the whole of the churchyards of ancient town churches. But the competition between the Church and the travelling and other lay actors still went on. For one thing, the comic element was excluded from religious plays acted in churches or churchyards. For another, early in the fourteenth century the clergy were forbidden to have any plays except those which represented the Nativity, the Passion and the Resurrection. Payment of lay actors for their help in religious plays in churches and churchyards did not mend matters ; and, when trade gilds began to compete with representations of their own plays on the feast of Corpus Christi, plays performed in churches had to take second place. Yet these plays went on until the end of the sixteenth century.

The source from which much information is derived about plays arranged by parish priests and their lay helpers in the middle ages, and performed either in the churches and the churchyards or on some other public site such as a market-place, is found in the accounts, where these have survived, of the churchwardens of ancient parish churches. At first, these accounts were written on rolls of parchment, but with the use of paper they began to be kept in books. Beginning with the accounts of the church of St. Michael, Bath, in the year 1349, the churchwardens' accounts which have survived provide, until they begin to be plain and bald statements of money received and spent, some of the most interesting side-lights on that part of the daily life of the parishes which had its focus in the parish churches. Except for a few scattered pieces of information, little is known about these plays before the middle of the fourteenth century. A schoolmaster of Dunstable, Geoffrey by name, who lived not long after the Norman Conquest, wrote the first miracle play which has come to light in this country. It was about the life of St. Catherine, who in the fourth century was tortured between spiked wheels —hence the name " Catherine wheels " for a kind of firework still popular on Guy Fawkes's day—and then beheaded because she would not renounce the Christian faith. The abbey of St. Albans lent the costumes to Geoffrey—a sure proof that miracle plays were performed at this great abbey 900 years ago. But the performance ended in a riot, and both the stage properties and Geoffrey's house were set on fire and destroyed. The sadder and wiser author then turned monk and died abbot of St. Albans. Thus disastrously ended an early attempt to use religious drama as a means of teaching the ordinary man, woman and child.

From the middle of the fourteenth century, however, until the end of the sixteenth, and at Wootton, Hampshire, for a century afterwards, religious plays were arranged by parish priests and their people in aid of parish funds. References to these plays in the accounts of churchwardens shew that they were performed at various seasons. At Braintree, Essex, in the year 1523, a play on the life of St. Swithun helped the funds of the church by the sum of £3 13s. 7½d. ; a St. Andrew's play brought in £3 17s. 8d. two years later ; and, nine years later, a play on St. Eustace no less than £8 2s. 8½. These profits were far greater than the sum of only 7s. taken in the parish of Hedon, in the East Riding of Yorkshire, in the year 1340, even when allowance has been made for the decreased value of money in the interval. Plays were popular in the parish of St. Margaret, Southwark, as the following items shew :

1453–4. Peid for a play upon seynt lucy day and for a pley upon seynt margrete day . . . . . xiijs.
  (This would be the cost of the manuscript copy.)

1458. Upon seynt lucy day to the clerkes for a pley . vjs. viijd.
  (This would be the pay of the actors.)

1460. To the Mynstrell for the procession . . . xvjd.
  (This would be the pay of the musician.)

1460. For hyryng of the Germentes . . . . xiiijd.

1466. To Harry for his Chyldren upon Seynt Lucy day . xijd.
  (A reference to acting by children.)

At Ashburton, Devonshire :

1528–9. For painting cloth for the players and making their tunics and for making staves for them and crests upon their heads on the festival of Corpus Xti . . ixs. ixd

1533–4. Recorded and alowed to the pleirs of crystmas game that pleyd in the churche . . . . . ijs.

1534–5. To the pleyers of Exeter playyng a Chrissmas game ijs.

1536–7. For a hed of here [a wig] and other thynges for the players . . . . ijs.

1537–8. For a pair of silk garments for Herod on Corpus Xti daye . . . . xijd.

1542–3. For ij devils heads and other necessary things for the players . . . . ijs. jd.

1555–6. For a payr of glovys for hym that played God Almighty at Corpus Xti daye . . . . . ijjd.

1558–9. For a payr of glovys to hym that played Christ on Corpus Xti daye . . . . ijjd.

St. Lawrence's, Reading, usually presented its plays not in the church but on a piece of ground, not far away, called Forbury.

1507. Rec. of the Sonday afore Bartylmastyde [St. Bartholmew's tide] for the play in the Forbery . . . ixd.
  To the labours for setting up the polls for the schaffhold . . . . ixd.
  To the Bereman [bear-man] for ber for the pley in the Forbury . . . . xd.

For ij ells di [i.e., 2½ ells] of cros-cloth for to make Eve
a cote .   .   .   .   vd.
For makyng of a dublett of lethur and j payr of hosyn of
lethur agaynst Corpus Xti day .   .   .   viijd.

This parish used to present an Easter play every year.

1534. Payd to Mr. Laborne for reformyng the Resurrecion
play .   .   .   .   viijs. iiijd.
1535. Payd to Mr. Laborne for a boke of the resurrection play
for a qu'r of paper and for byndyng thereof . ixs. ixd.

On St. Margaret's day in the year 1511, twenty-seven
neighbouring parishes, including the parish of Royston,
joined the parish of Bassingbourne, Cambridgeshire, in
presenting a play, each parish bringing an offering
towards the expenses. The sums varied from 10d. to
12s., the latter sum being paid by the parish of Royston.
Twenty-one years later, Weybridge, Essex, was joined by
twenty-three other parishes in the presentation of a play
on the Sunday before Whitsunday. These gatherings
were made the excuse for feasting. At Weybridge, the
players and their friends consumed, in flesh meat alone,
" a quartere of ij beffes, 7 cawys [calves], 6 shepe and
8 lambys ".

At various places, on May Day and on other occasions
during the summer, the populace gave itself up to enjoy-
ment provided by companies of entertainers who, dressed
in character costumes, took the parts of Robin Hood,
Maid Marian, Little John and Friar Tuck, with their
friends in Sherwood Forest. The expenses of the players
were paid out of the parish accounts, on condition that
the collections taken by the entertainers, who seem to
have " passed the hat " round during the performances,
were paid to the churchwardens in aid of church funds.
Naturally, the amounts of the takings varied very much.
Robin Hood usually collected the largest sum. At
Croscombe, Somerset, the whole of the takings varied,

over a period of several years, from 1480 to 1527, from less than 20s. to about £4. " Camyth in Robyn Hode and Lytyll John ", runs the account for the year 1500–1501, " and presyntyd in xvs ", apparently for both of them ; and that year was not a very good one, for the whole of the proceeds came to little more than 20s.

The following entries from accounts speak for themselves :

Reading, St. Lawrence.

1502. Rec. of the May play callyd Robyn Hod . . vjs.
1504. Recd. of the gaderyng of the said Robyn Hod in mony xlixs.
     Payed for a cote to Robyn Hod . . vs. viijd.
     Payed to a Taberer on Philips Day and Jacob for his wages mete and drink and bed . . . viijd.
1505. For Robin Hods cote and he's house. . vjs. vijd.
1506. For a supper to Robyn Hod and his company xviijd.
1557. For the yeough tree . . . . . iiijd.
     For fetchinge the summer pole . . . . ijd.

At Betley Hall, Staffordshire, there is a window of the second half of the fifteenth century which represents, round the motto : " A merry May ", figures dancing to music played on a pipe by a musician, who beats his own drum, a jovial monk being one of the dancers. In ancient time in this country, May-Day, the first day of May, was made a holiday so that the arrival of spring might be greeted with joy. The maypole, which can still be seen on some village greens, was the centre of the festivities, which were attended by the chimney-sweeps as a sign that their " slack time " had come with the disuse of household fires until the autumn. Even London had its maypoles, the last being removed early in the eighteenth century and used at Wanstead Park, Essex, to support a giant telescope belonging to Sir Isaac Newton.

CHAPTER IX

PLAY-ACTING

(2) MYSTERY PLAYS AT YORK AND COVENTRY

THE feast of Corpus Christi was founded by Urban IV in 1264 in honour of the sacrament of the Body of Christ. The observance spread westwards surely if not swiftly ; and, at Paris in the year 1313, the feast was celebrated with solemnity and dignity for eight days, in the presence of Edward II and Isabella of France, king and queen of England. The celebrations included the representation, in plays, of the glory of the blessed and the tortures of the damned. It may have been one result of this that a miracle play in English, *The Harrowing of Hell*, was written. The play, a short one of only 250 lines, describes the descent of Christ into the lower world in the interval between His Crucifixion and His Resurrection to release the good souls held there since the days of Adam and Eve. In the play, a conversation takes place at the mouth of hell between Christ and the Devil, Christ enters, the doorkeeper runs away, and the Devil and his followers flee in confusion. This was one of the favourite subjects of paintings in the middle ages. It was at about this time—a little earlier at Chester—that, in many cities and towns, the observance of the new feast began to be made by representations of plays in long cycles. Only four of these cycles have survived in anything like completeness, those connected with Chester, Coventry, Wakefield and York. They are composed of a varying number of plays on subjects connected with the Old Testament, the New Testament (the birth, Passion and Resurrection scenes, with very few taken from Christ's ministry), and often scenes from the life of the Virgin (her death, assumption and coronation), the whole series ending with the Last Judgment, another favourite subject of paintings. In these plays the medieval man received his instruction in the Bible. It was Chester that set the example of a cycle of plays to be acted on the feast of Corpus Christi. This cycle contained 47 plays, compared with 48 at York, 42 at Coventry and 32 at Wakefield. The manuscript of the Chester plays as it now exists was probably written about the year 1400. Fortunately, much more information about these plays remains in a manuscript now at the British Museum. It is headed:

> Now of the playes of Chester called the whitson playes, when they weare plaied and what occupacions bringe forthe at theire charges the Playes and pagiantes.

This interesting record states that the plays were written by :

> one Rondoll a monke of the Abbaye of St. Warburge in Chester, who redused the whole history of the byble into Englishe storeys in metter [metre], in the englishe tounge ; and this monke, in a good desire to doe goode, published the same. then the firste mayor of Chester namely Sir Iohn Arneway knighte, he caused the same to be played anno domini 1329.

This document therefore assumes that the plays were written by Ranulph Higden, author of *Polychronicon*, who is said to have travelled to Rome three times before he could get permission from the pope for the plays to be presented in the English tongue. As one authority, however, asserts that the Chester plays were being performed as early as the end of the reign of Henry III, a whole century before they could have been performed if the Higden authorship and journeys are taken as facts, there is sufficient contradictory evidence to justify doubt of both authorities. The document proceeds :

The playes weare diuided into 24 pagiantes or partes, and euery Companie brought forthe their pagiante which was the carriage of place which they played in. And yerlye before these were played there was a man fitted for the purpose which did ride, as I take it, vpon St. George daye throughe the Cittie and there published the tyme and the matter of the plays in briefe, which was called " the readinge of the banes " [banns]. They were played vpon monday, tuesday and wednesday in witson weeke.

The places or stations at which the plays were performed in turn are then given, a start, quite properly, being made at the gate of the abbey. It is not clear from the manuscript how many stations there were ; but if the number of plays is correctly given as twenty-four—even on this point there is no agreement—the number of stations on each of the three days could not have been more than eight.

Information is given as to how the plays were stage-managed :

These pagiantes or cariage was a highe place made like a howse with ij rowmes, being open on the tope ; the lower rowme they apparrelled and dressed them selues, and in the higher rowme they played ; and they stoode vpon 6 wheeles. And when they had done with one carriage in one place they wheeled the same from one street to an other . . . keaping a direct order in euery streete ; for before the firste carriage was gone the seconde came, and so the thirde, and so orderly till the laste was donne, all in order, without any stayeings in any place ; for, worde being broughte how euerye place was neere done, they came and made no place to tarye till the laste was played.

The form of proclaiming the banes or curses, which is contained in another manuscript, is interesting, contain-ing, as it does, a warning that those players who take the part of " gods " will not be seen except in a cloudy covering :

And now God in shape or person to appeare.

As time went on, however, protests were made about the

irreverence which crept into other Chester plays, such as

> the diuell in his fethers before the butchers, a man in woman's
> apparell, with a diuill waytinge on his horse called cuppes and
> cans, god in stringes, with other thinges.

The records prove, however, that the plays were acted regularly though perhaps not every year, as in certain years what are called Midsummer plays were acted instead, from 1328, when it is stated that the plays were written by Higden, to 1611.

Much more is known about the York plays. The manuscript of them, almost certainly the " official " copy once in the possession of the corporation of the city, was once in the possession of the family of Lord Ashburnham, and is now in the British Museum. The book contains 270 leaves, of which six are blank, this being due to the copying of the plays at different times, the last play in the book not being copied till towards the end of the reign of Queen Elizabeth. Most of the manuscript, however, belongs to the first half of the fifteenth century.

The first proclamation relating to these plays required, in the name of the king, the lord mayor and the two sheriffs of the city, that, except those officials who were entitled to have swords carried before or after them, no man should bear arms during the procession on the feast of Corpus Christi on the day following the day on which the plays had been acted, that no alteration should be made in the places at which they were to be presented, that the actors and the taperers should be ready to take their parts at the early hour of 4.30 a.m., and that the pageants should follow each other during the day without delay. For failure to observe these instructions the fines varied from half-a-mark (6s. 8d.) to 100 shillings.

No description of the stages used at York has survived

even if any description was ever made. The present description is founded mainly on the account of the stages used in the Chester plays. The stage had two rooms, the upper for acting, the lower for a dressing-room. The two were connected by means of a trap-door, a device which was convenient not so much for the entrances of the players, who usually entered from the back of the stage, as for the reception of those who, in the play of the Last Judgment, were condemned to hell. Naturally, the stages were decorated with paint and covered in stuff of various kinds. The Coventry gild of cappers took a carpenter round with them in case of accidents. The scenery was primitive and scanty ; so were the stage properties. An ark of reasonable size had to be used in the play about Noah and the Flood. Small boxes of the style of sentry-boxes were used for palaces such as those of Herod and Pilate, and for the Upper Room, the Synagogue and even the Temple. Such properties as crosses, spears, tools and weapons were well and artistically made at a time when good craftsmanship was the rule. Horses and asses were represented by dummy figures made of hoops and canvas. Clouds and trees and tombs were usually painted on the background. The noise of the earthquake in the Crucifixion scene was produced from below by means of stones in a barrel. Dummy figures of angels were kept floating in the air by being attached to windlasses. When the moment of the Resurrection came, a bright light was produced by setting fire to a lump of resin, and the end of the world at the Last Day by means of a burning globe. The costumes were by no means cheap and nasty, for every gild would have amongst its actors well-to-do men of business, and there was much rivalry amongst the gilds for the honour of producing the best play. False hair and beards were of various colours, though mostly gold and white. Christ was dressed in a long coat of fine sheepskin " woven without seam from the top to the bottom ". Herod, who brandished a large sword and was dressed like a Saracen, was usually in a passion ; if he shewed signs of mildness, his attendant, a boy, had to beat him into a condition of fury with a bladder attached to a stick. While angels were put into white surplices and had golden hair, demons wore ugly masks and made hideous noises. The Devil wore a coat of rough hair, had a red beard and was given horns and a tail. Lost souls, about to be sent to hell through the trap-door, were dressed in striped garments of black and yellow, and had their faces blackened, as if by fire and smoke.

In these plays, comedy was mixed with tragedy and pathos. Clowning and buffoonery are found, the forerunners of Shakespeare's clowns and the modern comedian. It seems natural that Noah and his wife should quarrel because she did not believe that the flood would come, and that she should refuse to go into the ark until her husband had given her a beating. One of the plays in the Wakefield series is so ridiculous that it has been called " the first farce in the English language ". But also there was much beauty and pathos, as in the scenes in which the Virgin is with her Child and Abraham is preparing to slay Isaac.

The standard of acting and of presentation that was expected was not low. The proclamation already referred to demanded

> good players, wel arayed and openly spekyng ;

and the council decided

> that verely in the tyme of lentyn there shall be called afore the maire for the tume beyng iiij of the moste connyng discrete and able players within the Citie, to serche, here and examen all the plaiers and plaies and pagentes thrughoute all the artificers belong-

ing to Corpus Christi Plaie. And all suche as thay shall fynde
sufficiant in personne and connyng to the honour of the Citie
and worship of the saide Craftes, for to admitte and able, all
other insufficiant personnes, either in connyng, voice or personne
to discharge, ammove and avoide. And that no plaier that shall
plaie in the saide Corpus Christi plaie be conducte and reteyned
to plaie but twise on the day of the saide playe ; and that he or
thay so plaing plais nor ouere twise the saide day vpon payne of
xl s. to forfet vnto the chaumbre as often tymes as he or they shall
be founden defaute in the same.

The requirement that no player should " plaie but
twise on the day of the saide plaie " cannot have meant
that none of the players should appear more than twice
in the day. This would have placed an undue strain on
the gilds to provide a far greater number of actors than
they were required to provide already, and would have
added to the number of rehearsals and the difficulty of
making costumes to fit people of different sizes. The
likely meaning is that no individual might appear in more
than two parts in any one play.

At first, the plays were presented at three stations on
one side of the river and at nine on the other. Very
soon this order was revised, probably in the interests of
finance. In 1417, citizens were allowed to bid against
each other for the privilege of having the plays represented in front of their houses. The city authorities
would welcome this change in the arrangements, for the
cost of production increased with the rising cost of living.
Doubtless, too, those who bought the right to have
stations in front of their houses would not be above
charging for admission to their small windows. In 1554
the number of stations was sixteen. Rents paid for the
sites varied, in 1519 from 12d. to 4s. 4d., probably according to the size of the sites. One expense which fell on
the city was the payment of a messenger, a kind of " city
crier ", for two journeys round the city to " cry " the

news that the plays were to be presented. The only recorded royal visit to the city while the plays were in progress was that of Richard II in 1397. The king was given the seat of honour at the gate of the priory of Holy Trinity, Micklegate, the starting-point of the plays and of the procession on the day following. For his extra work in preparing for the royal visits, the porter of the priory was given the sum of 4d.

How were the expenses of presenting the plays met? Chiefly by contributions from the members of the gilds, on each of whom a levy was made called " pageant-silver ". There is no indication in the few *compoti* that have survived that collections were made from those who witnessed the plays, though it would be strange if this obvious way of helping to meet the expense were ignored. Those in business in the city for a time, such as foreigners, were required to contribute as what may be called " co-opted " members of the gilds. The girdlers' gild required contributions from those " of the church ", that is, members of religious orders, or secular clergy, who made such things as

bokes, claspes, dog colers, chapes and girdilles.

Each of these was required to pay towards the cost of the production of their play twice as much as was paid by each member of the gilds. It may be inferred that the ultimate authority of the city could be invoked to support such claims. In 1483, when probably certain arrangements had to be revised, four producers promised the mayor that they would :

by the assent of all the Innholders of this seid Citie take apon them to bryng furth yerly durying the term of viij yere then next folluyng the pagent of the Coronacion of our Lady perteyning to the said Innholders and also to reparell the said paghent so that they that holdys Inys and haith no syns [i.e. inn-signs] pay as wel, and as moche yerely to the reparacion of the said pagent and bryngyng furth of the same, as the said Inholders that haith syns doyth, i.e., iiij*d.* each.

In the list of the plays and of the companies responsible for them which the book of the plays contains, there are only forty-eight plays. In the list made in 1415, however, there are fifty-seven. The reason is that the two lists were made at different times, the latter, as has been pointed out above, at various times as the plays were officially registered. The Corpus Christi plays had an uninterrupted course from the time when they started until towards the end of the fifteenth century, when competition began between them and the play of the Lord's Prayer and that of the gild of Corpus Christi on the Creed. It is not easy to assign a reason for the competition, for the whole of the year was open to those who wished to perform other kinds of plays. It was urged by a writer on the Towneley or Wakefield Mysteries in 1837 that :

> these mysteries are highly curious as affording us a specimen of the amusements of our unpolished ancestors and of the manner in which they endeavoured to combine instruction with entertainment. Whether it succeeded may admit of question. In them we have the most disgusting ribaldry joined with the deepest pathos, the most revolting blasphemy in connexion with the most sacred mysteries of our religion.

It may be doubted whether this judgment could be sustained in any serious inquiry into the matter. It is not easy for us to get, as it were, inside the mind of the medieval man, who seems to have treated his religion in a much more familiar and homely way than has been usual since the Reformation. It is more than likely that long familiarity with the mystery plays was breeding contempt. It was no ordinary burden on a gild to produce one of these plays year in and year out for two centuries. Further, the spirit of the middle age was dying, even if slowly. The plays belonged to the "old learning", and one sign of the times was the beginning of a change in the attitude towards the feast of Corpus Christi. In any case, the competition between the mysteries and the other plays went on intermittently from the end of the reign of Henry VIII till 1580, when the plays of Corpus Christi came to an end. Their supporters struggled for their continuance, but it is not surprising, regard being had to the conflict of religious opinion at the time, that the Church decided against their continuance. While supporters of the claims of the old plays sometimes gained temporary victories by persuading the lord mayor and the council to agree to a presentation of their favourite plays, the city authorities brought matters to a head on two occasions by appealing, on the first, to the judgment of the dean of York (Matthew Hutton) and then to that of the archbishop of York (Edmund Grindal). On the play of the Creed, Matthew Hutton wrote :

Salutem in Christo. My most humble dewtie vouched. I have perused the bokes that your lordshipp with your brethren sent me, and as I finde manie thinges that I muche like because of th' antiquities, so see I manie thinges that I can not allowe because they be disagreing from the sencentie of the gospell, the which thinges, yf they shuld either be altogether cancelled or altered into other matters, the wholle drift of the play shuld be altered, and therefore I dare not put my pen unto it, because I want both skill and leasure to amende it, thoghe in good will I assure you yf I were worthie to geve your lordshipp and your right worshipfull brethren counsell suerlie mine advise shuld be that it shuld not be plaid, ffor thoghe it was plawsible to yeares agoe and wold now also of the ignorant sort be well liked yet now in this hapie time of the gospell I knowe the learned will mislike it, and how the state will beare with it I know not. Thus beinge bold to utter mine opinion unto your lordshippe, I committ you and your brethren to the tuition of God's spirit.

> Your Lordshipps in Christ to commaunde,
>
> MATTH. HUTTON.

To the right honorable my Lorde Mayor of York and the right worshipfull his brethren, geve this.

The council decided :

> to have no play this yere, and the booke of the Creyde play to be delyveryd again.

The play was however represented again in the following year. But the letter of the dean and the action of the council on it shews how opinion was tending. On Corpus Christi day three years afterwards (1572) the play of the Lord's Prayer was due for presentation. A message was sent to the archbishop (Edmund Grindal) that his grace :

> be requested to have a copie of the bookes of the Pater Noster play, wherupon it was aggreed that his grace shall have a trewe copie of all the said bookes even as they weare played this yere.

For three years the archbishop neither returned the books nor delivered his judgment. On July 8th, 1575, the council asked two of its aldermen (Mr. Allyn and Mr. Maskewe) and two others (Mr. Robert Brooke and Mr. Andrewe Trewe) to :

> goe and require of my Lorde Archebishop his grace all suche bookes as perteine this cittie now in his grace's custodye, and that his grace will apoynt twoe or thre sufficiently learned to correcte the same, wherein the lawes of this realme ther are to be reformed, and if ther leysure will serve to goe about the premisses before Lammas next.

Nothing more is recorded till the spring of the year 1579, when the council gave its consent to the perform-

ance of the Corpus Christi play in accordance with the
ancient custom, but that first of all :

> the booke shalbe caried to my Lord Archebisshop (no longer
> Grindal, who had become archbishop of Canterbury, but Edwin
> Sandys) and Mr. Deane to correcte, if that my Lord Archebisshop
> doe well like theron.

It may be presumed that nothing happened in answer
to this request ; and, when the people petitioned the
council that on the day of the annual election of the new
lord mayor the Corpus Christi play should be acted, all
the satisfaction they got was a reply from the lord mayor
that " he and his brethren would consider of their
request ". No more references to any of the plays are
to be found in the records of the city, and it seems to be
certain that the acting of all the medieval plays now
ceased. It was in 1580 that the Coventry plays were
seen for the last time. The wonder is that during
a period of religious controversy they had lasted as long
as they did. By this time, English drama had entered
into the most glorious period of its history. That Shakespeare knew about the medieval plays is evidenced by his
references to them. When the religious plays came to
an end they had a more-than-worthy successor in the
Shakespearean dramas.

Here are some examples of the style of the author who
composed the plays. After creating Adam and Eve, the
Almighty says to them :

> At heuene and erthe firste I be-ganne,
> And vj daies wroughte or y wolde reste,
> My werke is endid nowe at manne,
> Alle likes me wele, but this be beste.
> My blissynge haue they euer and aye.
> The seunte day shal me restyng be ;

> Thus wille I see, sothly to say,
> Of my doyng in this degre,
> To blisse I schal you brynge
> Come forthe ye two with me,
> Ye shalle lyff in likyng
> My blissyng with you be.

The scene when Abraham is about to draw the knife to slay Isaac, his son, is full of pathos :

Abraham. Now, my grete god, Adonay,
> That all this worlde has worthely wroght,
> For-gyffe the sone, for his mercye,
> In worde, in werke, in dede and thoght.
> Nowe sone, as we ar leryd [taught],
> Our tyme may not miscarie.

Isaac.   Nowe fare wele, all medilerth [the world],
> My flesshe waxis faynte for ferde ;
> Nowe, fadir, take your swerde,
> Me thynke full lange ye tarie.

At the crossing of the Red Sea, the king of Egypt, finding himself in the water, cries out :

> Owte ! ay herrowe ! devill, I drowne !

Egyptian. Allas ! we dye, for alle our dede.

Israelitish Now ar we wonne fra waa, and saued oute of the see.
boy.   Cantemus domino, to god a sang synge wee.

Pilate, the braggart as he is often represented to be in these plays, makes no small claim for himself :

> For sir Sesar was my sier,
> And I sothely his sonne,
> That exelent emperoure exaltid in hight,
> Whylk all this wilde worlde with wytes had wone,
> And my modir hight Pila that proude was pight [set],
> O Pila that prowde and Atus her fadir he hight.
> This pila was hadde in to Atus
> Nowe renkis [knights], rede ye it right ?
> For thus schortely haue I schewid you in sight,
> How I am prowdely preued Pilatus.

Herod is represented as being equally blustering and cruel. When at the trial of Jesus before him a soldier reminds him that Jesus claimed to be a king, Herod replies:

> Thanne is it litil wonder yf that he be woo,
> For to be weried with wrang sen he wirkis wele.
> But he schalle sitte be my-selfe sen ye saie soo,
> Come nerre, kyng, into courte, saie can ye not knele?
> We schalle haue gaudis full goode and games or we goo.
> How likis tha? wele, lorde? saie, what! deuyll neuere a dele?
>
> .   .   .   .
>
> Say, may thou not here me? oy, man, arte thou woode?
> Nowe tell me faithfully before yowe thou fore,
> Forthe frende, be my faith, thou arte a fonde foode.

> *One of the*   My lorde, it astonys hym, your steuen [voice] is so
> *attendants.*   store [strong],
>   Hym had leuere [rather] haue stande stone still ther
>   he stode.

> *Herod.* And whedir the boy be abasshid of Herrowde byg blure
>   (bluster),
>   That were a bourde [jest] of the beste, be manhoundes
>   bloode.

And the end of the speech of the Almighty at the close of the last play, which represents the Last Judgment:

> Nowe is fulfillid all my for-thoght,
> For endid is all erthely thyng,
> All worldly wightis that I haue wroght,
> Aftir ther werkis haue nowe wonnyng,
> Thei that wolde synne and sessid [ceased] noght,
> Of sorowes sere now shall thei sing,
> And thei that mendid thame whils thei moght,
> Schall belde [shelter] and bide in my blissing.
> *Et sic facit finem cum melodia angelorum transiens a loco ad locum.*

The cycle of plays called *ludus Coventriae* (the play of Coventry, for it is only one play, intended to be acted throughout in one " performance ") will now be described.

The play is introduced in a *Proclamation*, as it is called, a long prologue of 528 lines, rendered necessary on account of the length and the comprehensiveness of the play. In this the only actors are a first, a second and a third *vexillator* or standard-bearer. The opening words, spoken by the first *vexillator*, are :

> Now graycous god groundyd of all goodnesse,
> as thi grete glories nevyr be-gynning had,
> So thou socour and saue all tho that sytt and sese
> and lystenyth to oure talkyng with sylens stylle and sad.
> Ffor we purpose us pertly stylle in this prese [present],
> the pepyl to plese with pleys ful glad
> now lystenyth us louely bothe more and lesse
> Gentyllys and yemanry of goodly lyff lad
> this tyde
> we shal you shewe as that we kan
> how that this werd ffyrst be-gan
> and how god made bothe molde [world] and man
> Iff that ye wyl abyde.

The audience are then told by the characters the subjects of the plays which they are to see. Two sections may be quoted :

> The iij^{de} pagent is now yow tolde,
> the ffourte pagent of Noe shal be
> how god was wroth with man on molde [earth]
> because fro synne man dede not fle.
> He sent to Noe An Angel bolde
> A shyp ffor to makyn and swymmen on the se
> vpon the water both wood and coolde,
> And viij sowles ther savyd shulde be,
> And j peyre of everich bestys in brynge.
> whan xl^{ti} days the flode had fflowe
> than sente Noe out a crowe,
> and After hym he sent a dowe
> that brouth ryth good tydyng.
>
> in the xxviijth pagent shal judas
> that was to cryst a ffals traytour
> with wepyng sore evyr crye Alas
> that evyr he solde oure savyour.

He shal be sory ffor his trespas
And brynge agen all his tresour
all xxx pens to sere Cayphas,
he shal them brynge with gret dolowre
Ffor the which cryst was bowth [bought],
Ffor gret whanhope [despair] as ye shal se
he hangyth hym self vpon a tre,
Ffor he noth trostyth in gods pece,
to helle his sowle is browth.

The link between the Old Testament and the New
Testament section of the episodes is supplied by means of
short verses, most of them of four lines, spoken in procession by prophets and kings, who were in the direct line
of descent from Isaiah to the Virgin, the names of all
being found in the genealogical tables in St. Matthew i.
and St. Luke ii. One by one, the characters occupy
the stage, there being no stage direction ; each character
appears for a few moments only while he speaks his part.
Here are two or three extracts :

Isaiah.   I am the prophete callyd Isaye,
        Replett with godys grett influens,
        and sey pleynly be spyryte of prophecie
        that a clene mayde thourgh make obedyens
        Shall bere a childe which shal do resystens
        Ageyn foule Zabulon the devyl of helle,
        mannys soule ageyn hym to defens
        Opyn in the felde the fend he shall felle.

Solomon. I am Salamon the secunde kynge,
        And that wurthy temple for sothe made I,
        which that is fygure of that mayde thyngs
        that shal be modyr of grett messy [mercy].

Jonah.   I jonas sey that on the iij^de morn
        ffro deth he shal ryse ; this is a trew tall [tale]
        fyguryd in me the which longe beforn
        lay iij days beryed with in the qwall [whale].

Joel.   And I Joel knowe full trewe that is
        god bad me wryte in prophesye
        he wolde sende down his sprytt i-wys
        On yonge and olde ful sekyrlye [surely].

The Old Testament characters end with king Amon,
the gap between him and Anna, wife of Joachim, being
bridged in a short general statement which includes the
families of the three Annes and their husbands, the
parents respectively of the three New Testament Maries.
Modern critics do not accept this account, but until long
after the middle ages its truth was not doubted.

The section in which the betrothal of the Virgin to
Joseph is described is followed by the eleventh section in
the series, called " The Parlement of Heaven ".   It
begins :

        Ffoure thowsand sex vndryd foure yere I telle
        Man ffor his offens and ffowle foly
        Hath layn yerys in the peynes of helle
        And were wurthy to ly ther-in endlesly,
        But thanne shulde perysche your grete mercye.
        good lord, haue on man pyte
        haue minde of the prayour seyd by Ysaie,
        lete mercy meke thin hyest mageste.

Those taking part in this interlude include God the
Father, God the Son and God the Holy Ghost, and the
four " daughters " of God, namely, the Virtues of Mercy,
Truth, Justice and Peace, personified as in the morality
plays.   When the Virtues have interceded with the
Father on behalf of man, the Father replies :

        Ffor the wretchydnes of the nedy
        And the porys lamentacion,
        now shal I ryse that am Almyghty ;
        tyme is come of reconsyliacion.
        Me prophetys with prayers haue made supplicacion,
        my contryte creaturys crye all for comforte,
        All myn Aungellys in hefne with-owue cessacion
        they crye that grace to man myght extorte.

The four " daughters " of God then speak, after which
the Son says :

> It peyneth me that man I mad[e],
> that is to seyn peyne I must suffre fore ;
> A counsel of the trinite must be had
> Which of us shal man restore.

> Ffadyr he that shal do this must be both god and man.
> lete me se how I may were that wede,
> And syth in my wysdam he began,
> I am redy to do this dede.

Finally, the Father says :

> Ffrom vs god Aungel Gabryel, thou shalt be sende
> In to the country of Galyle,
> the name of the cyte Nazareth is kende,
> to A mayd weddyd to A man is she
> Of whom the name is joseph se
> Of the hous of davyd bore
> The name of the mayd ffre
> Is Mary that shal Al Restore,

> Say that she is with-owte wo and ful of grace
> And that I the son of the godhed of here shal be bore.
> Hyghe the thou were there A pace
> ellys we shal be there the be-ffore.
> I haue so grett hast to be man thore
> In that makest and purest virgyne.
> Sey here she shal restore
> Of yow Aungellys the grett Ruyne.

This long dialogue has its fulfilment in the birth of
Christ and the well-known Gospel events which surround
it, including the Adoration of the Shepherds, the Visit
of the Magi, the Presentation in the Temple, the Massacre
of the Innocents, the death of Herod, and the Disputation
in the Temple. The dialogue between the boy Jesus
and the doctors in the Temple departs from the silence of
the New Testament as to the exact subject of the discussion by giving details of the questions, which are put

to the Child by two doctors. This episode is one of the most interesting of them all. The doctors refer to the knowledge—surely in prospect of centuries to come and not in reality—of reading, writing, orthography, grammar, cadence, prosody, music, dialectic, sophistry, logic, philosophy, metaphysic, astronomy, calculations, necromancy, augrim (algorism), asmatryk (arithmetic), geometry, physics, rhetoric, and canon and civil law. The Child replies :

> Omnis sciencia a domino deo est,
> Al wyth and wysdom of God it is lent
> Of all your lernynge with-inne your brest
> thank hyghly that lord that hath you sent ;
> thorwe bost and pryde your soulys may be shent [harmed],
> but god may make at hese entente
> of all your connynge many man yow lech [heal]

When He refers to the Incarnation the doctors are puzzled. The second doctor remarks :

> This childys doctryne doth passe oure wytt ;
> Sum Aungel of hevyn I trowe that he be,
> But blyssyd babe of oo dowte zitt [yet]
> We pray you enforme us for charyte
> Which toke flesch of the personys thre
> Ageyn the fende [fiend] to holde suche batayle.

There follows a discussion on the Trinity, in the middle of which (in a stage direction) they place Jesus between them on a high stool, a position which He occupies in a well-known illumination in a medieval psalter. The discussion turns to the parentage of the Child, Who says :

> I am of dobyl byrth and of dobyl lenage,
> Ffyrst be my fadyr I am with-oute gynnynge,
> And lyke as he is hendeless in his hygh stage,
> So shal I also neuyr nor haue endynge.

> Ffor be my fadyr kynge celestyall,
> Without begynnyng I am endles,
> but be my modyr that is carnall
> I am but xij yere of age that is expres.

In the midst of the discussion Mary and Joseph appear and claim the Child, the first doctor adding the last words in the episode :

> O blessyd jhesu with yow we wende
> of yow to haue more informacion ;
> Fful blyssys is your modyr hende
> of whom ye toke your incarnacion.
>
> we pray yow jhesu of consolacion,
> At oure most nede of yow to haue ;
> all that hath herd this comsummacion
> of this pagent your grace then saue.

The only incidents in the Gospel story between the birth scenes and the Passion which are dramatised in this cycle are the Baptism of Christ by John the Baptist, the Temptation, the woman taken in adultery and the raising of Lazarus.

The first of the two Passion plays follows, introduced by a demon, who claims to be

> your lord lucifer that out of helle cam,
> Prince of this werld and gret duke of helle.
> Wherfore my name is clepyd sere [sir] satan,
> Whech Aperyth among yow.   A matere to spelle.
>
> I am Nourisher of synne to the confusyon of man,
> To bryng hym to my dongeon ther in fyre to dwelle.
> He so evyr serve me, so reward hym I kan
> that he shal syng wellaway ever in peynes felle.
>
> Ffor I began in hefne synne for to sowe
> Among all the Angellys that weryn so bryth,
> And ther fore was I cast out in helle ful lowe,
> Not withstandyng I was the fayrest and berere of
>   lyth [light].

After the long speech of Lucifer, John the Baptist urges all to avoid sin by keeping to the middle path of right, and to do penance for sin " agens the comyng of oure lorde ". A stage direction then runs :

Here shal annas shewyn hym-self in his stage be-seyn after a busshop of the hoold lawe in a skarlet gowne, and ouer that a blew tabberd furryd with whyte and a mystere [mitre] on his hed after the hoold lawe, ij doctorys standyng by hym in furryd hodys and on be-forn hem with his staff of A-stat and eche of hem on here hedys a furryd cappe with wich shall be his massan-gere. Annas thus seyng :

> As a prelat I am properyd to provyde pes,
> And of jewys jewge the lav.e to fortefye.
> I Annas be my powere shal comawnde dowteles
> the lawys of moyses no man shal denye
> Hoo excede my comawndement.

The deliberations of the council of the Jews, presided over by Annas, follow, at which it was decided to arrest Jesus. One member of the council says about Him :

> He is An eretyk and a tretour holde
> To sesare and to oure lawe sertayn,
> Bothe in word and in werke and ye beholde
> He is worthy to dey with mekyl peyn.

The course of the cycle is continued in the entry into Jerusalem, the Last Supper, the conspiracy of the Jews with Judas, and the betrayal. The series of incidents which compose the first Passion play ends with verses spoken by the two doctors who had examined Jesus in the Temple, now converted :

> O Thou Altitude of Al gostly Ryches,
> O Thou incomprehensible of grete excyllence,
> O Thou luminarye of pure lyghtnes,
> Shete out Thi bemys on-tyl this Audyens.

> O Ffily Altissimi clepyd by eternalyte,
> Hele this congregacioun with the salve of the ;
> And we prey the spiritus paraclyte passyon
> With the ffyre of thi love to slake All detraccion.

To the pepyl not lernyd I stonde as A techer,
Of this processyon to geve informacion,
And to them that be lernyd As A gostly precher,
that in my rehersayl they may haue delectacion.

The second play is to some extent complementary to
the first. The stage direction at the head of the first
incident runs :

What tyme that processyon is enteryd in to the place and the
herowdys takyn his schaffalde and pylat and annas and cayphas
here schaffaldys. Also than come ther An exposytour in doctorys
wede thus seyng.

This is what Pilate's wife says to her husband :

Pylat I charge the that thou take hede,
deme not jhesu but be his frende ;
yf thou jewge hym to be dede,
thou art damdnyd with-owtyn ende.

A fend Aparyd me beforn
As I lay in my bed slepyng fast ;
Sethyn the time that I was born
was I nevyr so sore A-gast.

As wylde fyre and thondyr blast
he cam careng on to me ;
he seys thei that bete jhesu or bownd hym fast
with-owtyn ende dampnyd shal be.

ther-fore A wey here-in thou se
and lete jhesu from the clere pace ;
the jewys thei wole be-gyle the
and put on the All trespace.

Pilate replies :

Gramercy myn wyf for evyr ye be trewe ;
your cowncel is good and evyr hath be.
now to your chawmer ye do sewe
and all shall be weyl dame as ye shal se.

After the trials are over the procession to Calvary is formed. When it arrives there Veronica is introduced :

> A ye synful pepyl why fare this
> Ffor swet and blood he may not se
> Allas holy prophete cryst jhesus
>
> *(and sche whypyth his face with her kerchy)*
>
> Careful is myn hert for the.

And Jesus replies :

> veronyce thi whipyng doth me ese ;
> my face is clene that was blak to se.
> I shal hem kepe from all mys-ese
> that lokyn on thi kerchy and remembyr me.

The " lokyn on thi kerchy " was the image of the face of Christ, after the appearance of which Veronica received her new name, Veronica. And the direction for nailing Jesus to the cross runs :

> than shal thei pulle jhesu out of his clothis and leyn them togedyr and ther thei shul pullyn hym down and leyn hym Along on the cros and after that naylyn hym heron.

There is much imaginary conversation in the play, but much of it very natural and beautiful. After the Body was taken down from the cross there is a conversation between Mary and Joseph :

> *Joseph.* Lo mary modyr good and trewe,
> here is thi son blody and bloo.
> ffor hym myn hert ful sore doth rewe,
> kysse hym now onys eer he go.

> *Mary.* A Mercy Mercy myn owyn son so dere
> thi blody face now I must kysse
> the face is pale with-owtyn chere
> of meche joy now shal I mysse
> ther was nevyr modyr that sey this
> so here sone dyspoyled with so gret wo
> and my dere chylde nevyr dede A-mys
> A mercy fadyr of hefne it schulde be so.

Joseph. Mary your sone ye take to me
       in-to his grave it shal be browth.

Mary. joseph blessyd evyr mo thou be
       for the good dede that ye han wrowth.

     (*here thei shal leyn cryst in his grave.*)

While the sepulchre is guarded by soldiers, who go to
sleep, the soul of Christ has a conversation with Abraham
and Belial, and His spirit passes into His body, which
rises and appears to Mary Magdalene. The confusion
of the soldiers when they discover that the body has disappeared is graphically described. The first soldier says :

       Awake awake
       hills gyn quake
       And tres ben shake
       ful nere a-too
       Stonys clevyd
       wyttys ben revid
       Erys ben devid
       I am servid soo.

The second soldier says :

       he is a-rysyn this is no nay
       that was deed and colde in clay
       greet woundyr it is to me
       He is resyn by his owyn myght
       And fforth he goth his wey ful ryght
       how shul we now qwytte
       Whan Pylat doth us se.

And Pilate says :

       What What What What
       Out upon the why seyst thou that
       Ffy vpon the harlat
       how darst thou so say
       thou dost myn herte ryght greet greff
       thou lyest vpon hym fals theff
       how shulde he rysyn ageyn to lyff
       that lay deed in clay ?

Pilate meets Annas and Caiphas, and suggests this story to account for the disappearance of the body of Jesus :

> Jentyl knyghtys I yow pray
> A bettyr sawe that ye say
> Say ther he was cawth away
> with his dyscyplis be nyght
> Sey he was with his dyscyplis ffett (fetched ; i.e. stolen)
> I wolde ye worn in youre sadelys ssett
> And haue here gold in a purs knett
> And to rome rydyth ryght.

And one of the soldiers replies :

> We wyll not prate
> no lengere now
> now we haue golde
> no talys shul be tolde
> to whithtys [people] on wolde
> we make the A vow.

The appearance to the three Maries, to Mary Magdalene, to Cleophas and Luke and to Thomas follow. And Christ appears to convince Thomas, who says :

> My god and my lorde, nyght and every morn
> I Aske mercy lorde ffor my grett trespas.

The series of episodes or scenes in this second Passion play ends with the Ascension, Pentecost, the Assumption of the Virgin and the Last Judgment. The appeal of the *animae dampnandae* (damned souls) and the answer are both brief :

> Souls. Ha Ha mercy mercy we crye and crave
> A mercy lorde for oure mysdede
> A mercy mercy we rubbe we rave
> A help us good lord in this rede.

> God. How wolde ye wrecchis Any mercy haue
> Why Aske ye mercy now in this nede
> What haye ye wrought your sowle to saue
> to whom haue ye don Any mercyful dede
> Mercy for to wynne.

A final appeal of the condemned souls is apparently fruitless ; but here the manuscript comes to an untimely end, and the answer has been lost.

It has been pointed out that this cycle of plays is an advance on earlier cycles in many ways. It contains far more stage directions, all of which add to the dramatic quality of the play. Here are a few, in addition to those that have already been quoted :

> and forth-with he smytyth of Malcheus here (ear) and he cryeth help myn here myn here and cryst blyssyth it and tys hol.

> here shal A messenger com in-to the place rennyng and criyng Tydyngs tydyngs and so rownd Abowth the place jhesus of nazareth is take Jhesus of nazareth is take and forth-with helyng the prynces this seyng

> > All heyle my lordys princys of prestys
> > Sere cayphas and sere Annas lordys of the lawe
> > tydyngs I brynge you reseyve them in your brestys
> > Jhesus of nazareth is take ther-of ye may be fawe [glad].

> > he shal be browth hedyr to you A-non
> > I tell you trewly with A gret rowth
> > when he was take I was hem Among
> > and ther was I ner a kachyd a clowte.

> here thei pulle of jhesus clothis and betyn hym with whyppys.

> > Jhesus thi bonys we shal not breke
> > but we shal make the to skyppe
> > thou hast lost thi tongue thou mayst not speke
> > thos salt a-say now of this whippe.

> > Serys [Singly] take these whyppys in your hande
> > and spare not whyl thei last
> > and bete this tretoure that here doth stonde
> > I trowe that he wyl speke in hast.

> and qwan thei han betyn hym tyl he is alle blody than the herownde seyth.

The introduction of the dialogues between the Almighty and His " daughters " and the addresses of Lucifer are rare features in plays of this kind. And at times the audience must have been thrilled (as, for example, when Pilate's wife was having her dream) by a stage direction which runs :

> her shal the devyl gon to Pilatys wyf the corteyn drawyn as she lyth in bedde and he shal no dene make but she shal sone after that he is come in makyn a rewly noyse comyng and renning of the schaffald leke a mad woman.

This Coventry play was presented in one place, not, as with the plays at York, by different companies each of whom had to move their stage and stage properties from place to place. It was an undertaking of no small magnitude to present in one day the whole of the series of incidents which form *ludus Coventriae*. In the Early English Text Society's edition the whole cycle occupies 377 pages in a smallish type. The mere reading of them at one sitting would take not less than eight to nine hours.

Even though the stage scenery was probably so simple as not to take much time in being shifted, there must be added to the time for speaking the words a good deal more time for intervals for rest and the moving of scenery that had been used for a scene and would not be needed again for some time. It would be impossible for the whole of the episodes to be presented in much less than nine to ten hours, and, though one actor might play several parts, not many fewer than forty to fifty would be needed to sustain all the characters. Further, at times as many as thirty people would be on the stage at the same time. The play would naturally be continuous, and, while a few people might sit through the whole session, most people would retire for meals and such work as had to be done even on a holiday.

In addition to this cycle, Coventry could boast of another, a civic cycle, written for performance under the direction of the city's authority. William Dugdale, the antiquary who wrote, amongst other books, *The Antiquities of Warwickshire* (published in 1656), and lived through almost the whole of the seventeenth century, asserts that this series existed ; indeed, two plays from it were destroyed in a fire at the Birmingham Public Library in 1879. This cycle was probably written before the one which has just been described. Henry VIII was once present at a presentation of the *ludus Coventriae*, which was then staged outside the house of the Grey Friars at Coventry—probably in their courtyard. It is likely that at this time the friars supplied the actors, or at any rate the chief ones.

It is evident to anyone who will read all the cycles of plays that they vary in quality of dramatic interest, in literary merit and in poetic quality. *Ludus Coventriae* reaches a high level in the first two of these. It is based on what were then considered to be first-rate sources, such as John Lydgate, the monk of Bury St. Edmunds, England's foremost poet of the fifteenth century, and *legenda aurea* (the Golden Legend). In the plays there is great dignity. Buffoonery and vulgarity are entirely absent, and there is no " playing to the gallery ". Some of the plays are uncommon of their kind, there being no surviving parallel to the plays of the Conception of the Virgin, Mary in the Temple, the Betrothal of Mary and Joseph, and the trial of Mary and Joseph. Further, during the trials of Christ on the stage, none but " yf he be knyght or gentylman born " was allowed to touch the person who was taking his part. Perhaps as poetry these plays do not reach as high a level on the whole as other cycles ; but they display great pathos and a rare understanding of the needs of dramatic representation.

In addition to the cycles of plays to which reference has been made, other medieval plays were acted by a people who had always been fond of acting. Single plays or collections of plays of varying sizes were acted at Braintree, Bungay, Canterbury, Chelmsford, Hull, Ipswich, Leicester, Lincoln, Malden, Newcastle-on-Tyne, Norwich, Shrewsbury, Winchester, Worcester and places in Scotland such as Edinburgh and Aberdeen. The total number of separate plays must have been counted by scores if not hundreds. These plays were acted at gatherings of various kinds, at which people were both willing and able to make their own means of amusement to an extent which is being forgotten in days when people pay to be entertained. Social and sporting gatherings, entertainment of guests in country houses, visits of notabilities, such as that of the Emperor Sigismund to Windsor Castle in the year 1414 to receive the insignia of the Garter, and religious festivals of various kinds—all these occasions were marked with performances of plays. What are called "morality" plays, in which the vices and the virtues were personified, attracted the more thoughtful and serious-minded. It is much to be desired that there should be written a book that would contain a full account of this side of the life of the medieval man and woman, for it is in the pastimes as well as in the occupations of people that their tastes and their characteristics are revealed.

CHAPTER X

THE BOY-BISHOP

ONE of the most curious of medieval religious customs in this country was that of the boy-bishop. It was observed in churches or chapels of all kinds, whether monastic, or collegiate, or parochial. It was finally abolished in the year 1559, after a life of between three and four centuries, during which it was part of the annual observance of the Christmas festival.

The Christian Church has always included human beings of all ages. From very early times, children have had their own patron saint in St. Nicholas, or, to give him the name by which he is more commonly and more popularly known, Santa Claus. The Santa Claus story is a story by itself, and is not one of the stories about St. Nicholas which have been handed down. The story that established St. Nicholas as the patron saint of children is the horrible one of the innkeeper who, running short of food during a famine, killed three boys on their way to school at Athens, pickled their flesh and stored it in a cask. Nicholas, bishop of Myra, passing by, raised the three boys to life again. In medieval pictures in glass and in manuscripts, he is often represented with the cask at his side, out of which three boys are climbing. This story spread by word of mouth over the districts which were being won to Christianity, and in the calendar of the Church December 6th was given to St. Nicholas as his feastday. Henry VI, who was born on the feast of St. Nicholas, adopted St. Nicholas as his patron saint, and, in honour of " our Lady and St. Nicholas ", founded Eton College and King's College, Cambridge. It is not surprising to learn that, at both these colleges, March 25th (Lady Day) and December 6th (the feast of St. Nicholas) are still observed as Founders' Days, and that observances connected with St. Nicholas, including the ceremony of the boy-bishop, were made at Eton College. Of churches which are now, and some of which were then, cathedral churches at which the custom of the boy-bishop was observed, Canterbury, York, Durham, Exeter, Gloucester, Hereford, Lichfield, Lincoln, London (St. Paul's), Salisbury, Newcastle-on-Tyne and Norwich, with Winchester College and the college at Rotherham, provide records of it. Included in this list are a few which were formerly monastic churches. Very many parish churches also made the observance.

Every year on the feast of St. Nicholas at these churches, most of which had boy-choristers, the choristers met to choose one of their number to be the boy-bishop. At York, where the names of several boy-bishops can be seen in the later medieval acts of the chapter, the boy who was the best singer was chosen, if he was also good-looking. In a few places, such as Eton College, Bristol (the church of St. Nicholas), and Heddon (near Newcastle-on-Tyne), the boy performed his duties on the day of his election. At Heddon, on December 6th, 1299, the boy-bishop said Vespers in the presence of Edward I, who was on his way to Scotland ; and the king made gifts to the boy-bishop and those who assisted him. Towards the end of the thirteenth century, however, it was ordered that the duties of the boy-bishop should not begin until after Vespers on December 27th (the eve of the feast of the Holy Innocents) and should end with Vespers on the day after. On December 26th fell and still falls the feast of St. Stephen, the day for deacons, St. Stephen being a deacon ; on December 27th the feast of St. John the Evangelist, the day for priests ; and on December 28th the Feast of the Holy Innocents, the day of the boy-bishop and the children.

In every place, elaborate provision was made for the annual custom. In 1245, twenty-eight small copes were bought for the use of the boys of St. Paul's Cathedral, and half-a-century later a magnificent mitre and a pastoral staff. A gold " episcopal " ring was provided at York and Salisbury. At all places, the cope worn by the boy-bishop was more splendid than those worn by the other boys. In 1481, Thomas Rotherham, archbishop of York, who is thought to have been for a short time a schoolboy at Eton, gave to the college of Jesus at Rotherham, his native place, a mitre of cloth-of-gold for the " barnes bishop " (i.e., the bairns' bishop). At York, the names of a number of boy-bishops are known. At Magdalen College, Oxford, the college provided each year a feast in the college hall for the boy-bishop and his companions, and made a present to the boy-bishop of a pair of gloves. The Northumberland Household Book gives a long list of the vestments and the ornaments of the boy-bishop :

Contenta de ornamentis episcopi puerorum.

Imprimis, j myter, wel garnesshed with perles and precious stones, with nowches of silver and gilt, before and behind.

Item, iiij rynges of silver and gilt, with four redde precious stones in them.

Item, j pontifical (the book to be used by the boy-bishop in the services which he conducted) with silver and gilt, with a blew stone in hytt.

Item, j owche broken, silver and gilt, with iiij precious stones and a perle in the myddes.

Item, a crosse with a staf of coper and gilt, with the image of St. Nicholas in the myddes.

Item, j vesture, redde, with lyons of silver, with brydds of gold in the orferes [orphreys or borders] of the same.

Item, j albe to the same with starres in the paro [parure].

Item, j white cope, stayned with tristells and orferes of redde sylke, with does of gold and whytt napkyns aboute ther neckes.

Item, iiij copes of blew sylk, with redde orferes, trayled with braunchis and flowres.

Item, j steyned cloth of the ymage of St. Nicholas.

Item, j tabard of skarlet and a hodde therto, lyned with whitt sylk.

Item, a hode of skarlett, lyned with blue sylk.

At Magdalen College, Oxford, the ornaments and the vestments included tunicles, of various colours, albs of blue damask and red silk, and a banner of St. Nicholas. Other places have left records of copes and mitres, " a lytyll chesebyll (chasuble) for Seynt Nicholas bysschop ", nine copes for the attendants, books with silver clasps, and, at Westminster Abbey,

the myter of seynt Nycholas bysshoppe, the grounde therof of whyte sylk garnysshed complete with ffloures gret and small, of sylver and gylte, and stones complete in them, with the scripture, Ora pro nobis sancte Nycholas, embroidered theron in perll, the sydes sylver and gylt, the toppys of sylver and gylt, and enamelyd with ij labelles of the same and garnysshed in lyk maner and with viij long bells of sylver and gylt, weying all together xxiij unces . . . and a gret blewe clothe with kyngs on horsebake for saynt Nicholas cheyre [chair].

In Salisbury Cathedral there is an effigy of a boyish-looking figure in episcopal vestments which some have taken to be that of a boy-bishop buried in the cathedral. Be that as it may, the ceremonies of the boy-bishop are described with care in the *Sarum Processionale*, many copies of which, printed in the first half of the sixteenth century, have survived. The boy-bishop was chosen by his fellow-choristers on the feast of St. Nicholas and performed his " episcopal " functions in the cathedral until the night of the feast of the Holy Innocents. During those days—just over three weeks—the status of the members of the cathedral foundation was turned upside-down. The boy chosen was the bishop; his fellow-choristers became canons; the canons became the junior members of the foundation and gave up their seats, as the bishop did his throne, to the boys, and took the lowest places in the processions, the boys taking the highest place followed by the boy-bishop and his chaplains at the very tail of the processions. There is some uncertainty as to whether he always said or sang the Mass. The proclamation of Henry VIII which suppressed the institution makes it clear that he did perform this most sacred office of the Church, though it seems to be unbelievable that he did. At Salisbury, on the eve of the feast of the Holy Innocents, the boy-bishop went in procession to the altar of the Holy Innocents or of All Saints (apparently either being used), all wearing copes and carrying lighted tapers, where a solemn service took place, the boy-bishop censing the altar first of all. The procession was then re-formed, and wended its way, through the screen between the choir and the crossing, to the choir, " the canons resident bearing the incens and the book, and the petit canons [i.e., the vicars-choral, who were the deputies of the canons for singing the daily offices] the tapers, according to the rubric ". The choir service being ended, the boy-bishop said :

Benedicat vos omnipotens Deus pater et filius and spiritus sanctus.

[God the Father, God the Son, and God the Holy Ghost, bless you.]

At some places these solemnities were followed by a feast at the house of the head of the foundation attached to the church—abbot, prior, dean or provost—one of the boy-bishop's chaplains saying grace, of course in Latin. On the following day, the feast of St. Nicholas, the same topsy-turvy order of proceedings was continued. At St.

Paul's Cathedral, the boy-bishop was allowed to choose his host for the evening from amongst the dean and the canons, taking with him, if he chose the dean as his host, two chaplains, two taperers, five clerks, two apparitors or vergers, and four " canons " ; the boy who for the time was " dean " had three attendants ; and the boy who was a " canon " had two only.

The next ceremonies were reserved for the feast of the Holy Innocents, when a similar service at the second Vespers was solemnised in the choir, the boy-bishop dismissing those present with his blessing. And, according to the Salisbury record,

> all this was don with that solemnitie of celebration and appetite
> of seeing that the statute of Sarum was forced to provide that
> no man whatsoever, under pain of anathema, should interrupt
> or press upon these children at the procession spoken of before,
> or in anie other part of their service in anie waies, but to suffer
> them quietly to perform and execute what it concerned them to
> do. . . . In case the chorister bishop died within the moneth,
> his exsequies were solemnised with an answerable glorious pomp
> and sadness. He was buried, as all other bishops, in all his
> ornaments, as by the monument of stone, spoken of before, it
> plainly appeareth.

At the High Mass on the feast of the Holy Innocents, the boy-bishop was required to preach a sermon to the whole cathedral body. At most if not all the places at which the ceremony of the boy-bishop took place, there were sermons prepared for him so that he might choose one to read. Nowhere was he allowed to preach one of his own making. While records of the existence of collections of these sermons have survived, practically all the sermons themselves have perished. In 1328, the almoner of St. Paul's Cathedral bequeathed to the cathedral

> all the quires of sermons for the feast of the Holy Innocents,
> which in my time the bishops of the boys used to preach.

At St. Paul's, too, Erasmus wrote a sermon for use on this occasion.

The statutes of the school founded in connexion with St. Paul's by John Colet in c. 1512 direct that the scholars " every Childremas day " shall

> after be at the hygh Masse and each of them offer a peny to the Chylde-bishop, and with them the maisters and surveyors of this scole.

At Bristol, the mayor and the members of the corporation attended the church of the corporation on College Green,

> to here Masse and to here the boy-bishop's sermon and haue his blessing.

A few extracts from one of the extant sermons, " pronownsed by John Stube, querester " in Gloucester Cathedral in 1558, one of the last preached in this country, may be given. The text was St. Matthew xvii. 3.

> Except yow will be convertyd and made lyke vnto lytill children yow shall not entre in to the kyngdom of heuen.

The discourse begins :

> Among all the conclusions in holy Scryptur, which are many and marvellous, Ryght worshypfull audience, this is not the lest to be marvellyd as, doubtyd and dreadyd of all yow that are no childer, but men, women and yonggolds, of years and discretion, yow specially whych alow no construccion of the Scryptures but only the letter as it lyeth, thys I say whych our Saviour Chryst procouncyd wyth his own mouth, saying, " Except yow wil be convertyd ". As he wold say, lytill ones shall entre to the kyngdom, but other shall not ; and so all seme to be excludyd from the kyngdom but only childer, and such as are litill ones lyke vnto childer.

After reflexions on the Protestant martyrs and on scriptural stories of martyrs such as Abel, the Holy

Innocents and St. Stephen, the preacher addressed exhortations to elders and children :

Yow that are of the elder sort . . . must nede reforme your corrupt maners, which are dissonant and disagreeable with the incorrupt maners of childer, and frame your affections therafter, so that yow be convertyd into the better, or else yow kan not loke for the kyngdom of heauen . . . Yow must nede gyve over your stowt corage that bolden yow to syn, and yow must becum meke as childer. If yow will cum to heavyn yow must not disdayn to becum and to be cowntyd as childer. . . . I report me to yow how many witless childer and childysh people were in thys realme of late years and yet are in many places, which waveryd in ther faith and were caried hyder and thyder, from one opinion to another, as childer ar caried with an apple or wyth a puffe of wynd, as thei that have strength to resist nothing, which is reproveable in men that should have constancie and discretioun.

Now for yow childer, both boys and wenches, that beare the name of childer, I gather this lesson of the wordes of our Saviour, that is it is for yow most necessary to kepe the innocency of your childhood and other vertues proper unto that tendre age, and not to learn the vices and evill qualities of your elders, leste yow lose the kyngdom which is appoynted unto yow by name . . . I have hard say of my elders that a child was wont to continew an innocent untill he was 7 years old, and untill 14 he was provyd to be of such vertue and honest nurture that he deservyd the love and prayse of all people ; and now we shall not fynd such a one at 7 as was then at 14, nor at 5 as was then at 7, nor scant at 3 as was then at 9 or x years old : this is great odes, but is this a good hearyng ? Tell me, yow boys, yow childer, yow litill ones, are yow not ashaymd of your partes that yow are so sone corruptyd ? so sone rype, and so sone rottyn ? so late innocentes, and so sone lewd lads ? deservyng nother love nor prayse of any honest person. What yow are I kan not tell ; but, on my honestie, I am both ashamyd of it and sory for it, that you should so slandre the name of childer and deceive your elders, which have an eye unto yow to mote and folow your maners, as thei are advertysed by the wordes of Christ.

Where then, the preacher proceeds, can he find children whose example is to be followed ?

In the citie ?   I dare not warrant yow to folowe the childer of the citie, no not the yongest of all, if thei be ones owt of ther mothers handes and ken run abowt the streates and speake all thinges perfittly ; for thei have be scolyd at home that of them as yong as thei are yow may learne as evill properties as yow have all redy of your own . . . as to swere with a grace . . . with a stomake to curse bitterly, to blaspheme, to lye, to moke ther elders, to nykname ther equalls, to knowledge no dutie to ther betters, and such other many mo. . . .

Which then ?   The childer that go to scole in the grammer scoles under a master ?   A man wold think yea, because thei are scoles set up purposly for the good educacion of childer . . . yet I dare not warrant to folow the childer of the gramer scoles, for, how so ever it happ, nurturyd thei are as evill or rather worse then the other.   Yf yow will have a profe herof, mark ther maners in the temple and at the table ;   mark ther talkes and behavior by the wayes at such tymes and houres as thei leave scole and go home to ther meales, specially on holydays and campos dayes (i.e., days for football matches), when thei are sett a littil at libertie.   I will say no more ;   but mark them, for I have lost my mark except yow find the most of them most ongracious grafftes, ripe and redy in all lewd libertie.   I will not wish yow to folow such.

Which then ?   The queresters and childer of the songe-scole ? Beware what yow do, for I have experience of them more then of the other.   Yt is not so long sens I was one of them myself but I kan remembre what shrewness was used among them, which I will not speake of now ;   but I kan not let this passe ontouched how boyishly thei behave themselves in the church, how rashly thei cum into the quere without any reverence ; never knele nor cowntenaunce to say any prayer of Pater Noster, but rudely squat down on ther tayles, and justle wyth ther felows for a place ;   a non thei startes me owt of the quere agayne, and in and out agayne, and thus one after another, I kan not tell how oft nor wherfor, but only to gadd and gas abrode, and so cum in agayne and crosse the quere fro one side to another and never rest, withowt any order, and never serve God nor our Lady with mattyns or with evynsong, no more than thei of the grammer scoles ;   whose behaviour in the temple is as it were in their scole ther master being absent, and not in the church God being present.   I will not wysh you to folow such.

Parents come under the lash of the preacher again, this time for not teaching their children, any more than they are taught in the schools. Fond mothers, he says, spoil their children by striking the cushions instead of their children :

> O fond, fond mothers ! what falt have the quyssion don to be bettyn ? what falt have the rodd don to be brent ? Your child have done the falt, why do not he smart of the rodd ? Why do you spare the child ? What hurt can the rodd do to your child ? Ys it not an old and a tru saying, The rodd breakes no bones ? . . . Such mothers shall wepe here after to see the ontowardness of such childer, when the childer will not wepe with the mothers for company as yow mothers do not with them.

The youthful moralist then has a word for the school-masters.

> Yow scolemasters have a good order in your scoles for breaking Priscian's head or syngyng out of tune. I wold yow would take the same order for breakyng of God's comandements and on-tunynge of God's harp, which soundeth in all his wordes. Yf a scoler of the song scole syng out of tune, he is well wrong by the ears or else well beaten. Yf a scoler in the gramer scole speak false Latyn or Englysh forbyddyn, he is taken withall of one or the other and warnyd custos to be beatyn. I wysh that yow wold take the like order for the evil behaviour of your scolers, that if any be takyn with a word of blasphemy, a word of ribaudry, with a manifest lye, and such talk or dedes as are contrary to the laws of God and the Holy Churche, or wrong by the ears for it and after be correctyed as the custom is usyd.

After acknowledging that one so young as he may be regarded as taking upon himself too much in so speaking to his elders, the preacher acknowledges that

> I was sumtyme as yet the most of them are, shrewd ynough for one, but I paid well for it and have now left it, and I may now alledge for myself the wordes of S. Pawl : " When I was a chyldysh boy, my discrecion was therafter, my wordes and dedes were therafter, the fancys and desires of my hart were therafter ; but

now that I have cum to be a man I have cast off all the boy's
touches ",

a free translation of 1 Corinthians xiii. 5.

On the completion of the ceremonies in the church, it
was the custom for the boy-bishop to hold, after the
manner of a bishop in real life, a " visitation ".   On his
visitation, a real bishop, having sent to each parish in
the district which he proposed to visit officially a list of
questions to be answered, met the incumbent and the
churchwardens in order to deliver his judgment on their
replies to the questions, which they were bound to
observe and obey.   The bishop was then entertained by
the lord of the manor or some other prominent person.
The boy-bishop had none of these powers, but he was
always sumptuously entertained.   These visitations might
last a month and might cost a great deal of money, which
the boy-bishop and his attendents hoped to collect from
the religious houses and the parishes which they visited.
In the diocese of York, the earl of Northumberland was
in the habit of entertaining the boy-bishop at his houses
at York and Beverley.   At Winchester, the children of
the neighbourhood were invited to the feast, at which the
boy-bishop and his attendants sat in the highest places.
One record tells of a man who, for the love of his son at
school, kept the feast of St. Nicholas with great solemnity.
His son became a boy-bishop, so it fell to him to give
him a feast.   At times there might be as many as one-
hundred boys at such a feast, and all present were bound
to pray for the good estate of the benefactor in the next
life as well as in this.

The only detailed information at York of a boy-
bishop's visitation is taken from a *compotus* or account-
roll of the year 1396 which no longer exists.   It was
made by John of Cave, who was the boy-bishop in that
year.   The receipts came from three sources, (1) offer-

ings in the cathedral church, comprising collections on
Christmas Day (12*d*.) and the feast of the Holy Innocents
(24*s*. 1*d*.), and a silver spoon, a silver ring and a silk
purse ; (2) subscriptions from the canons, of whom six
gave 40*s*. 4*d*. ; and (3) offerings from citizens, including
the abbot of the great Benedictine abbey of St. Mary,

Conferring the tonsure

which amounted to 10*s*., and from people in the places
which were visited, an amount of £5 14*s*. The total
receipts therefore were considerable, and must be multiplied by at least thirty to be expressed in the currency
of the present day.

Naturally, the expenses were not small. The great
supper on the eve of the feast of the Holy Innocents cost
nearly 16*s*., of which 21*d*. was spent on ale, 2*s*. 3*d*. on

wine, 9½d. on mutton, 4d. on sausages, 2s. 6d. on two ducks, 2s. 3d. on twelve chickens, and 2s. 2d. on a plover. Grocery and spices cost 11d., pears 5½d., honey 2½d., mustard, 1d., candles 2½d., flour 2d., bread 11d., and the cook 6d.

On Thursday, January 4th, the party paid a call at Kexby, on the Hull road five miles from York, where they received from Sir Thomas Utrecht 3s. 4d. On the feast of St. William (January 7th), the bishop and his train set out on a longer journey. Provision had been made for this and similar journeys, for which already there had been paid 4s. 3d. for a torch which weighed twelve pounds ; 9d. for a cap ; 3d. for a pair of gloves ; 5d. for a pair of spurs ; 18d. on the making of the boy-bishop's overcoat ; 2s. 6d. for lamb's wool for the over-coat ; 6s. for furs ; 8d. for faggots ; 7d. for sea-coal ; and for various other items similar amounts.

On the way to the next place of visitation, Kirkham and district, the boy-bishop's cap had to be mended, and this cost 1d. Breakfast had to be paid for before the start, at a cost of 10d. But they did well in offerings. The prior of Kirkham gave the bishop 2s., and the prior of Malton half-a-mark or a noble, 3s. 4d. 20s. and a gold ring came from the countess of Northumberland, who was staying at the earl's house at Leconfield, near Beverley. The prior of Bridlington, the prior of Watton, the rector of Bainton and the prior of Meaux, 3s. 4d. each. At Beverley a new girth for the bishop's horse cost 1d. At Ferriby (North) the prior, not being as well-off as the other priors, could spare only 20d., but Sir Stephen Scrope raised 6s. 8d. for him, and the prior of Drax 2s.

Next to St. Mary's Abbey, Selby was the most import-ant abbey in the north, both abbots being authorised to wear mitres. But the abbot of Selby offered only 3s. 4d., half of what his brother-abbot of St. Mary's had managed to produce. Other religious houses visited includes those of Nostell, Monk Bretton, Pontefract, Rievaulx (where only 2*s.* was received), Byland (also 2*s.*), New-brough (2*s.*) and Marton, 11 or 12 miles north of York (2*s.*). They also received offerings from certain noble ladies : Lady Marmion, of Tanfield, gave them a noble, a gold ring and a silk purse ; the lady of Harlsey, not far from the newly-founded Carthusian monastery of Mount Grace, half-a-noble, and the Lady Roos of Hamlake (Helmsley) Castle, a noble.

Day by day the expenses of the journeys mounted up. The boy-bishop and his retinue could not visit the great religious houses and offer nothing at the Masses which they heard. At Bridlington Priory they offered 2*d.* in the church and gave 1*d.* in alms. A new girth was required there, which cost 1*d.*, and the old one was repaired for ½*d.* A horse-comb was also needed, at a cost of 2*d.*, probably because the one with which they started had got either lost or damaged. " Ferilay " had to be paid for the service of ferries at Melsam, Drax and Harlsey—4*d.* each time. The horses had to be fed ; at Selby this cost 4*d.* At Ferriby the horses had to be shod, as also at Fountains and Newbrough, where in all 1*s.* 3*d.* had to be paid. At Leeds, stabling and fodder cost 13*d.*, and the board and lodging of the party 17*d.* ; at Ripley the supper cost 16*d.*, and the hay and oats for the horses 12½*d.* Only the boy-bishop was given wine on the visitation, and this cost 8*d.* for the whole tour.

Much had to be spent on the service of the attendants. " Wages of servants " is one heading ; under it, Nicholas of Newsome, a tenor singer, received one mark, though what and why he sang is not clear ; his horse cost 2*s.* for the hire ; Robert Dawtry, acting as steward, received 2*s.* 1½*d.*, and his horse cost 2*s.* ; John Baynton sang the

" middle-voice " part and received 2s. ; and other
singers received similar amounts. John Schapton, who
supplied two horses, charged 10s. 2d. ; Thomas Mare-
schale, for one horse, received 3s. 4d. ; Richard Fewler,
for two horses, 5s.

At York there were expenses on the two chief days of
the festivals and on their eves. These totalled nearly
12s.—2s. to the succentor of the vicars-choral who formed
the choir ; 12d. to the sub-chancellor ; for wax for the
candles, 12d. ; for the clerks of the vestments for setting
out the vestments and re-folding them, 12d. ; for the
sacrists for preparing the chapels and the altars, 12d. ;
4d. for adorning the chair in which the boy-bishop sat ;
and 3s. 4d. to the master of the choristers. When everything had been paid, there was a credit balance of
£6 14s. 10½d., which was the property of the boy-bishop
for that year. This was more than the master of
a grammar school then received in a year.

It must not be supposed that nowhere was any protest
made against the continuance of what can hardly have
been always and everywhere an edifying spectacle. At
Salisbury in 1319 both the visitation and the festivities in
the church were alike forbidden. At Ottery St. Mary,
in the same century, the bishop forbade the boys attached
to the church there to leave the parish on a visitation.
On July 22nd, 1541, Henry VIII issued a proclamation
that

> Whereas heretofore dyuers and many superstitious and chyldysh
> obseruances have be vsed, and yet to this day are observed and
> kept . . . and children be strangelie decked and apparayled to
> counterfeir priestes, bisshops and women . . . and boyes do singe
> masse and preache in the pulpitt . . . rather to the derysyon than
> the true glory of God or honor of his sayntes. The Kynges
> Maiestie therefore myndinge no thinge so moche as to aduance
> the true glory of God without vaine superstition wylleth and
> commaundeth that from henceforth all such superstitious

obseruations be left and clerely extinguished throwout his realmes and dominions, for as much as the same doth resemble rather the vnlawfull superstition of gentilitie than the pure and sincere religion of Christe.

For a short time the ceremony was revived under Queen Mary Tudor. The bishop of London ordered the clergy of his diocese to obey the queen's wishes, and in 1554 a grand parade took place in the city, which included the boy-bishop and his retinue. The revival however was short-lived ; for, at the beginning of the reign of Queen Elizabeth, the order of Henry VIII was repeated, and the observance came to an end.

George Hall, bishop of Chester 1662–1668, remarked on the festival of the boy-bishop :

What merry work it was in the days of our holy fathers . . . Children were wont to be arrayed in chimeres, rochets and surplices, to counterfeit bishops and priests, and to be led, singing and dancing from house to house, blessing the people, who stood grinning in the way to expect that ridiculous benediction ; yea, that boys in holy sport were wont to sing masses and to climb into the pulpit to preach to the simple auditory.

And he adds that the practice was " stoutly forbidden " by Henry VIII.

Yet, in spite of the bishop's evident satisfaction that the observance had come to an end long before his time, it is true that many boys who afterwards became eminent had taken part in them. Amongst these can be counted five popes, Wulstan (bishop of Worcester), Eata (bishop of Lindisfarne), and four other bishops. The records of York Minster shew that several boys who were chosen as boy-bishops in the early sixteenth century were afterwards ordained and joined the staff of the Minster. Perhaps the ancient ceremony had its good points ; perhaps it deserved better than to be described by one writer as " the foolish mummery of ignorant monks ".

CHAPTER XI

GEOGRAPHY AND MAPS—I

AS with the study of other sciences, the study of geography begins with the Greeks, though for a complete study of the origins of this science it would be necessary to go further east to the Arabs. The earliest surviving map—it is little more than a diagram—dates back to the beginning of the twenty-seventh century B.C. It represents the earth as flat and circular, surrounded by a broad belt of water ; and only two or three cities are marked, the chief of which is Babylon. This map was the result of the observation of a man who realised that, as far as he could see with his eyes, the shape of the earth was circular, that apart from a few hills its surface was flat, and that, somewhere beyond the horizon, the dome of the sky met either the earth or something else to which it was attached or out of which it sprang. And, as the man was a Babylonian and knew the river Euphrates, he considered that his city was at the centre of the world and that somewhere beyond where he or anybody else was ever likely to reach were hills of snow in which the great river rose. If an intelligent child who knew no geography were asked to make a drawing of what he or she could see from a hill—earth and sky—the result might be something like the map drawn by the ancient Babylonian.

As soon as men began to be interested in the earth, they realised that they could not understand much about its position in the universe without the help of the sun, the moon, the planets and the fixed stars. It is not to their discredit that they came to wrong conclusions, such as the belief that the earth was at the centre of a vast system of unknown bodies. Rather is it to their credit that they realised the interdependence of geography and astronomy.

Our starting-point is Ancient Greece of the second century B.C., where for the first time we touch solid ground with a remarkable man, Eratosthenes of Cyrene, who, as librarian of the famous library of Alexandria, had both the opportunity and the aptitude for a study of any branch of learning then known. Before his time, more than one theory of the shape of the earth had been held. Homer's world was flat and circular; that of Anaximines, who died in the sixth century B.C., was flat and rectangular and rested in space on a cushion of air; in *The Clouds* of Aristophanes, the view is implied that the earth was flat and oval, one axis being twice as long as the other. Anaximander, a pupil of Anaximines, discovered that the axis of the earth is inclined at an angle to the plane of the ecliptic. Concluding from the shadow cast by the earth on the surface of the moon during an eclipse that the earth must be spherical, and that on that account its circumference at the equator could be calculated, Eratosthenes took as the length of a degree the distance between Alexandria and Syene, which he supposed to be on the same meridian, and from that calculated the length of the circumference of the earth. His reckoning was too small by fifty miles; but he had shewn the way in which scientific calculations might be made and had earned the honour of being the first true geographer. He arrived at the idea of lines of latitude and longitude and thus laid every cartographer who came after him under a load of debt to him. His world was contained in an oblong of about 6,000 miles from east to west and about 4,500 miles from north to south. Mistakes he made; but he left enough knowledge of the technique of map-making to enable his successors to build on solid foundations. The superiority of his map over any surviving medieval map is obvious by a comparison of the two.

Much of his work we know only through another notable Greek geographer, Strabo, who lived from 64 B.C. to A.D. 20. His treatise on geography in seventeen books, nearly all of which have survived, has been paid the compliment of being described as " an encyclopaedia of information, a historical geography and a philosophy of geography ". He forms the bridge between the Greeks and the Romans, and his works were frequently printed towards the end of the fifteenth century and afterwards. Geographers came and went, and some of them formed correct ideas. Crates of Mellus (second century B.C.) divided the surface of the earth into four quarters by means of two great seas, the one running north and south, and the other running east and west ; and Marinus of Tyre made his own calculation of the length of a degree of longitude, using frequent lines of longitude and latitude in plotting the positions of places. These however were men of ordinary ability compared with their predecessors and their successor, Ptolemy (second century A.D.), who stands between the ancient and the medieval world as the last of the ancients. Born in Egypt, as a young man teaching at Athens and Rome his own discoveries in plane and spherical trigonometry, he migrated to Alexandria about the middle of the second century A.D., and in the place where, four centuries earlier, Eratosthenes had worked he took up the study of astronomy and geography. He was so successful that, as has been said of him, what Euclid did for geometry, Apollonius for conic sections, and Nicomachus for arithmetic, Ptolemy did for astronomy. The results of his work he put down in his *Almagest*, written in Greek, an epoch-making book, for— wrongly as it turned out—he settled for fifteen centuries that the earth was the centre of the solar system. The portion of his book that deals with geography was frequently translated into Latin during the middle ages, and when printing was invented was issued as a printed book, few copies of which are free from printers' errors, probably owing to the large demand for them.

As a geographer, too, Ptolemy had his limitations. But he was the first cartographer to adopt the principle, afterwards more fully and accurately copied by Mercator, of the projection on a flat surface of markings on a spherical surface. His map, part of which is reproduced opposite page 185, shews the world as he knew it, from Scandinavia (*insulae scandiae*) in the north to the supposed source of the Nile in the south, and from the western coasts of Europe and Africa in the west to the bounds of the Indian Ocean in the east. Further, the map, instead of being circular, is fan-shaped, like an open military or ecclesiastical cloak. The upper boundary, in latitude 60 degrees north, is part of a circle of latitude ; and the lower boundary in the south, at latitude 20 degrees, is also part of a circle of latitude. The 0° parallel of longitude, which forms the western boundary of the map, runs through the so-called Fortunate Islands, now called the Canary Islands. The 180° parallel of longitude forms the boundary of the map on the east. At every ten degrees of latitude and longitude there is a parallel, so that the whole map contains 144 " squares ". It is covered with names, but errors are numerous. Ptolemy was not a very good cartographer ; his interest lay chiefly in how to get the foundations of maps correct and how best to represent a sphere on a plane surface. It was unfair to him that the only portion of his work that was not driven underground during the middle ages was that on astronomy. Thereby, for centuries, students were deprived of much.

Long before Ptolemy's time, fresh surveys of the eastern

world were being made, as, for example, those which
preceded and followed the campaigns of Alexander the
Great, through whose conquests much that had before
been unknown was revealed about the world in which he
lived.   At Baghdad, also, the study of astronomy and
geography was being encouraged not only by a translation
of Ptolemy's work into Arabic but also by the frequent
interchange of ideas between Arabia and India.   From
Arabia and India it was not difficult to explore the Indian
Ocean to its furthest limits eastwards.   We learn from
Marco Polo that charts of the Indian Ocean were made.
When Vasco da Gama crossed the ocean from the east
coast of Africa to Calicut, he did so with the help of an
Indian pilot.   The competence of the Arabs as surveyors
is shewn by the calculation of the angular " distance "
between Baghdad and Toledo—51 degrees 30 minutes,
an error of only three minutes, whereas Ptolemy's error
was six times as much.

The Romans used maps for their campaigns of conquest, one such being made for Nero's campaign in
Armenia.   A map of Italy was engraved on marble.
A map of the whole empire, begun while Julius Caesar
was alive and finished in the time of his successor, was
copied and placed in the portico of the house of the
emperor's sister, Octavia.   A copy of a Roman road-map
was made by an English monk of the thirteenth century.
The Romans however were not great geographers.   The
elder Pliny (23–79 A.D.), called " the naturalist ", was
unquestionably the greatest Roman geographer.   In
naturalis historia (natural history) a mighty work in thirty-
seven books, he told the story of the universe, which he
described as " boundless, uncreated and indestructible ".
He passes in review the earth, the sky, meteors, earthquakes, man, birds, beasts, fishes, insects, trees, fruits,
flowers, bees, honey and farming.   In spite of his ration-

alism, he did not avoid superstitious and unreasonable tales. But he did describe the world as he saw it ; and his book on natural history is one of the greatest of early times.

Then came a gap in the study of geography. Very soon, Europe was in the throes of dissolution. As the Roman Empire grew weaker and at last fell, the Christian Church grew stronger. Orosius, who lived in the fifth century, was the first Christian geographer worthy of the name. The immediate object of his treatise, *historiarum adversus organos libri septem* was to combat the pagan view that the troubles of the world, such as the fall of the Roman Empire and the incursions of the " barbarians " into Europe, were due to the Christian faith. Those portions of his book that were devoted to a description of the world were translated into Anglo-Saxon by Alfred the Great. The influence of Orosius was reflected in several medieval maps, notably the Hereford map, which will be described later in this book, and in *imago mundi*, a work of the twelfth century which at one time was attributed to Anselm. The standpoint of Orosius was orthodox. While the Greeks, the Romans and the Arabs were not bound by the cosmology and the ethnology of the Old Testament, Orosius was compelled by his belief in the literal accuracy of the Bible to interpret facts as a believer in the Bible had learned them. Biblical ethnology made a new start with the Flood, which, if the account of this great deluge as given in the Bible is true, must have destroyed every living thing that did not seek refuge in Noah's ark. There could not therefore be any human beings left anywhere except in the basin of the Mediterranean sea and in western Asia. It was universally believed that anybody who tried to find his way to new lands would have to cross impassable seas and would perish either by drowning or from the effects of the tropical climate. According to Acts xvii. 26, God had " made of one blood all nations of men for to dwell on all the face of the earth ". There could not be, therefore, any human beings on the earth except the descendants of Noah.

Cosmas, an Egyptian monk of the sixth century, wrote a learned treatise, *topographia christiana* (Christian Topography), to prove that the earth could not be spherical. It was, he stated, of the same shape as the tabernacle of God which the Israelites had carried with them through the wilderness on their way to the promised land, namely, rectangular, twice as broad as it was high, and with openings for four seas. Geography, therefore, had become a branch of theology. Nearly nine centuries afterwards, the project of Columbus to sail westward in search of Cathay was condemned by an assembly of divines at Salamanca as being not only insane but even profane. No progress in the scientific study of astronomy or geography was therefore likely to be made.

The traditional view of the earth was reflected in the map of Isidore (bishop of Seville 600–636), which, owing to its shape, has been called " a T within an O ". Here is the outline of it in diagrammatic form :

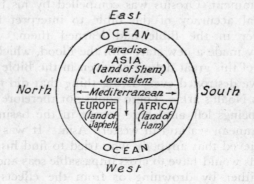

The Inhabited World in the time of Strabo

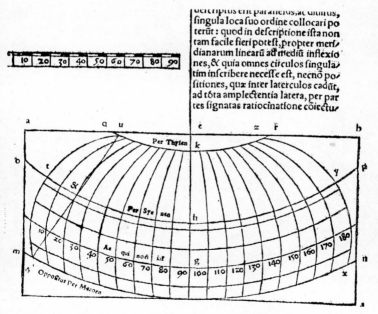

Ptolemy's Lines of Latitude and Longitude

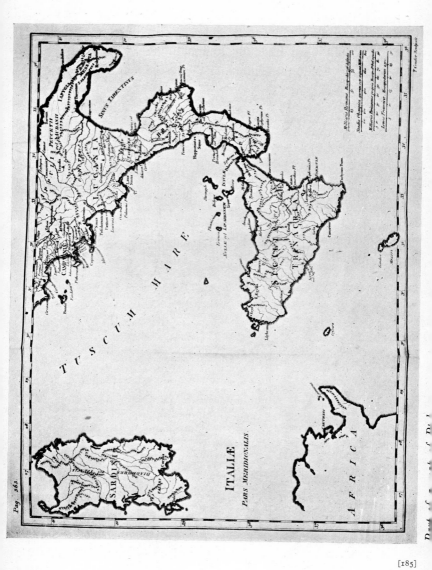

ITALIÆ
PARS MERIDIONALIS.

This idea was based on the threefold division of the world between the three sons of Noah, whose names were Shem, Ham and Japheth.

One source of knowledge, however, that of those who had travelled far and had returned to tell their stories, could not be gainsaid. From various sources, rumours of these stories reached this country long before any Englishman formed the ambition to travel far afield. Indeed, as travellers and navigators the English were behind other peoples. They were too far off the beaten track for stories of the wonders of the world told by those who had seen them to arrive in this country in large numbers. Yet much was being learned elsewhere. From the ninth to the thirteenth century, the conquests of the Mohammedans were opening up new worlds. The encouragement given to travellers by the caliphs of Baghdad had results of the same kind. Returned crusaders brought back stories of what they had seen, while the encouragement given by Robert, count of Sicily, to Edrisi, an Arabian geographer of the twelfth century, had the effect of popularising the works of the Arabian geographers. Probably working with a small silver globe to represent the world, Edrisi divided it into seven zones " horizontally " and eleven " perpendicularly ". Each of these seventy-seven divisions he then described from the point of view of its climate and its natural features.

In this country, very little attention was paid to the study of geography until the thirteenth century. Before the Norman Conquest, almost the only surviving evidence of any interest in the subject is provided by the map in a copy of a work of Priscian the grammarian (who has been referred to in the chapter on Education), now in the British Museum, and Alfred the Great's translation of part of the work of Orosius. The map has been regarded as of tenth-century workmanship. It has one or two unusual features, Jerusalem being not in the centre but at some distance to the south, and Ceylon (named Taprobane) being in the place of honour usually reserved for the " earthly paradise " (that is, the Garden of Eden). The eastern ocean, now known as the Indian Ocean, the Red Sea and the Persian Gulf are painted red, all being included in *Erythraeum* (or Red) *Mare*. The number of names is comparatively few, and some of them present a puzzle to the reader. A ferocious lion adorns the northeast of Asia, the legend being, *hic abundant leones ; mons aureus* (the golden mountain) is the place where pygmies fought the cranes for the possession of the gold ; Noah's ark rests on the Armenian mountains ; and Babylon, Caesarea Philippi, Tarsus, Alexandria, Rome, Carthage, Padua, Ravenna, Constantinople, London and Winchester are marked. The dog-headed men, placed in the Hereford map in northern Europe, are here placed in the south-west of Africa, which then was somewhere not far from the Gold Coast, Africa not having then been explored very far south. This map is the oldest surviving English map by about two centuries.

At least three English maps of the twelfth century survive, the most important and interesting being in the manuscript that contains the famous geographical treatise *imago mundi*. The map, it has been claimed, was drawn by Henry, a canon of the cathedral church of Mainz, early in the twelfth century. The fact that the manuscript accompanying the map is in an English hand and was owned by the Benedictine monastery of Salley (modern form Sawley), a few miles north of Clitheroe, may point to the English authorship of the map also. The resemblances between this map and the Hereford map are so remarkable that they cannot be attributed to coincidence. This is a much smaller map, an oval of

9 inches by $7\frac{1}{2}$, whereas the Hereford map is circular and very much larger.

We now come to the thirteenth century, in almost any activity of the medieval man the most interesting century of medieval England. At once we meet two remarkable Englishmen, Roger Bacon and Matthew Paris. These two men were very different from each other, the one a friar who was suppressed for his unorthodoxy, the other a monk who held an honourable position in his monastery of St. Albans and was the friend of Henry III. Roger Bacon was born in Somersetshire at about the time when Magna Carta was signed. After studying in the new *scholae* at Oxford, he went to Paris, where the Franciscan and Dominican orders had become the pioneers of learning as the founders of the university of Paris. He did not enter the Franciscan order till he was 36 years of age, by which time he had acquired fame as a scholar and had already been suspected of unorthodoxy. For ten years he was put under restraint by the general of his order, John of Fidenza (afterwards canonised as St. Bonaventura), who ordered that his activities should be supervised. Pope Clement V, however, having been interested in Roger's studies while he had been papal legate in England, asked him to send for his perusal a treatise expressing his views. Within two years the manuscript was ready—the well-known *opus majus, opus minus* and *opus tertium*, which he sent to Rome by the hand of his young friend and pupil, John. As a result the pope, before his death in 1268, by which time Roger was more than 50 years old, made it possible for him to return to Oxford so that he could both write and lecture. The fourteen years from 1278 to 1292 he spent in prison for his heretical opinions, and he died two years after his release, a worn-out old man of nearly 80 years of age. His life had covered four-fifths of the thirteenth century.

Roger's literary output was great, and would have been greater still had he not, for two long periods, been deprived of his liberty. Of his greatest work, which was called the " encyclopaedia of the thirteenth century ", the fourth book is devoted to mathematics and geography. He held the belief, universal during nearly the whole of the middle ages, that the earth was the centre of the solar system, but with that belief his respect for astronomical tradition ended. Not a cartographer himself, he believed that the only method of determining the correct relative position of any point on the surface of the earth was by the use of lines of latitude and longitude. His calculation of the length of a degree of longitude at the equator was within a quarter-of-a-mile of being correct. He believed that every one of the four quarters into which the globe is divided by two great circles, the one at the equator and the other through longitude 0°, was inhabited, and that therefore there was land, hitherto unexplored, far to the west. This belief had no small influence on the decision of Columbus, in his search for Cathay, to sail westwards. Roger Bacon was one of the earliest of English scientific thinkers and one of the most distinguished of a long line of scholars and writers on geography and topography whom this country has produced.

Bacon's great contemporary, Matthew Paris, monk and historiographer, was one of the greatest of all Englishmen. For most of his life he lived in the Benedictine monastery of St. Albans, then at the height of its renown. He is remembered chiefly for his work as a historian. In his work, he included two maps of Great Britain, that is, England and Scotland. These are the earliest of their kind. The shape of England is recognisable, but that of Scotland is more than passing strange to the eye. The two walls, that of Hadrian to the south, and that of Antoninus Pius to the north, reminded those who used the maps of the ancient barriers between the two peoples, barriers which in the time of Matthew Paris shewed no signs of ever being broken down. As a map, however, the Scottish part of it was of little use. In the south, only Edinburgh and Glasgow amongst places of consequence are marked, with the district of Galway, or Galloway. The two firths are joined by a narrow channel, which makes the northern part of the country an island. The drawing of this northern part can have been the result only of a guess on the part of one who had probably never heard of the wild grandeur and majesty of the mountains and the lochs and the islands of Scotland. The whole district is named, tersely, *Scotia ultra marina*. On the extreme north, Sutherland, called southern land, can be identified. Though St. Andrews was then the seat of an ancient bishopric, it is not marked, the ecclesiastically-minded cartographer surprisingly passing it over in favour of its neighbour across the Tay, Dundee. Dumbarton will be recognised under its medieval name, *Dunbrumen*.

England is better and more fully treated, except for the east coast, which is represented as a succession of inlets, whereas there are only three considerable estuaries, those of the Thames, the Humber and the rivers of East Anglia. Names, most of them in their Latin form, which can be recognised include those of Durham, Northallerton, Boroughbridge, York, Lincoln, Norfolk, Suffolk, Wymondham, London, Nottingham, Sussex, Thanet, Dover, Southampton, St. Albans, Evesham, Salisbury, Somerset, Dorset, Cornwall, Devon, Bath, Bristol, Oxford, Gloucester, Worcester, Llandaff, Menevia (St. Davids), Karmerdia (Caermarthen), Snowdon, Bangor and Chester. Round the frame, the existence of the following countries is indicated by the intrusion into the frame of portions of them : Norway, the Orkneys,

Holland, Brabant, Germany, Flanders, Normandy and Ireland. Islands marked include the Orkneys, Coquet, the Scillies, Anglesey and Columbkill (Iona, the island of St. Columbkill or Columba).

Apart from its shape, it is perplexing to find the south-east corner of England occupied by Norfolk and Suffolk; the Medway and the Thames emptying themselves into the sea at the south coast; the county of Kent, with Rochester, Canterbury and Dover, to the south of London; and Thanet marked as an island between the mouths of the Thames and the Medway. Essex lies west of London, not east; and Sussex west of Essex, Chichester being placed in Dorset or Somerset. The chief towns in the south-west of England are, on the whole, correctly marked, but Corfe is on the Bristol Channel. It may be that Matthew the cartographer had in mind not scientific accuracy but the desire to shew how simple and direct was the journey, from almost any part of the country, to London and thence to Dover. From New-castle-on-Tyne, the route to London is almost as straight as an arrow, through Northallerton, Pontefract, Doncaster, Blyth, Newark, Leicester, Northampton, St. Albans, London, Rochester and Canterbury; or from Beaulieu along the coast in virtually a straight line; or from Worcester south-east to Gloucester, Oxford and Northampton.

Some of the legends on the map are worthy of mention. Suffolk is described as the part of England which belonged to the king of the North-folk. The people of South Wales are described as uncultivated and warlike, as are those of Wales in general.

In the well-known Canterbury psalter, one of the treasures of the library of Trinity College, Cambridge, written by Eadwine, a monk of the priory of Christ Church, there is a plan of the priory and its grounds which shews the water-system of the priory. This is one of the earliest plans of its kind. During the fifteenth century, encouragement was given to map-makers by owners of large landed estates, such as noblemen and monastic and other religious foundations, who found maps of their lands useful in more ways than one. These maps demanded for their usefulness and accuracy much skill in surveying. Early in the sixteenth century, with the foundation, by Henry VIII, of the Brethren of Trinity House, maps and charts began to be made to guide mariners through the perils of shoals, tides and currents on their approach to the numerous ports round much of the coast of this country. Thus began the history of this body of men, friends of the sailor, who still continue their beneficent work.

The early part of the reign of Edward III saw the production, by an unknown cartographer, of a portion of a map on which, for the first time, roads were marked, with the distances in miles between one place and the next. Like practically all medieval maps, this one was arranged with the east at the top. From Salisbury to London, the route, about eighty miles in length, lay *via* Winchester, Farnham, Guildford and Kingston. The great road to the west passed through Maidenhead, Reading, Hungerford, Marlborough, Chippenham and Bath, as it still does. The New Forest is marked by a single tree, Oxford by a large Gothic church, and Woodstock not by Blenheim Palace, which was not then built, but by a small aisleless building, probably a little church. London was dignified by a strong castle, probably representing the Tower. Names not very far from London are easily recognised in their medieval forms, such as Croidon, Dorkyng, Colbrok, Wycomb, Walynford, Abyngdon and Alesbury. There are no lines of latitude and longitude. Yet the triangulation, by which alone the exact relative positions of places can be determined, was well done, even though it is extremely unlikely that the cartographer had the use of an astrolabe. Little more than half-a-century after this map was drawn, Chaucer was writing his treatise on the astrolabe to " litell Lowis my sone ".

The appetite for news of far-off peoples and countries was stimulated in the fourteenth century by the incredible adventures of Marco Polo. Accompanied by his two protectors, his brothers, who had done the journey before, the young Marco ultimately travelled not only to Cathay (China), the domain of the Great Khan Kublai, but, at the behest of the Great Khan himself, to the border of Tibet, Karakoram, Cochin China and the south of India. In his book, dictated to Rusticiano of Pisa, Marco tells the story of his adventures, a story which reached this country towards the end of the fourteenth century. Jerusalem was no longer at the very centre of the world.

Though the effects of them were not seen immediately, the adventures of Marco Polo foreshadowed, even if they did not at once provide, more work for the cartographers. The excitements of the fourteenth century were succeeded by even more, if not more romantic, discoveries in the next two centuries. Indeed, these discoveries and the beginnings of settlements of Europeans in the newly-found world—of Spaniards in South America, Mexico and the West Indies, of Dutch in South Africa and the East Indies, and of Anglo-Saxons in North America and, later, in Australasia—form one continuous story.

This is not the place in which to recount the remarkable adventures of the intrepid navigators whose story adds light and colour to the wasteful dynastic and ecclesiastical disputes of the middle ages and the beginning of the modern period. All that can be done here, except for a reference to the discoveries of such picturesque navigators as Prince Henry of Portugal, Bartholomew Diaz, Vasco da Gama, Christopher Columbus and, most daring of them all, our own Francis Drake, is to indicate how the map was added to as the result of their daring. In their minds mainly were certain objects—first, to prove that the world was a sphere by sailing westwards and arriving at places which previously had been reached by sailing eastwards ; second, to discover any, and what kind of, countries and people there might be on the way ; third, to enrich the old world at the expense of the new ; fourth, to gather into the fold of the Church more faithful followers of the one and only true God ; and, fifth, to arrive once again, as Marco Polo had done, at the romantic Cathay, where all was gay and bright, where human beings had no troubles, and where riches poured down on people without their doing anything much except pick them up.

Underlying this romantic strain, however, was a harder strain, the love of adventure into the unknown, and the hope of adding to the store of the world's knowledge of itself.

In turn, it was the Portuguese, then the Spaniards, then the English and, after a long interval, the Dutch, who took the lead in voyages of exploration. Owing first to dynastic quarrels and then to the long, complicated and uncertain chain of events between about 1530 and 1560, the English were late in the field. Indeed, it was not until the issue between England and Spain became clear-cut that Drake's voyage round the world could be undertaken not only as a bid for trade and commerce but also as an act of defiance to the king of Spain.

The Portuguese, the Spaniards and the English were the peoples who were best placed for voyaging abroad, to north, south and west. All three had an Atlantic sea-board, and all three were maritime nations. Up to the beginning of the fifteenth century, the rich commerce of the east had been far more easily accessible, by land, to the Mediterranean peoples than to those whose seaboards were on the Atlantic. Ancient trade-routes across Europe, from north-west to south-east, were connected with ports which themselves were the starting-points of trade-routes by land to thè Persian Gulf. It was on one of those routes that Joseph had been sold to the Midianites. The discovery of the new sea-route to the west and of that round the Cape of Good Hope to the east and the much later cutting of the Suez Canal combined to destroy the use of this ancient land-route between Europe and the east. With the opening of sea-routes across the oceans of the world, new problems arose, the gravity of which we in this century realise as nobody before us could realise.

This is not the place in which to tell the stories of these voyages of exploration. Within little more than two centuries of the exploits of Marco Polo, the world had grown in size, as it were, from a tiny child into a giant. With the world, the map also had grown. The world now—not long after the middle of the fifteenth century— was open to all from the far east to the far west, and from the far north to the far south. Only two of the great land masses, Australia and New Zealand, had not yet been found. The medieval world was dying, and the modern world was just being born.

The exciting discoveries of the navigators did not however produce any effect on the maps that were being made in the monasteries. Columbus, Bartholomew da Diaz and Vasco da Gama had been dead for some years when a *cosmographia* was written by a monk which contained a map of the world. It was of the well-known shape, a **T** within an **O**, the **O** being not a circle but an oval.

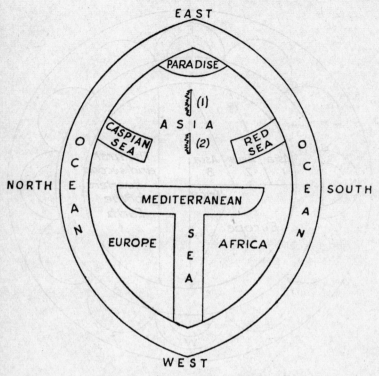

From another cartographer, at the same time, there came a map which represented no advance on those of the thirteenth century. News, however, travelled slowly in those days.

Round the rim of the circle is an inscription to the effect that the names in the semicircular spaces on the outer edge of the inner ring are the names of the twelve winds that blow, whereof four are the cardinal or chief, and the other eight subsidiary.

The first surviving map to be made at the end of the fifteenth century was made on a globe, 20 inches in

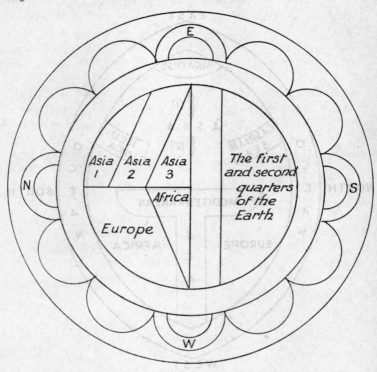

diameter, by Martin Behaim, a Nüremberger, and, it
has been claimed on his behalf, also a navigator. One-
half represents Asia ; the other half, Europe and Africa. In
his representation of the Mediterranean, and in Asia,
Behaim closely followed Ptolemy. Naturally, between
the western coasts of Europe and Africa and the continent
of Asia, there is a broad expanse of sea, the continent of
America not having then been discovered. But the
Pacific Ocean, or rather the western part of the enlarged
Atlantic Ocean, is dotted with islands, Cipangu (Japan)
being the largest. Behaim started his lines of latitude

and longitude where, thirteen centuries earlier, Ptolemy had left off.

When Columbus returned from his earlier voyages, Juan de la Coza, who had accompanied him, designed a chart of the new islands. In quick succession, other charts and maps followed, one map, issued in 1507, marking, for the first time, America and Asia as two separate land-masses.

At about the same time, two globes were made, known as the Lenox globes because they are kept at the Lenox Library, New York, which, though only 4½ inches in diameter, shew the four known continents, the West Indies, the islands of the Pacific, and the middle of Africa marked as desert. But, as in all early maps, inaccuracies appear which are the result of faulty surveying. This surveying can, however, be done only on the spot ; and this was too much to expect from a cartographer who had to rely solely on others for his information.

Mercator's Projection

Though not within the medieval period, this ingenious device ought to be referred to. It will be remembered that Ptolemy was the first to use the idea of a projection from a spherical surface on a flat surface. This idea was extended to the whole globe by Gerhard Krämer or Mercator (1512–1594), born at Louvain. All who read this book will be familiar with maps made in this way. They will realise that the effect of the use of the projection is that, as distances increase from the equator to the poles, the great circles of latitude are more and more proportionately increased in size, each becoming, when projected on a cylinder of paper which touches the globe all round only at the equator, a great circle, whereas, in fact, the only great circle, the one that forms the path of 0° latitude, is the one at the equator. So, on Mercator's projection, the poles become as large as the equator. But there is no other way of representing the surface of the earth on a flat plane than the way of a projection of some kind. Since the time of Mercator, other and similar methods of projection have been devised. When Mercator was only 25 years old, he plotted a map of Palestine, following this attempt with a map of his own country. Other maps appeared in quick succession— Europe (in six sheets, in 1512), the world (in two globes, each barely 5 inches in diameter, less, that is, than one-quarter of the diameter of Behaim's globe), and—his greatest work—an atlas and marine chart of nine maps engraved on copper, issued at Duysburg in 1568 and " copyrighted " in a warning to any who might be tempted to make unjustifiable use of his ideas. On the map of the world, to the north of North America, where there could be no names of places, he engraved three figures, those of Peace, Justice and Piety.

Mercator's map of the world differs much from the one that we know. Drake had not yet made his great voyage round the world, and very few parts of the world had been carefully plotted. But to set his map side by side with the Hereford map or that of Ptolemy is to reveal how much progress had been made, not in some such period as a thousand years but, so far as the west was concerned, in less than two hundred. In that time the medieval man had given place to the person who, comparing himself with his grandfather, would have regarded himself as being a very modern person. And in fact he was not far wrong, for his way of looking on the world had been revolutionised within less than fifty years.

CHAPTER XII

GEOGRAPHY AND MAPS—II

LET us now glance at the construction of a medieval map. Jerusalem was regarded as being in the very centre of the earth. Had not Ezekiel written (v. 5) : " This Jerusalem I have set it in the midst of the nations round about her " ? Both Rabanus Maurus and Isidore had described the city as *umbilicum regionis totius* (the navel of the whole world). When Marco Polo's discovery of the actual existence of Cathay in the very far east shifted the centre of gravity of the map, it was easy to alter the position of Jerusalem a very little and to accommodate China on the very edge of the circle of the land-mass which was the world and to compress something that nobody had ever seen or heard of. And, as the sons of Noah had inherited from their father the whole earth, it was argued that Asia, the portion of Shem as the eldest son, ought to occupy one-half of the map—in accordance with the principle of primogeniture—and Africa and Europe, the portions respectively of Ham and Japheth, the other half.

Between Europe and Africa, which were about equal in size, lay the Mediterranean Sea, then almost literally in the middle of the land-masses which constituted the world. Asia came to an end, on the east, at the mouth of the Ganges, which emptied itself into a vast eastern ocean ; the coasts of Africa and Asia could not stretch far south owing to the supposed existence of the impassable sea and the hot climate ; and the Caspian Sea, regarded as an arm of the impassable ocean to the north, marked the northern limit of the possessions of Japheth.

Yet Roger Bacon knew that the Caspian was an inland
sea. North-westwards, Europe stretched as far as Norway,
Sweden and Denmark, while Iceland and the Faroe
Islands were regarded as *ultima thule*, six days' sail north-
wards from Britain. Here, to the north, the world
ended.

In shape, this odd world varied. As the earth had
" four corners " some cartographers, such as Cosmas,
a monk of Alexandria in the sixth century, made its shape
rectangular, and of course flat ; others, including Ralph
Higden, inclined to the view that the shape must be oval
or ovoid ; while Matthew Paris, following Ptolemy, made
it the shape of an open military or priest's cloak. The
commonest shape, however, was circular, with Jerusalem
in the centre of the circle. And all round it lay a circular
ocean, of limitless breadth, to sail the waters of which
would endanger not only physical life but also spiritual
life in the world to come. Inside this circle and its land-
masses were four inland seas, which we now call the
Mediterranean, Caspian and Red Seas and the Persian
Gulf. The Hereford map shews also the Baltic Sea and
the Bay of Biscay, but as small and subsidiary.

The most curious feature of this map still has to be
pointed out. The east was placed at the " top " of the
map, where modern maps place the north ; and the
other compass points occupied corresponding places.
The reason for this was that the original home of the
human race, the garden of Eden, the " earthly paradise ",
was in the east. In *Polychronicon*, Higden asks, in reference to the garden of Eden, *an sit, ubi sit, qualis sit* (whether
it exists, where it is, what it is like). Out of it flow
(Genesis ii. 10–14) the four great rivers of the world—
Euphrates, Tigris, Nile and Ganges, as they are now
called. In order to provide for the appearance of these
rivers on the earth, they were supposed to flow under the

Ptolemy's Map of England and the neighbouring countries

A Map made in the Thirteenth Century

sea which separated Eden from Earth, and to emerge in
fresh sources, thence to form great rivers. When Columbus arrived at the mouth of the Orinoco, he was sure that
he had discovered " the fount of Paradise ", and he
was afraid to go any farther, seeing that no mortal might
penetrate to the " earthly paradise ".

Such, then, was the arrangement of the medieval
map. Granted the literal truth of the Bible, there was
much to be said for it. But such a map, with no lines
of latitude and longitude, may well have been described
as " a chaos of error and confusion ". This, however,
did not seriously trouble the medieval geographer. His
map was a reflexion not so much of scientific as of scriptural and ecclesiastical truth. The heavens declared the
glory of God ; and the glory of God knew no bounds.
No fable was too incredible to be believed. Nothing on
this earth was too strange for God to have created.
Because the Isle of Thanet was composed of soil that was
fatal to serpents, it was the Isle of Thanatos (Greek for
death) ; and the Canary Isles were the home of a breed
of huge dogs (Latin, *canis*, dog). So examples might be
multiplied. The sources of the information on which
these maps was based were various—biblical, classical and
legendary. The names themselves are largely in their
Latinised forms, for Latin was the ecclesiastical language,
and geography and cartography were religious studies.
Troy, Carthage, Rome, Rhodes (with its Colossus)
and the Pillars of Hercules (guarding the entrance to
the straits of Gibraltar) are marked, with illustrations
to help the imagination of the seeker for knowledge,
though to the modern mind the mistakes in the location
of these and other places are so great as to be ludicrous.
The Nile rose in west Africa, emerged in Egypt and
flowed into the Mediterranean. Men with four eyes
each, and men with only one foot, which they could use

as umbrellas, not only existed but had been seen by travellers with fertile imaginations. The hard crust of credulity had to be broken before it was discovered that the real wonders of the world were so wonderful that truth was stranger than fiction. It was not until towards the end of the middle ages that the first glimmerings of scientific truth once again, after being eclipsed for centuries, began to shine. The light which they shed on the world opened the way to a new period.

The Hereford Map

In many respects this celebrated map is one of the most remarkable of its period. In size, it is the largest except one, in contents the most comprehensive, in orthodoxy unimpeachable, and in fame unsurpassed even if approached. Further, it can be dated almost exactly, and the name of its maker is known, for, considerately for a medieval man, he left it in a six-line verse, which, written in medieval French, can be seen in the lower left-hand spandrel of the sheet on which the map is drawn :

> Tuz ki cest estoire ont
> Ou oyront ou lirront ou veront
> Prient a Jhesu en deyte
> De Richard de Haldingham e de Lafford eyt pitie
> Ki lat fet e compasse
> Ki ioie en cel li seit done

This may be translated :

> May all who this fair history
> Hear or read or see,
> Pray to Jesus in Deity to have
> Mercy on Richard of Haldingham and of Lafford
> Who made and fashioned it ;
> To whom be joy in heaven.

Lafford is Sleaford, Lincolnshire ; and Haldingham is Holdingham, a hamlet in the ancient parish of Sleaford,

a mile or so to the north-west of Sleaford.   It is generally
agreed that Richard was Richard de Bello, canon and
treasurer of Lincoln Cathedral, whose prebend (that is
to say, estate and church from which he derived most of
his income as a canon of the cathedral) was that of
Lafford, which he held for some years before 1283, when
he left Lincoln.   It is a just inference that the map was
finished before his connexion with Lincoln Cathedral
came to an end, that he took it with him to Hereford, and
that when he left Hereford he presented the map to the
cathedral there.   The representation of Lincoln Cathedral on the map as a far bigger church than Hereford
Cathedral has been regarded as additional evidence that
he was at Lincoln when he made the map, though this
does not follow, for Lincoln Cathedral is larger than
Hereford Cathedral.

That Richard was a geographer of some knowledge is
shewn not merely by the existence of the map but also
by his mention, in inscriptions on the map, of no fewer
than five geographers—Pliny the Elder, Orosius, Solinus,
Isidore of Seville, Marcian Capella, and Ethicus (or
Ethnicus).   He relied on Orosius for the outline of the
world, the source of the Nile, and the names of mountain
ranges in Asia and Africa, on Solinus for the description
of the marvels and the fabled animals, on Isidore for the
" earthly paradise " and the divisions of Asia and Africa,
on Capella for the islands of the Mediterranean, and on
Ethicus for the northern parts and for the existence of
a remote island in the southern seas.   Pliny was his
authority for the size of the countries.   But whether he
knew the actual works of these and others of his predecessors or copied from references to them in later works
cannot be regarded as certain.   He must have known
imago mundi and one of the maps (contained in a copy of
a psalter) now in the British Museum ;   and he must

have had access to a copy of the bestiary (a book of fabled animals and birds which was one of the most popular allegorical books of the middle ages) and one of the Herbal (a book of properties of plants, chiefly for medicinal use). There is no reason to doubt that the map has been in Hereford Cathedral since Richard brought it there early in the fourteenth century. It is carefully preserved in a case in which it has the protection not only of plate glass but also of folding doors. The size of the map itself, which is on vellum, is 65 by 53 inches, the vellum being stretched over a framework of oak. Black ink of the finest quality was used for the outlines and most of the inscriptions, vermilion for the capitals and some of the names, gold leaf for some of the larger letters, blue for rivers, and (apparently) green for seas, lakes and fountains, though the green (if that was the colour) has faded to brown. The circle which contains the map is enclosed in a framework in the shape of an isosceles triangle, the border being ornamented with a zigzag design, floral and other decorations, and star-shaped flowers.

Contents

While in itself a modern map is one of the most fascinating of all things to study, and becomes more interesting as it increases in size, it is intended to be used in connection with a separate descriptive work. A medieval map, however, was to some extent both chart and text-book. This will be realised as the description of this amazing map progresses. Believing the universal tradition that Julius Caesar appointed three surveyors to survey the Roman Empire, though it is known to all who are familiar with the New Testament that it was Augustus who ordered that " all the world should be enrolled " (St. Luke ii. 1), Richard had the following inscription placed round the inner edge of the map :

A Julio Cesare orbis terrarum metiri cepit. A Nocodoxo omnis oriens dimensus est. A Teodoto septentrio et occidens dimensus est. A Policlito meridiana pars dimensus est.

(Julius (a mistake for Augustus) Caesar ordered the whole world to be measured. The east was measured by Nicodoxus, the north and the west by Theodotus, and the south by Policlitus.)

The use of the table of winds described in Isidore's *de natura rerum* is an indication of the reading of the compiler of the map. Three winds (*septentrio, circius* and *boreas*), came from the north ; three (*subsolanus, vulturnus* and *eurus*) from the east ; three (*auster, eurusnorhus* and *auster-africanus*) from the south ; and three (*favonius, Africus* and *chorus*) from the west. At the circumference of the earth, the sea surrounds the land. The positions of the various seas, as indeed of everything on the map, appear to us to be fantastic, but some are shewn more or less in the relationship to one another which modern knowledge has not much altered—the Arabian Sea, the Red Sea, the Persian Gulf, the English Channel and the North Sea, the Baltic and the Caspian (this an inland sea, as in Ptolemy), the Mediterranean and the Black Sea.

As might be expected at a time when everybody believed that the rule of God was a stern reality, and that the Last Judgment was the most certain of all future events, the space between the top of the land-mass and the frame is occupied with a representation of the Doom or the Last Judgment, one of the commonest represent-ations in medieval art. At four points in the outer frame, at the places at which the pins would have been placed had the map been pinned to a board, the four letters M O R S (Latin for *death*) are seen. The medieval man was not allowed to forget that he was mortal and that for his deeds in this life he would one day be judged.

Paradise, a circular island fortified with a wall from which issued flames, is easily recognised, with its four rivers. Adam and Eve are eating the fruit of the forbidden tree, and the gates of the garden are ominous reminders that if there was a way in there was also a way out. India can be recognised by its great rivers, Indus, Chenab, Jhelum, and Ganges, its satellite, Ceylon, and the " elephant and castle " ; the tower of Babel *in terra Bablonie* is prominent ; *civitas Ninivei* stands on the Tigris ; the Euphrates and the Tigris, joined into one river, empty themselves into the Persian Gulf ; but Damascus is set on mount Gilead, and the Jordan is given two sources, *fons Jor* and *fons Dan*. It is not surprising to find that much attention is paid to Palestine, and, naturally, to Jerusalem, with its proud position at the centre of the map. The length of the country is given as

a Dan usque Beersabee cxl milia passuum longitudine
(from Dan to Beersheba 140 thousand paces in length),

that is, 140 miles. Many familiar names are seen—those of the twelve tribes, Tyre, Joppa, Lydda, mounts Carmel, Ephraim and Tabor, Nazareth, Bethlehem and Bethel. Jerusalem is surrounded by a wall, outside which is mount Calvary, crowned by a representation of the Crucifixion, and the mount of Olives is prominent. Jericho has the inscription :

usque ad civitatem Jericho ducebat Moyses pupulum Israel
(Moses led the people of Israel as far as to Jericho) ;

not quite true, for he died in sight of the promised land, not in it. On mount Sinai, Moses is seen receiving the two *tabule testamenti* (tables of the covenant) from Jehovah.

The wonders of Egypt deserve some notice. They include (a) a satyr (a horned creature with the head of a bird and the feet of an animal, and holding a club) ; (b) the sphinx (*avis est penna serpens, pede, fronte puelle* with the wings of a bird, the feet of a serpent and the front of a young woman) ; (c) the centaur (*fauni semi-caballi homines* men half-fauns, half-horses) ; (d) a breach in the Red Sea where the Israelites crossed it, the phoenix (*phoenix avis : hec quingentis vivit annis : est autem unica avis in orbe*—the phoenix-bird ; it lives for 500 years, the only one of its kind in the world) ; (e) a crocodile bestridden by a man ; (f) the city of Rameses (*hic congregatus populus Israel in Ramesse ; exiit de Egypto altera die post pascham* here the people of Israel met in Rameses ; they went out of Egypt on the day following the Passover) ; (g) the Pyramids (marked by their old name, *orrea Josephi*, the granaries of Joseph) ; (h) a salamander (which could withstand fire) ; (i) the mandragora (a plant which grew out of a human head and had properties against poison) ; and (j) the delta of the Nile (*in hoc triangulo id est delta inferioris Egipti CCL civitates esse artim Ysidorus attestante*— in this triangle, i.e., the delta of lower Egypt, containing, according to Isidore, 250 cities).

Of the Pyramids, the fabled traveller, Sir John Mandeville, wrote :

> Sum Men seyn that thei ben Sepultures of grete Lordes, but that is not trewe, for alle the comoun rumour and speeche ys of al the peple there, bothe far and neer, that thei ben the garneres of Joseph.

Of the man with one foot, which he could use as an umbrella, Sir John wrote :

> In that contree ben folk that han but oon foot, and thei gon so fast that it is marvaylle and the foot is so large that it schadewethe all the Body aghen the sonne, whanne they wole lye and reste hem.

So must end the description of Asia (Egypt always being regarded as part of Asia). We turn now to Africa, then indeed a " dark " continent, being largely unexplored and therefore largely unknown. Its boundaries made it a very small country compared with Asia, as it consisted of little more than the northern portion which bounded the Mediterranean Sea on the south. The dimensions of the country are described in an inscription which is written near the Nile :

> The length of Africa from the Ethiopian Sea to Alexandria, through Meroe and Syene, is ten times seven times twenty-five military miles, and in breadth three times seven times ninety miles.

The Ethiopian Sea was an imaginary sea to the south of Ethiopia, a country which in its turn lay to the south of Egypt.

Libya had been known to the classical geographers, and Augustine of Hippo had ruled his diocese from Hippo in that country. Tripolitania too was known. Cape Bon, marked here as *Mons Mercurii*, is placed opposite Crete, while Cape Farina is placed at an enormous distance from it—an instance of astounding ignorance on the part of Richard the cartographer, who, however, to do him justice, had probably never been out of England. Carthage (*Cartago Magnä*) is represented by a large building. On the other side of the Mediterranean, Gibraltar is marked as *Mons Calpel*. The more southerly parts of Africa were not ever guessed at until the voyages of the Portuguese navigators during the fifteenth century.

The Nile was believed to have its source near Mount Hesperus, well to the west. It then disappeared, and reappeared as a lake which discharged itself on the borders of Egypt, when again it disappeared underground. Pliny and other ancient geographers believed that its basin was inhabited by monsters as well as by strange human beings, some of whom were not merely deaf but even without ears ; others, like their fellows in Asia, could not open their mouths and so had to be fed through reeds which were forced between their lips and teeth ; others walked on all fours ; others had their mouths and eyes not in their heads but in their chests ; others had four eyes each—though Pliny says that this was merely a way of describing their phenomenal eyesight ; others were troglodytes (cave-dwellers), or serpent-eaters. There were ants which dug for gold-dust with their feet. But one race of Ethiopians was known who had only one eye and ate of the flesh of lions and tigers. With legends such as these, it was not likely that a medieval geographer could remain immune from such credulity as exhibits itself on medieval maps.

Off the coast of Africa were the *fortunate insule : sex sunt* (Fortunate Isles, six in number), amongst which were the Madeiras and the Canaries, commonly regarded as elysium because of their delightful climate. In this group was the island of St. Brandon, of which one ancient writer remarks that it is

the faryest countree eastwarde that ony man myght se and was so clere and bryght that it was an hevenly sight to beholde ; and all the trees were charged with rype fruyte and herbes and full of flowres, in whiche londe they walked xl dayes, but they could se none ende of that londe, and there was always daye and neuer nyghte, and the londe attemperate ne to hotte ne to colde.

Expeditions were made to find this island, but they were unsuccessful because it did not exist. Still further east were the Hesperides (*insule Hesperidum*), probably the Cape Verde Islands. All these islands find a place on the Hereford map.

The Mediterranean Sea

This, the most important of all the seas of the medieval world, deserves some notice here as it was imagined by Richard the cartographer. Being well known to all European map-makers from the earliest times, it was always more or less correctly represented in general shape. The Adriatic, the Aegean and the Black Sea, with the sea of Azov, are almost always marked, even if not correctly or proportionately represented, with the Bosphorus and the Hellespont. The islands in the Mediterranean also were known. Sardinia is described in the Hereford map as " Sardinia, called *Sandialotes* from its likeness, in shape, to a human foot ". Palermo is marked as the capital of Sicily ; Venice is an island ; the Colossus at the entrance to the harbour of Rhodes is seen, even though it had collapsed within little more than half-a-century of its erection in 224 B.C. ; and several of the islands of the coast of Greece find a place.

Europe

The outline of Europe is hardly anywhere to be recognised for the familiar shape which we know it to take. Often, Greece is hardly visible as a peninsula ; Italy has " heel and toe ", but not in the familiar shape ; and Spain is hardly a peninsula. The Bay of Biscay, the English Channel, the North Sea and the Baltic exist, but in shapes very different from their real shapes. The channel between Britain and the mainland of Europe stretches almost from Spain to the coast of France, and is of almost uniform width. The rivers are less open to criticism, but the Tagus does not find a place, and two imaginary rivers, the Coruus and the Arfaxas, are placed between the Dnieper and the Don, with their mouths in the Black Sea. But many European rivers are named—Moselle,

Rhine, Seine, Oise, Loire, Sarthe, Garonne, Gironde, Dordogne, Rhone and Ysere; Gaul is divided into three parts, according to Richard as well as to Julius Caesar— *Gallia Celtica*, *Gallia Belgica* and *Aquitania*; several divisions of southern France and of the Netherlands are recognised; and many French and other towns appear, such as Paris, Rouen, Rheims, Soissons, Laon, Noyon, Cambrai, Boulogne, Liége, Aix-la-Chapelle (Aachen), Metz, Ghent, Cologne, Worms, Mainz, Coblentz, Verdun, Strasburg, Basle, Nüremberg, Chartres, Le Mans, Orleans —historic places which have found their way into history books for centuries.

What is called on the Hereford map *Germania* is the region across the Rhine to the boundary of modern Russia, which is undefined except by a range of mountains on the shore of the Baltic. Most medieval geographers regarded the Vistula as the boundary of Germany towards the east. South to north, the country extended from the Danube to the Baltic. The map distinguishes upper from lower Germany, the former being called " Germany, upper, which is Slavonic ", and the latter, " Germany, lower, which is Saxon ". The chief rivers include the Main, the Ems, the Oder, the Vistula and the Danube. It is the source of the Rhine, however, which is marked, *hic surgit fons Danubie* (here rises the spring-water of the Danube). German towns include Bremen (then the seat of the only archiepiscopate in the country), Hamburg, Magdeburg, Oldenburg, Prague and Ratisbon. The political divisions of the two Germanies, north and south, are marked, those in the south being Saxony, Noricum, and Pannonia, and their chief towns, Augsburg, Ratisbon, Vienna and Pesth.

East of Germany, names become scarce. Hungary is identified by the river Theiss and the Carpathians, the country called *Hungaria* being relegated to a position in the north-east of Russia. The Slavs occupy the country north-east of the Carpathians, while the border of Russia is made to look as forbidding as possible by the sketch of a bear.

Richard's knowledge of the north-west of Europe was scanty. Denmark or Jutland did not exist for him. The boundary of the Danes and the Saxons, as he calls it, is placed to the north-west; Scandinavia is a peninsula, but is very far west of the Baltic Sea, and only Norway amongst the countries is named, as *Noreya*. Beyond the bounds of Norway, to the east, are the words : *in hoc tractu sunt cinophales*, the reference being to a race of dog-headed men. One of the early Christian writers examined the question of the existence of these curious beings, and came to the conclusion that they did not belong to the human race.

But, not far from Scandinavia, the map recognises the existence of thirty-four islands (*Orcades insulae XXXIIII*— thirty-four Orkney Islands), which were known to Orosius, who held that they were inhabited. The correct number of these islands is fifty-six, about one-half being uninhabited. And the Faroes, Iceland and Thule (was the last the Shetlands?) also find a place.

The British Isles

And what had Richard to say about his own home ? The first impression that a medieval map of our own islands conveys is that surveying was in its infancy when the map was made. The Hereford map shews Great Britain as far too large compared with the seas which surround it, and the protrusion of East Anglia is not recognised as existing. Conway and St. David's (called by its ancient Roman name *Menevia*) are so close to each other that Wales is almost non-existent. The description of the shape of Great Britain from the pen of Gerald of

Wales, the medieval historian, runs : " It is oblong, and broader in the middle than at the ends "—a definition of an oblong that would not have satisfied Euclid. There can have been little excuse to place Winchester opposite Nantes, across the sea, or the mouth of the Thames opposite the mouth of the Seine ; or the Lincolnshire coast opposite Cambrai ; or Aberdeen opposite the mouth of the Ems. These, however, are the freaks of the medieval cartographer, who was between the upper and nether millstones of ecclesiastical tradition and poverty of surveying-instruments.

The names of the two large islands which form the British Isles, or rather the main portion of them, are given as *Britannia Insula* and *Hibernia*, the former being divided into *Scotia*, *Wallia* and *Anglia*, the south-west being called *Cornubia*.

Of the hills of England there is no mention, with the solitary exception of Clee Hill, in Shropshire. Of the Welsh mountains, only Snowdon is noticed. Of the group of rivers which form the Humber, only the Derwent and the Don and the Trent are named. The Severn and the Dee are represented as rising in Clee Hill. The Great Ouse is not visible, though the Tamar, the Exe, the Avon, the Medway, the Thames, the Colne, the Nene, the Witham, the Tyne and the Tweed appear, even though one or two of these are smaller than the Great Ouse.

The only divisions of the country that are named are Cornwall, Lincolnshire (*Lindeseya*) and Northumbria (from the Humber to the Tees). Most, though not all, the cities then of cathedral rank are marked, but not Chichester, Norwich and Salisbury. Some of the larger monasteries also are ignored, perhaps because Richard was not a monk, but a secular priest. Yet Kirkham, an Augustinian Abbey on the banks of the Derwent in

Yorkshire, is named. Castellated buildings denote the sites of London, Chester, Nottingham, Newcastle-on-Tyne, Northampton, Shrewsbury and Dover. Glastonbury finds a place in the map probably because of its reputation as the traditional burial-place of King Arthur. Only three Welsh towns can be found—Caernarvon, Conway and St. Davids. The first two of these had played a part in the then recent conquest of Wales by Edward I, an event through which Richard had lived.

Islands off the coast include the Isle of Man, the Farne Islands, and several that cannot now be identified by their names or their positions. Two islands called *Svilla* are marked, one off the south coast of Ireland, which may be intended for the Scilly Isles, and the other off the north coast of Scotland. Two unidentified islands, *insula avium* and *insula arietum*, present difficulties in the way of their identification. The former, the " island of birds ", which contains " a fayre tree, full of bowes, and on every bough sate a fayre birde, and they sate so thycke on the tree that unnethe only lefe of the tree myght be seen," may be connected with the legend about St. Brandan, who was told by the birds that they were fallen angels ; the latter, the " ilonde of shepe, where every shepe was as grete as an ox and there is never colde wether but ever sommer ", is possibly meant for the Fortunate Isles, the abode of the blest, the medieval name for the Madeiras and the Canaries (see p. 181).

Scotland

Edinburgh, St. Andrews (later the seat of an archbishopric), Perth, Aberdeen and Roxburgh are prominent, Perth being marked under its ancient name, " the City of St. John ". The south is called " Lothian ", the present name for the eastern part of the south of

Scotland ; and the Grampians are marked as Muneth (mountains ?).

Ireland

Richard knew of only two rivers in Ireland—the Shannon and the Boyne, the latter being made to run across the whole island, perhaps to mark the boundary between Ulster and the south. Dublin, Bangor (now in ruins), Armagh and Kildare are noticed. It is clear, however, that neither Scotland nor Ireland, both of them foreign countries to Richard and his contemporaries, interested the people of that day.

CHAPTER XIII

HISTORY—I

ABOUT Ranulphus or Ralph Higden, compiler of one of the best-known histories during the middle ages, not much is known. He had a long life of about eighty years, sixty-five of them being spent as a monk of the Benedictine abbey of St. Werburgh at Chester. He died on March 12th, 1364, so that his life occupied most of the reigns of the first three Edwards. For a monk, he travelled far afield, in the three neighbouring counties of Shropshire, Derbyshire and Lancashire. Apart from what can be gleaned about him from his great work on history entitled *Polychronicon*, not his only book but his chief claim to fame, this is all that can be said about his life. But he was one of the great historians of the middle ages. Whether he was the author of the well-known cycle of Chester Plays, by name Don (for *Dom*, the title of every Benedictine monk) Rondle Heggenet, who, it is said, undertook a journey to Rome in the hope of getting the Pope's consent for his plays to be acted in the abbey in the native tongue, will probably never be known. If he did write the plays, his output was indeed great, and would place him amongst the most versatile men of his time. He shewed his ingenuity in the initials of the opening letters of chapters 34 to 42 of his history, which form the word RANULPHUS, his own Christian name.

It was then as easy for a monk to write in Latin as in English, probably more so. Higden's first " edition " he carried to the end of the reign of Edward II, the point at which some of the manuscripts end. Later, he

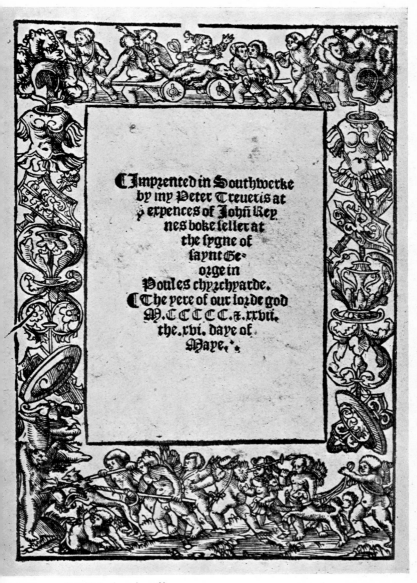

¶ Imprented in Southwerke
by my Peter Treueris at
y̆ expences of Johñ Rey
nes boke seller at
the sygne of
saynt Ge=
orge in
Poules chyrchyarde.
¶ The yere of our lorde god
M.CCCC.i.xxvii.
the.xvi. daye of
Maye.

Colophon of "Polychronicon"

good in the staple. And on that other syde the duke of Somersete beynge in Guysnes gate people to hym whiche came oute and scarmuched with them of Calays / and they of Calays with them / whiche enduryd many dayes. Durynge this day ly scarmuchynge moche people dayly came ouer vnto thyse lordes.

Then on a tyme by ye aduyse of coun sell the lordes at Calays sente ouer mayster Denham with a grete felyshyp to Sandwyche / whiche toke ye towne / and therin the lorde Ryuers and ye lorde Scales his sone / and to ke many shyppes in the hauen / and broughte them all to Calays / of whi che shyppes many maroners of theyr free wyll came to Calays to serue ye erle of warwycke. And after this ye erle of warwycke by ye aduys of the lordes toke all his shyppes and manned them well / and sayled hymselfe in to Irlonde for too speke with the duke of Jorke. And to take his aduyse how they sholde entre in too Englond agayn And whan he hadde be there / and done his erandes / he retorned agayn towarde Calays / and broughte with hym his moder the Countesse of Salysbury. And compynge in the westcountree vpon the see the duke of Excetre Admyrall of Englonde / beynge in the grace of Dyeu accompanyed with many shyppes of warre / mette with the erle of warwycke and his flote / but they fought not. For the substaunce of the people beynge with the duke of Excetre ought better wyll and more fauour to the erle of warwyck than to hym. And so they departe and came to Calays in sauftee. blessyd be god. Then

le lordes had gote these shyppes frõ Sandwyche / & take ye lorde Ryuers And his sone ordeyned a garnyson at Sandwiche to abyde & kepe ye towne. And made one Mountforde cappytayne of the towne. And that no mã ne vytaylle / ne marchaunt that sholde goo in to Flaundres sholde not goo to Calays. Thenne they of Calays seenge this / made out mayster Denham & many other to goo to Sandwiche. And soo they dyde / & assayled the towne by water & by londe & ga te it. And broughte moutforde theyr capptayn ouer see to Rysebank / and there smote of his hede And yet dayly men came ouer to them out of all partyes of Englonde.

Capitulum   xlj

And after this the sayd erles of Marche / of warwyck and of Salysbury came ouer see too Douer is moche people: And there ca me a londe. To whom all the countreye drewe. And came to london at myd. And for to lete the lordes of ye kynges councell knowe the ptcouth And more ouer theyr entente / assem bled them. And told them that they entended none harme vnto the kynges persone. Sauf that they wolde put from hym suche persones as were about hym. And so departed from London with a grete puysaunce to ward Northãpton where the kyng was acompanyed with many lordes

A page of "Polychronicon."   (Printed in 1527.)

added a further portion, to the year 1342. His work became in such great demand that it was translated into English by John Trevisa (1326–1412), a Cornishman and Fellow successively of Exeter College and the Queen's College, Oxford. Trevisa undertook the labour of translation for the benefit of his patron, Lord Berkeley, and finished it on April 16th, 1387, less than twenty-five years after the death of Higden. In addition, he made in the course of the translation useful notes, and continued the chronicle to the year 1380. A second translation into English followed early in the fifteenth century, made by an unknown scholar. Further evidence of the demand for copies is provided by the printing of Trevisa's translation by William Caxton in 1482, by Wynkyn de Worde in 1495, and by Peter Treveris in 1527. Caxton had already printed in the year 1480 a summary compiled by himself. *The Descrypcyon of Englond*, extracted from the chronicle, was printed five times between 1490 and 1528. Higden therefore has claims to have written a " best-seller " the demand for which was for some years continuous. In the most recently-compiled list of medieval books that have been traced to monastic and other medieval libraries, about twenty-five manuscripts are listed as still existing.

The plan of the work is as follows :

(1) a description of the countries of the then-known world—a kind of *mappa mundi* in words, which begins with (a) a prologue in praise of historians, by whose work alone a knowledge of the lives of famous men had been handed down to posterity ; followed by (b) a list of forty historians from whose writings information had been obtained, including Josephus, Livy, Pliny the Elder, Suetonius, Augustine, Orosius, Isidore of Seville, Bede, William of Malmesbury, Henry of Huntingdon, Alfred of Beverley, Giraldus Cambrensis (Gerald of Wales), John of Salisbury and Florence of Worcester ;

(2) a summary of the seven divisions of the work, namely, (a)

from the creation of the world to the destruction of the Temple by Nebuchadnezzar ; thence to (*b*) the captivities of Israel and Judah ; (*c*) the birth of Christ ; (*d*) the English invasions of Britain ; (*e*) the Danish invasions ; (*f*) the Norman Conquest ; and (*g*) the beginning of the reign of Edward III ;

(3) the empires and the religions of the world, and the methods of chronology adopted by the Hebrews, the Greeks, the Romans and the Christians ;

(4) the size of the world ; the three great continents of Europe, Asia and Africa ; the great oceans surrounding the earth ; the three great gulfs (the Mediterranean, Caspian and Red seas) ; and Paradise, aloof and apart from the world in the inaccessible east ;

(5) Asia and its divisions, including, as was the custom in those days, Egypt ;

(6) Africa and its peoples ;

(7) Europe and its countries of Greece, Italy, Germany, France, and Spain ; the islands of the Mediterranean and the Atlantic, including Ireland, Scotland, Wales and England, the description of England being the most detailed of all ; and

(8) history from the creation of the world to the accession of Edward III.

Such is Higden's grand plan. The habit of the author to prefix every statement which he makes, long or short, with the name of the historian from whom he borrowed it, has laid him open to the charge of being little more than a copyist. The reader of the summary given above will be able to draw his or her own conclusions whether in the end the means taken by the author was or was not justified. At any rate, though he did copy, and copy freely, he did not try to hide the fact. His work is the most fully-documented work of its kind in the whole of the middle ages, and he deserves no ordinary commendation for his years of study of the historians whose works were found in the library of his monastic home.

We will now follow the course of Higden's narrative,

some of it in the words of the translation printed by
Peter Treveris in 1527 and published, with the original
version and Caxton's English version, in the Rolls Series
(1876–1886). We make a start with ancient Rome.

Survey of the World

It is not possible to describe even in outline the course
of this comprehensive survey of many countries and many
ages. All that can be done is to indicate, with the help
of extracts from the translation printed by Peter Treveris
in 1527 and published eighty years ago in the Rolls
Series, the general style of the book, with special reference
to our own country, its description and its history. We
make a start with ancient Rome.

> Iulius Cesar, by counsaile of the senatoures and elder men of
> Rome, lokede and serchede stories and bookes of his yeres of
> doynge and dedes and ordeyned wyse men and redy to mete and
> discreue all the worlde aboute. Then from Iulius his tyme to
> Sauturnus tyme, two and thritty yere, messengeres, wise men and
> wel i-taught in the practike of geometrie, konnynge and profit-
> able to mete and to gesse highnesse and lownesse, lengthe and
> brede and depnesse also, were rediliche i-sent into euery londe
> aboute to iuges and to chreuteynes, to lederes of londes, for they
> schulde mete and discreue londe and water, wodes and landes,
> valeies and pleynes, downes and hilles and the see stronde and
> euery place where eny man myght goo other ride other schip
> seilth ; and write and certifie the senatoures where and what
> wondres were i-founde.

This survey, he says, occupied thirty-two years. Being
skilled in geometry, the surveyors were competent to
make measurements of all kinds, and to report about
land, water, woods, valleys, plains, downes and hills
wherever it was possible to travel. In their journeys,
they saw 30 seas, 72 islands, 40 famous mountains,
370 noble cities, 57 great rivers and 125 different nations
of people. From India in the east to the pillars of

Hercules (the straits of Gibraltar) in the west, the earth measured 7,120 miles, and from the Ethiopian sea in the south to the mouth of the Thany in the north, 4,562 miles. The Mediterranean Sea was computed to be 15 furlongs in depth. The circumference of the earth measured 20,240 miles—this on the assumption that :

the proportion of the roundnesse aboute of a cercle is to the breadth as is the proporcioun of two-and-twenty to seuen.

And he concludes :

Then half the thiknesse of the erthe inward and doun right is thre thowsand two hundred and fyue and fourty myle and somwhat ouer as it were half a myle. So if helle is in the myddel of the erthe doun right, me [one] myghte knowe how meny myle it is to helle.

Of the sizes of the land masses, he writes :

Asia is most in quantite, Europa is lesse, and like in noumbre of peple, bot Africa is lest of alle the thre parties bothe in place and in noumbre of peple ; and therfore summe men that knewe men and londes acountede but twei parties of the erthe onliche, Asia and Europa ; and they acountede that Affrica longeth to Europa, for Affrica is narwe in brede ; and yuel doers, corrupte ayre, wylde bestes and venemous woneth [dwelleth] therynne.

Quoting Pliny, he says of Europeans compared with Africans :

Therfore it is that Europa norischeth and bryngeth forth men huger and gretter of body, myghtier of strengthe, taller and bolder of herte, and fairer of schap, than Affrica. For the son bene [beam] alwey abideth vppon the men of Affrica, and draweth out the humours, and maketh hem schort of body, blak of skyn, crisp of heer, and by drawinge oute of spirites maketh hem coward of herte. The contrarie is of northeren men, in the whiche colde with oute stoppeth smale holes and poorus and holdeth the hete with ynne ; and so maketh hem fatter, gretter and whiter and hotter with ynne, and so hardier and boldere of herte.

The ocean, the historian contends, surrounds the earth like a garland.

As for Paradise, three questions are asked : whether it exists, where it is, and what it is like. As evidence that it exists, four rivers flow out of it (see Genesis ii.), and some travellers had actually seen it. He goes on to say that, because at every eclipse of the moon the earth makes " a rounde schilde ", the earth must be round in shape. It will already have been noticed that Higden's ideas of the map of the world were those of his own time.

Paradise

Higden's description of Paradise is of an enchanting place. Its very name, he says, declares its beauty and loveliness, for does it not derive from a word meaning an orchard, and does not the Hebrew name for it, " Eden ", mean " liking " ? Therefore an " orchard of liking " must be a fair place. It contains everything that makes and preserves life. The air is neither too cold nor too hot. Did not Enoch and Elijah go there, and are they not still alive ? There the weather is always fair ; no tree ever sheds its leaves, no flower wilts, and the fruit of every tree is sweet to eat and goodly to look upon. The great Flood did not reach Paradise—so some say,

> by an excusacioun of spekynge that is i-cleped yperbolica, so that thei that so speketh wolde mene that Paradys in heyght passeth all other londes.

The way to Paradise which human beings must tread is, however, barred because of the sin of our forefather, Adam, for Paradise

> is i-closed al aboute with a firen wal, so that the brennynge therof arecheth to heuene, as some men wolde wene. Paradys is i-closed with that wal to holde out mankynde ; aungelles stondeth on that wal to kepe wel Paradys, that none euel goostes mowe come therynne.

It is tempting to dwell on the simplicity and the childlike faith of this monk of Chester. We may be pardoned for smiling to ourselves that such credulity should be found in a great literary figure of the middle ages ; but he was only the child of his time.

Babylon

The description of Babylon, taken from Orosius, is very striking. Called after Babel, the tower, this notorious city, the seat of more than one ancient empire,

> was i-build as a castel, and i-walled with foure walles square al aboute ; euerich wal was fifty cubites in brede, and foure tyme so moche in heithe ; the lengthe of euery wal from oon corner to another was sixtene myle. The walles were all aboute foure hondred and foure score furlong, that is, foure and fourty myle. The walles were i-made of brend [burnt] tile and of glewe in stede of morter, so that nother water nother fire myghte hem to schifte nother to dele. In the citee were an hondred gates and a diche with oute . . . The ryuer Euphrates ran by the myddel of the citee thorwoute. Neuertheles Cyrus, kyng of Persida, tooke the citee afterward and destroyed hit.

Of the Dead Sea, Higden remarks :

> That see bryngeth forth no thing that is quyk and on lyue [alive], so that he songeth nother water foules, nother fisshes ; so that what quik thing that it be that duppeth therynne, anon it lepeth vp agen ; and alle dede thinges swele with so fer forth that a lanterne with lyght fleteth and swymmeth alone. And if the lyght is i-queynt, it duppeth doun and dryncheth. . . . That was assaied and i-knowe in that grete princes tyme Vespasianus bi tweie men that were i-bounde hir hondes by hynde hem and i-cast yn here, but anon they were i-cast vp agayne.

Strange Tales

The legend of the race of Amazons is here told with relish ; namely, that when Alexander the Great asked tribute of his formidable band of women their queen replied :

Of thy wittes we wonder that thou desirest to fyghte with wommen ; for if fortune fauerith vs and thou be ouercome it is grete schame and vilonye whan thou are ouercome of wommen. Also if oure goddis beeth wrooth with vs and thou ouercome vs for to wynn the maystrie [mastery] of wommen thou getest but litel worschippe.

Alexander was so pleased with this witty sally that he granted to these gallant ladies their freedom with the words :

Wommen moste [must] be ouercome with fairenesse and loue, and nought with sternesse and drede.

Strange tales had been brought back from Ethiopia by those who had penetrated so far south of Egypt. Grisly and strangely-shaped men and women were found there, including troglodytes or cave-dwellers, and others who were " swifter than hertes ". Others cursed the sun for its great heat ; others ate serpents and adders, and hunted the lion and the tiger. Those who lived in dens and caves spoke with a noise more like grunting and chattering of teeth than speech. Others were what are now called nudists ; others had no heads or mouths, and had chests of iron. Some of the quadrupeds had no eyes, and dogs were often seen which were kings of human beings. In such a country it was not uncommon to meet with the basilisk, the unicorn, the camel (then no less strange to a European than the fabled beasts) and the dragon, all of which

haueth in here [their] brayn and hedes many precious stones.

The basilisk, the king of serpents, had power to slay beasts and fowls

with smyl and sight.

Europe. Rome

From Asia and Africa, the description turns to Europe, about which far more was known than about the other two land-masses. Rome has a chapter all to itself. After detailing the various legends which surround the foundation of the city, including the story of Romulus and Remus, Higden describes how the city was furnished with walls, towers, gates, temples, palaces, and other wonderful things. The towers on the walls numbered 361, and the walls extended for about 22 miles round the city, the area of which was about 42 square miles. The Tiber flowed through the city. In the Palace of Peace, Romulus built an image of gold to represent himself, of which it was said :

It schal neuere falle or [unless] a mayde bere a child.

And, adds the historian :

That ymage fel when Crist was i-bore.

Descriptions are given of the Pantheon (the site of which was occupied by the church of St. Maria Rotunda), the arch of Augustus Caesar on which his victories and great deeds were recorded, the Capitol, from which consuls and senators ruled the world, the image of Venus and various pillars on which stood statues of famous Romans, including that of Julius Caesar, which stood 250 feet high. Special mention is made of the image of the Colossus, which in length was 126 feet. This image " was somtyme in the ylond of Rhodus, fiftene foot highere than the highest place of Rome ". All Romans worshipped this image until it was destroyed by St. Gregory (pope 590–604). There was also a wonderful brazen image of a woman, which was so large that it was said that it would never be destroyed until a maid should bear a child ; and it fell down when the Maid Mary bore the Child Who was Christ.

So ends the description of Rome.

The account of the Roman institutions begins with a description of a Roman " triumph ", and ends with one of the characters of the Roman emperors. At his arrival in the city a victorious general was received by the whole populace in a triumphal procession in which his prisoners marched through the streets bound, while the victor was drawn to the Capitol in a chair drawn by five white horses.

The description of the other countries of Europe follows—from Greece, Gaul (" plaster of Paris " being mentioned), Spain, and the islands of the Mediterranean and the Atlantic. This brings Higden to his account of Ireland, Scotland, Wales and England.

Ireland

Mingled with much that is not only credible but doubtless true is even more that is tinged with the credulity of the times, which looked for magic everywhere. Ireland is represented as almost inaccessible on account of the rough seas which surround it.

The Irish Sea, says Higden, is

six score myle brood.

The country of Ireland is full of hills and water, and contains much more pasture than arable land. Wild life abounds, and so do honey, milk and wine. Higden denies the statement of Bede that the roebuck was hunted in Ireland, for he says contemptuously :

It is no wonder of Beda, for Beda knew neuere that ilond with his eyes, bot som tale tellere toldde hym suche tales.

Fish abound in the lakes, but St. Patrick had cleansed the country from

> venomous bestes and wormes.

As for the people, they are descended partly from

> Bartholarius with iij childer, of the stocke of Iaphethe son of Noe, in the iij yere after Noes flood.

Other ancestors of the people were the Casera, sons of Noah's daughter, and a family of Scythians. By right, Ireland belonged to Britain, so that when Henry II conquered the country he was merely taking what originally belonged to him. The people were lawless and uncivilised, at least in the view of Higden's authority, Solinus. They were cowards and full of deceit. Their old hags could change themselves into hares, and their conjurors could transform, by craft of " nygramauncie ", dead matter into swine, which, however, return to their original form if they pass by any water.

In spite of all this, however,

> many men telleth that in the north side of Irlond is the ilond of lyf ; in that ilond is no man that may deie ; but whan they beeth i-holde with hard siknesse they beeth i-bore out to the next ilond, and deie there.

In this wonderful country there are places where the dead lie without corruption. At Ossory, in the south, every seven years, at the prayer of a holy abbot a wedded couple were outlawed by being turned into wolves for seven years, at the end of which they returned to their own shape and were succeeded in this terrible imprisonment of transformation by another unfortunate couple.

Finally, there is a sweeping condemnation of the men and the saints of the country. The men are more angry than other men, and the saints more vindictive. It is only fair to Higden to say that many of his uncomplimentary remarks about the ancient inhabitants of Ireland were inspired by the historians on whose works he relied.

The description of Ireland occupies five chapters. Scotland and Wales are given only one each.

Scotland

Scotland has had several names, says Higden—(1) Albania, from Albanactus, an early ruler; (2) Albania, a province of Scythia (from which the modern name is derived); (3) Pictavia, from the Picts; and (4) Hibernia. The Picts were so called because they painted their bodies—*picti* from *i-peynt*, which seems far-fetched. The people are light of heart, strange, and wild, " but by mellynge (mixing) of Englisch men they beeth moche amended ". They eat more flesh, fish, fruit and milk than bread.

The kings of Scotland are never crowned or anointed. The reason why St. Andrew is the patron saint of Scotland is that he had as the portion of land which he had to evangelise " the north contrayes of the worlde ".

Wales

The description of Wales is in verse. The name Cambria is derived from Camber, son of an early ruler, Brutus; the name Wales, from Gwalae, daughter of Ebrancus. Food is plentiful, so much so that Wales is spoken of as the pantry of the earth.

> Than Wallia was to mene
> For Gwalaes the quene,
> Kyng Ebrank his childe
> Was wedded thider mylde.

> And of that lord Gwaloun
> Withdraweth lettres of the goun
> And putte to L, I and A,
> And thow schalt fynde Wallia.

A simple way of explaining a place-name.

Flesh-meat and fish, beasts, tame and wild, the horse, the sheep and the ox—all these abound. The soil is fruitful, and on it grass, corn and herbs grow abundantly. There are woods and meadows, valleys and hills, the hills being rich in metals. The land flows with milk and honey, and mead and ale abound. North Wales and South Wales, however, differ from each other. The Welsh marches had customs that were English. In meat, drink and clothing they followed the English.

> They beeth clothed wonder wel
> In a scherte and in a mantel;
> A crisp breche wel fayn
> Bothe in wynd and in rayn.

Earlier than this, however, they were more hardy and simple in their habits. When they fight, they use bow and arrows, and short spears. They love music, playing skilfully the harp, the tabor, the pipe and the horn.

By degrees, as they mixed with the English, they began to till the land and to live in towns.

A disproportionate amount of the chapter on Wales is given to the story of the marvels which are to be seen there. At Brecknock, curious sounds and forms are to be seen and heard in a deep pool; at Pembroke, demons can cause earthquakes; near Cardiff is an island where unearthly sounds can be heard from a crevice; in Anglesey is a stone which, if any man should move it to any place, returns to its original place immediately. This was proved by the earl of Shrewsbury of the time of Henry I, who not only carried it away but fastened it to another stone with heavy iron chains, but all in vain, for the stone returned to its place.

It was natural that the mightiest mountain in Wales, Snowdon, should command respect and inspire awe. High up on its slopes was a lake, in the middle of which was an island which

> movede to and fro with the wynde, in so moche that drovers of bestes meruaile theyme to be caryede from oon place to an other sodenly.

Another lake contained fish of many kinds which had only one eye each. Lastly, there is a hill at which, no matter how great a sound is made, such as the blowing of a horn, nothing can be heard ; yet the hill is called the rock of hearing.

Trevisa's writing is pleasing throughout, but the descriptions of both Scotland and Wales are disappointing. We now turn to the description of England.

Britain

After the ilondes of occean now Bretayne schal be descreued. By cause of Bretayne alle the trauaile of this storie was bygonne. The firste poynt that me schal telle is of the names of the ilond ; thanne of the stede and place of the lengthe and brede ; the thridde of the worthynesse of the lond ; the ferthe of the mervayles and wondres that beeth there ynne ; the fifte of the chief parties of the lond ; the sixte of ilondes that beeth bisides that lond ; the seuenthe of the kynges of highe weies ; the eighthe of famous ryueres and stremes ; the nynthe of olde citees and townes ; the tenthe of prouinces and schires ; the elleuenthe of lawes and of the names of lawes ; the twelfthe of kyngdoms, of boundes, and of markes by twene kyngdoms ; the thrittenthe of bisshopriches and of bisshoppes sees ; the fourtenthe how many manere of men haueth woned and i-dwelled in that lond ; the fiftenthe of longage, of maneres, and vsage of men of that lond.

With these words, Higden introduces his description of his own country. The earliest name for it, he says, following the tradition of his time, was Albion, chosen because of the

> white rokkes aboute the clyues [cliffs] of the see that were i-seie wide [seen from afar],

a reference to the white cliffs of Dover.   When the fabled king, Brut, whose existence was for centuries believed in, conquered the island, its name, Albion, was changed to Britain.   When the Saxon tribes arrived they called the island " Anglia " or " England ", after the name of another fabled person,

> Angela, a noble dukes doughter of Saxouns.

Higden also mentions the theory that the new name given to the island was due to its being

> as it were an angul, a corner, of the world.

Reference to the Hereford map will shew that for this suggestion there was something to be said, for the island was placed on the edge of the world as then conceived. He also relates the story, told by Bede, of the Anglian children in the slave-market at Rome.   And, because the country was separated from the land-mass which we call Europe,

> the ilond of Bretayne is nigh worthy to haue the name of another world.

The island was

> acounted an holy lond bothe in oure stories and als [else] in stories of grees [Greece],

because it

> lieth vnder the north nolle [head] of the world, hath light and bright nyghtes in the somertyme, so that ofte tyme at mydnyght men haue questiouns and doute where it be euentyde or dawnynge, that is for that tyme of the yere the sonne goth nought fer vnder the erthe by nyght, but passeth by the north side and cometh

sone in to the est aghe [again], and therfore ther beeth in somer
dayes ful longe of xviij houres longe, and the nyghtes of sixe.
And ofte in the wynter beeth longe nyghtes of xviij houres and
schort dayes of vj houres.

When sailors draw near to England they see a city
called Reptacestre. Bede mentions this place. Its
modern name is Richborough, on the coast of Kent,
and there are still Roman remains to be seen there.

The island is 800 miles long from north to south, and
200 miles broad from east to west, that is, from Menevia
(St. Davids) to Great Yarmouth. Bede is quoted as
estimating the coastline to measure

abowte eyghte and fourty sithe seuenty thowsand paas [paces],

a Roman mile consisting of one-thousand paces.
The vegetation, the rivers, the water-supply,

grete plenty of smal fische, of samon and of elys and grete fisches
as hit were of whales kynde and dyuers manere of schel-fische,

the salt-wells, the hot wells, the metals (brass, iron, lead,
tin and silver), the soil (good marl under the turf), the
corn, the sheep (" that bereth good wolle "), the cities,
the towers (" faire and noble and riche "), the great
rivers and streams, the stone-quarries, the clay for
making pottery—all these—are listed with pride. And
Higden, quoting Alfred of Beverley, adds with equal
pride, which we ourselves may share :

Englond is good lond, fruytful of the wolle, but in a corner
of the world ; Englond ful of pley, fremen wel worthy to pleye ;
fre men, fre tonges, hert fre ; fre beeth al theyr thinges ; here
lond is more fre, more better then here [their] tonge. Engelond
hight of lond, floure of londes al aboute ; that londe is ful payde
with fruyte and corn of his own.

> Straunge men that needeth
> That lond wel ofte releueth.
> What hunger greueth,
> That lond alle suche men fedeth.

More wonderful things, however, have to be recorded about this most attractive of countries. There are hot springs presided over by Minerva, in which people can take hot and perhaps medicinal baths. But the four greatest wonders in a wonderful country are listed :

The first is at Pectoun [the Peak ?]. There bloweth so strong a wynde out of chynes of the erthe that it casteth up agen clothes that me casteth yn. The secounde is at Stonhenge by sides Salisbury ; there beeth grete stones and wonder huge, and beeth arered an high as hit were gates ; so that there semeth gates i-sett vppon other gates ; notheles hit is nought clereliche i-knowe nother perceyued how and wherfore they beeth so arered and so wonderliche i-honged. The thridde is at cherdhole. There is grete holownesse vnder erthe ; of meny men haueth i-walked therynne and i-seie ryueres and stremes, but nowher konneth they fynd non ende. The ferthe is that reyn is y-seie raised vppon the hilles and anon i-spronge aboute in the feeldes.

Other wonders are pointed out, such as a den near Winchester out of which a strong wind always blows so that nobody can " endure forto stonde to fore that den ", and the strange behaviour of the river Dee, which flows under the city of Chester, changes its fords every month, and has plenty of salmon though there are none in the lake, called Pymbilmere, from which it flows. In no other country, he continues, are there so many

hool bodyes of men after hir deth in liknesse of euere lastynge lif that schal be after the day of dome, as it wel semeth in these holy seyntes Ethelred, Edmond kyng, Elphege and Cuthbert. I trowe that it is i-doo by special grace of God alle myghti.

The chief divisions of the island are then described as owing their names to the three sons of Brut, namely, Loegria (England), Cambria (Wales) and Albania (Scotland). Some held that in the days of Brut England did not extend beyond the Humber. Offa's dyke is mentioned :

> Also kyng Offa, forto haue a distinccioun for euermore bytweene the kyngdoms of Engelond and of Wales, made a long deche that streecheth forth oute of the south side by Bristowe [Bristol] vnder the hilles of Wales northward and passeth ye reuers of Seuarne and Dee almost at the hedes, and anon to the mouth of the ryuer Dee biyonde Chestre faste by the castle and renneth forth bytwene Colhille and the ministre of Basyngwerc in to the see. This diche is yit in many places i-seyn.

Of more importance are the "royal roads", which, according to the medieval historians, were not of Roman origin but were first cut to enable those who fled for sanctuary to reach their refuge unharmed.

The names of the four were the Fosseway, Watling-street, Ermine-street, and Ikeneild-street. Ancient towns mentioned include London, York, Canterbury, Worcester, Lincoln, Gloucester, Cirencester, Winchester, Cambridge, Oxford, Colchester, Dorchester, Silchester, Chester, Caerleon-on-Usk, Bath and Shaftesbury. The southern counties of Kent, Sussex, Surrey, Hampshire, Berkshire, Wiltshire, Somerset, Dorset and Devon, divided largely by the Thames from the rest of the country,

> were somtyme i-gouerned and i-ruled by that lawe that hatte Westsaxoun lawe.

The counties of Oxford, Warwick, Gloucester, Worcester, Hereford, Salop, Stafford and Chester,

> these eighte myddel and west schires were somtyme i-gouerned and i-ruled by that lawe that hatte Mercia in Latyn, and Mercheyne lawe in Englisshe.

And the remainder of the country was

> sometyme i-gouerned and i-ruled by that lawe that hatte Danelawe.

Ecclesiastical history follows, but to most people will be of less interest than what Higden has to say about the

speech of the people of his day. He laments that there
have been as many varieties of speech as there are nations.
While the Welsh tongue, he says, had remained comparatively pure, the Scottish tongue had been corrupted
by an admixture of the Pictish. English he divides into
northern, southern and midland. But the original
tongue had been corrupted through its contact with
foreign elements introduced by the Danes and the
Normans, some of the people using

> straunge whafferings, chiterynge, harrynge, and garrynge gris-
> bayting. This aparynge of the burthe of ye tunge is bycause of
> tweie thinges : oon is for children in scole agenst the vsage and
> manere of alle othere naciouns beeth compelled forto leue hire
> owne langage and forto construe hir lessouns and here thinges in
> Frensche, and so they haueth seth the Normans come first in to
> Engelond. Also gentil men children beeth i-taught to speke
> Frenshe from the tyme they they beeth i-rokked in here cradel,
> and kunneth speke and playe with a childes broche ; and
> vplondisshe men wil likne hym self to gentil men, and fondeth
> with greet besynesse for to speke Frensche, for to be i-tolde of.

Yet Higden advocates foreign travel. Children who are
being educated at " gramer scole "

> schulle passe the see and trauaille in straunge landes and in many
> other places.

It is a source of satisfaction to him that in his day
English was beginning to be taught in schools to the
exclusion of French.

Midlanders, he says, understand the speech of north-
erners and southerners better than these understand each
other. About the speech of Northumbrians and York-
shiremen he has uncomplimentary things to say :

> Al the longage of the Northumbres and specialliche at York
> is so scharp, slitting and frotynge and vnschape that we sotherne
> men may that longage vnnethe vnderstonde. I trowe that that
> is bycause that they beeth nygh to straunge men and naciouns

that speketh strongliche, and also bycause that the kynges of
Englond woneth [lived] alway fer fro that cuntrey ; for they beeth
more i-torned to the south contray, and gif they gooth to the
north contray they gooth with greet help and strengthe. The
cause why they beeth more in the south contray than in the
north is for hit may be better corne londe, more peple, more
noble cities and more profitable hauenes.

Higden takes the difference between north and south so
seriously that he refers to it again. The men of the
south are

esier and more mylde, and men of the north be more vnstable,
more cruel, and more vnesy ; the myddel men beeth somdele
partyners with bothe ; also they woneth [accustom] hem to
glotenye more than other men and beeth more costleye in mete
and in drynke and in clothynge. Me troweth that they took that
vyce of kyng Hardeknute that was a Dane, for he sette twyes
double messe and also at soper. The men beeth able to al
manere sleithe and witte, but to fore the dede blondrynge and
hasty, and more wys after the dede.

In fact, the vices of Englishmen are attributed to
drunkenness, neglect of God's house, and mixing with
Normans, Danes and Scots.

CHAPTER XIV

HISTORY—II

The History of England

I T is not possible to give more than a summary of this interesting series of chapters devoted by Higden to the history of his own country. As in duty bound, he gives prominence to religious history, but by no means to the exclusion of other kinds of history.

Alfred the Great

Alfred succeeded to " the hole kyngdom of west Saxouns ", which he held " nyne and twenty yere and ruled it nobilliche, but with greet travaille ". He was fair of shape, and more greatly beloved by his parents than were his brothers. He lived at his father's court until he was 12 years of age, but did not learn much up to that time, when he began to learn :

right wel, and helde Saxons poesy in mynde. He passed other men in craft of hontynge, and was a sotel maister of bildynge and of other werkes. He gadrede psalmes and orisouns to gedre in a litel book and cleped that book manual, that is an hond book ; he hadde the book with hym alwey. He kouthe his gramer but sympilliche, for that tyme was nought oon techer of gramer in his kyngdom. Therfore by counsail of Neotus the abbot whom he visited ful ofte he was the furste that ordeynde comyn scole at Oxenforde of dyverse artes and sciens, and procrede fredom and priveleges in many articles to that citee. He suffrede no man to stye up [i.e., take degrees or orders] to what manere dignitee it were of holy chirche but [i.e., unless] he were i-lettred. He tornede the beste lawes into Englisshe tonge. At the laste he auntred [adventured] to torne the psauter in to Englisshe. But he torned unnethe [translated] the firste party to fore his ende day [i.e., his last day].

And, adds the historian, Alfred frequented " full ofte ", when he was tempted to do wrong, temples of holy saints " erliche and late and at cokkes crowynge ".

Anxious to learn, he sent for Grimbald, the monk,

> a connynge man of lettrure and of song and prayed hym for to come to hym out of France into Engelond. Also he sente for Iohn, monk of Seynt Davy his abbey in Menevia [St. David's] for he schulde come to hym out of the unnetmeste ende of Wales to teche hym lettrure and clergie.

He encouraged his nobles to have their children educated, or, if they had no children, to free such of their bondmen as " hadde witte and were able to lerne " and to send them to schools. Over his officers and servants Alfred kept strict watch, and any that were found guilty of misdemeanours were dismissed from the court.

It will be noted that Higden repeats the unfounded assertion, then and for long afterwards accepted without question, that the university of Oxford came into existence in Alfred's time and by his foundation. His selection of facts is, however, on the whole judicious, and nobody will quarrel with his high estimate of one of the greatest Englishmen of all time.

Edgar the Peaceful

The portrait of this king is equally well drawn.

> He was anoynt kyng of the holy bisshops Donston and Oswold . . . he onede [made into one] the kyngdoms that were to deled [divided] and made therof oon kyngdom. He bare doun wickede men and chastede hem that were rebel. He loued wel good men and sobre ; he repayralde and amendede chirches. In meny places he dede awey clerkes that lyuede in outrage and dede there other monkes.

The last sentence refers to the expulsion of " clerks ", that is, secular clergy, and their replacement by monks.

In evidence of Edgar's zeal for monasticism, fostered by
Dunstan, Edgar built, we are told, more than forty
abbeys, the largest amongst them being Glastonbury,
Abingdon, Burgh, Thorney, Ramsey, Wilton and Winchester.   Higden relates that at the New Minster, hard
by the Old Minster at Winchester, the secular clergy
were turned away because of their evil lives, their habit
of squandering the revenues of the church, and their
neglect of their duty ; but, he adds,

> for the moste partie, monkes beeth worste of alle, for they beeth
> to riche, and that maketh hem to take more hede aboute seculer
> besynesse than gostely devocioun ;   therefore [as Jerome hath
> said] holy cherche was encrescede in possessiouns but hath
> decresced in vertues.

Edgar suppressed thieving, and compelled "Lud-
wallus, kyng of Wales ", to pay him a tribute every year
of 300 wolves, so that in four years not a single wolf
was to be found in the country.

Yet, apparently, Edgar was of such small stature that
the king of the Scots

> seide in his game that it semede wonder that so meny provinces
> were suget to so litel a man as Edgar was.   A mynstrel herde that
> worde and tolde the kyng ;   and he tolde nought his men but
> aroos up from the feste where Kynadius [the king of the Scots]
> was and hadde Kynadius to hym as it were for a greet counsaile,
> and ledde hym fer in to a wode and toke hym oon of tweie swerdes
> that he hadde brought with hym and spak to Kynadius and seide,
> Now thou hast leve to kythe thi strengethe and assaye whether
> of us tweyne schal be suget to other, for now we beeth here al
> alone :   hit is a foule thing for a kyng to iangle moche at the feste
> and nought fyghte in batayle.   Kynadius was aschamed and fil
> doun to Edgar his feet and prayed hym forgivnesse of that symple
> word that he had i-seide in his game.

Then follows a description of the navy that Edgar
gathered together.   It was grouped in four fleets, the

westerly to sail north, the northerly to sail east, the easterly to sail south, and the southerly to sail west.

In winter-time, Edgar rode through his kingdom, putting right those things that were wrong, and, finding that the Danes were great drinkers,

> made them stike nayles in the cuppes and marked the cuppes for they schulde drynke by mesure anon to the nayles.

The story is told here that when the king's daughter, Edith, who was a nun of Wilton, near Salisbury, was rebuked by Ethelwold, bishop of Winchester, for wearing

> gayer clothes than her professioun axede,

she replied :

> Goddes dome [judgment] may nought faille ; he is i-plesed onliche with conscience ; therfore I trowe that as clene a soule may be under thes clothes that beeth arrayed with golde as vnder thyn slit furrour skynnes.

The account of Edgar and his times ends with the story of Cnut, who, asserting that no child of Edgar could be as holy as Edith was reputed to have been, consented to the opening of Edith's tomb, and was startled to see her rise and make signs as though she would resist him.

> For that drede the kyng was astonyed, and fil doun to the grounde as thoygh he were i-sowe [in a swoon], and drowght [drew] breath at the laste and was aschamed and glad that he was i-saved and i-kept to do worthy penaunce.

Higden had the gift of being able to choose short and true estimates of his characters from the descriptions of them given by the large number of authorities which he consulted. Lanfranc and Anselm, both former abbots of Bec, in Normandy, where Edward the Confessor spent his early years, Higden describes as follows :

> two lanternes of the world, men of ful passynge letterature, of the whiche that one after the othre was i-made priour in the foreseid place, and afterward archebisshop of Canturbury.

Of another archbishop of Canterbury, Stigand, Higden
writes :

> A man forsothe as almost al other bisshoppes at that tyme in
> Engelond that was unlettred, but ful myghty in money and
> plesynge . . . ; wherfore he deserueth neuere for to gete his pal
> [pallium] to Rome though al that byenge and sellynge wirk
> moche there.

Harold

It will be remembered that, in support of his claim to
the throne of this country, William relied on a promise
which, he said, had been made to him by Harold.   The
story of this promise is related by Higden.   Driven by a
storm to land on the shore of what is now northern France,
Harold was delivered into the hands of William.   " Me
seith " (" they say "), continues Higden, that as the price
of his freedom Harold swore to marry William's daughter
and to hold England for him on the death of Edward
the Confessor.   Harold, however, " that was fuller of
wit ", seized the kingdom for himself, claiming that
Edward had designated him as his successor and pointing
out that, as by then his wife, William's daughter, had
died, he was no longer bound to William by his promise.

Harold began his reign well, for after his coronation
he abolished evil laws, made " good lawes and rightful ",
upheld holy Church, held religious men in reverence,
punished evildoers and defended the law.   His troubles
then began, for Tostig, his brother, sailed from Flanders
with twenty ships, took tribute from the Isle of Wight
and Kent, and burned towns in Lindesey (Lincolnshire).

The story of the campaign that led to the battle of
Stamford Bridge, seven miles east of York, where the
Derwent is still spanned by a bridge, is so well known
that no account of it need be given here.   Higden does
not as a rule spend much space on campaigns ; but in

this case the result of the campaign was decisive for this
country, and in giving details of it he displayed the judgment of a good historian.   Harold then marched south
to meet a new peril from the landing of duke William.
His forces were depleted by his losses at Stamford Bridge.
Meantime, William had landed.

> Thanne duke William com toward Engelond after Michelmasse
> day and londede at Hastynge in a place that hatte Pevenessey.
> In his goynge out of his schip he stode with his oon foot, and
> stiked in the sond and the knyght that was next cried to hym and
> seide : " Now, sire eorle, thu holdest Engelond, thu schalt right
> newliche be kyng."

While the English spent the night before the battle in
carousing, the Normans got themselves shriven, and the
next morning were " i-housled ", that is, received Holy
Communion.   How the battle was began by Talyfer the
Norman, and how Harold was

> i-hit with an arwe and lost his oon eyghe and was i-hurt in the
> brayne and fel downe in that place,

how, after the battle, William sent his body to his mother,
who had it buried in Waltham abbey, which Harold had
founded—all this is faithfully set down.   Higden repeats
the story of Gerald of Wales that

> Harold hadde many woundes and loste his left yghe with a strook
> of an arwe, and was ouercome and scapede to the contry of
> Chestre, and lyuede holily, as me troweth, an ankers lyf in seint
> Iames celle faste by seint Iohn his chirche, and made a gracious
> ende, and that was i-knowe bi his laste confessioun ; and the
> comyn fame accordeth in that sitie to that sawe [tale].

The earls of Northumberland (Edwin) and Mercia
(Morcar) and others went to Winchester and

> gaf hym pleges and swoor hym fewte [fealty] and dede hym
> suerte.

William I

Much information is compiled by Higden about William the Conqueror. He refused to be crowned by Stigand, whom he imprisoned at Winchester. He began his reign by levying on the whole people a tribute

grettere then thei myghte bere,

and by laying siege to and destroying Exeter, which held out against him. He built castles at

Snotingham, that we hatte Notyngham,

Lincoln and York, burnt the city of York,

with the mynstre of seint Petre,

and, when the Danes invaded the north by way of the Humber,

destroyed so that province that for greet honger men ete hors flesshe, houndes flesshe, cattes flesshe and manes flesshe.

Only Beverley, being the land, by tradition, of St. John of Beverley, was spared. The king then seized the treasures of all the religious houses in the north. In 1070 he appointed to the see of York, Thomas, a canon of Bayeux,

a faire man of face and of speche, who maide a faire cherche at York and made the chanouns riche and made songes of holy chirche.

In dealing with those who had taken refuge in the isle of Ely, the king

stopped out the goynge out in the est side and made a brigge of tweie myle in the west side ; than thei were i-closed with ynne and yilde hem to the kyng, and the kyng sente the bisshop to the abbaye of Abyngdoun to be there in warde ; there this bisshop deide for honger, for he wolde not ete for sorwe.

The bishop referred to here was Edwin (or Egelwine), bishop of Durham, an Englishman. To the see of Hereford William appointed Robert of Lotharingia, of whom Higden writes :

> He was connynge of al manere of artes and sciens, specialliche he knowthe skile Inabacus [in the use of the abacus], that is a table to make dyvers figures and schappes. He knewe the hours of the mone and of the other sterres and planetes.

The building of the first cathedral church of Sarum (Old Sarum) is chronicled. Osmund, the new bishop :

> bulde there a newe churche, and brought thider noble clerkes and konnynge of clergie and of songe. So that this bisshop hymself schonede not to write and lumine and bynde bokes. Also he made the ordynal of the service of holy chirche and cleped it the Consuetudinarius. Now wel nyh al Engelond, Wales and Irlond useth that ordynal. Also he endited seint Aldhelm his lif.

This refers to the " use ", or custom of daily worship, of Sarum or Salisbury which, except in the monasteries, was adopted in most parts of England and retained its supremacy over all uses to the Reformation. Monks were settled at Durham, abbeys were built at Shrewsbury and Wenlock, and the monks of Glastonbury had a quarrel with their abbot, who, they alleged, despised Gregory's song (the Gregorian tones introduced into this country by Augustine of Canterbury) and ruled unjustly. So fierce became the quarrel that :

> the abbot with his men of armes fel i-armed on the monkes and slowth tweyne at the hight awter and woundede eighteen and schot arewes to ymages and schrynes of the cherche. The monkes, as they were i-drove to by nede, defended hem self as wel as they myghte yn everiche side with foormes and stooles and candle-stikkes, and woundede some of the knyghtes. This cause was i-mooved tofore the kyng, and the abbot was i-chaunged and i-torned to his owne abbay in Normandie.

The reference to Domesday Book is as follows :

> Kyng William made to descriue al Engelond, for he wolde wite and knowe how muche lond everiche of his barons hadde, how meny knyghtes fees, how meny teme lond, how meny townes and men and how meny beestes. The lond was greved with meny mescheves and happes that fil for that drede ; that descripcioun was i-write al in oon volym and i-doo in the kynges librarie at Wynchestre.

A pestilence and the burning of St. Paul's Cathedral are recorded :

> That yere in Engelond was greet deeth of beestes and distem- perynge of the ayer, by the whiche meny men deide in the feveres and for honger. In the same tyme grisliche furye destroyede the principal citees of Engelond, and Seynt Poul his chirche and a greet deel of London.

Finally, the king is described :

> This William Conquerour was a wise man and a gileful, riche and coveitous, glorious and loved wel greet fame ; faire spekere with Goddes servauntes, and sturne to hem that wolde hem with stonde. In the province of Hamptoun, in the newe forest in space of thritty myle, he threw doun cherches and townes and put there wilde bestes. So that who took there a wilde best schulde lese his oon yghe [eye].
>
> Kyng William was of skilful stature, to greet and fat of body, and sturne of face, bare of forhead, greet of strengthe in brawne and armes, so that unnethe eny men myght bende his bowe ; but he wolde on his hors strecche forth his senewes and bende hit esiliche ynow uppon his owne foot. He had skilful strengthe and gaf hym self to moche to hontynge, so that he threwe doun cherches and townes to make wodes. He made grete festes and revells in the highe feestes of the yere. He hilde his mydwynter tide at Glowcestre, his Esterne at Wynchestre, Witsonday at Westmynstre, whan he was in Engelond. But he passede and over dede in gadringe of money of the people, other to with stonde his enemyes, other to make hym a great name, other to cese his covetise.

And, recording that during his reign Englishmen were

> i-made bonde, so that it was a schame and despite to be i-cleped
> an Englischeman,

the historian adds, with relish :

> To bere doun and destroye Englisshe men God had i-ordeyned a
> cruel man and sturne, that beeth of suche kynde that whanne
> thei haueth i-bore doun here [their] enemyes than they bereth
> doun hem self [themselves].

Comparatively few have heard the name of Stephen
Harding, one of the most saintly of Englishmen, the
founder of the Cistercian order. As was natural in a
monk, Higden gives much space to ecclesiastical affairs,
but in the case of Stephen Harding he is abundantly
justified. To Wulstan, a great bishop of Worcester, he
devotes about twice as much space as he does to Stephen
Harding, but as a Benedictine he would not be disposed
to pay overmuch attention to the founder of a rival
order. Harding was a monk of Sherborne who travelled
in Scotland and France, where he learned " liberal
sciens " and, out of his love of God, went to Rome. On
the journey, nothing kept him and his companion, who,
like himself, was a student in search of divine knowledge,
from saying the whole of the psalms, in Latin, every day.
Higden gives currency to the statement that Harding
had never heard of the Rule of St. Benedict, but it is
hard to believe this. At the abbey of Molesme in
Burgundy, of which he became abbot, Harding decided
to embark on a new venture, and with eighteen companions journeyed to Citeaux to found the Cistercian
order. In 1130, Walter L'Espec brought the new order
into England in the foundation of Rievaulx. Of the
dress of the Cistercians, Higden writes :

> These ben observaunces that semeth hard in that ordour :
> thei schal were no manere furres, ne lynnen cloth, ne wollen that

is smal and softe as stamyn, neither breches, but in the wey; oon of hen schal have on hym two curtell [kirtles] and a covel [cowl], and no more though it be wynter, but if thei wil thei mowe haue lesse in the somer tyme. They slepeth i-clothed and i-gerd, and aftyr matyns they goo neuere to bedde agen.

Some of the services are mentioned; and then, we are told,

After that they gooth to the hondwerk that they doon by day and maketh an ende therof withoute candel light; noon of hem schal be from hourse ["hour" offices, at certain hours of the day and night] nother from complyn but if he be sike. . . . The abbot is overal present with his flok, but onliche at mete, and that by cause of gestes, and than he is served but onliche with two messe. Noon of hem eteth blood, nother flesche, but yf he be sike. From the thrittenthe day of Decembre to the Estertide they eten but ones in the day; outake the Sonday they goon neuere out of cloystre but by cause of handwork. They speken in no place but to the priour other to the abbot. . . . After this Hardynge Stevene was abbot here [at Molesmes] and builde there sixe abbayes and bygan the seuenthe. That ordre encrescede so that tyme that the monkes of Cisterciens were spied of all monkes the myrour of hem that were goodliche best, and reproof and chastysynge of slewthe.

William II

Higden now takes his readers to England once again, and to the reign of William Rufus. He tells a story of the way in which, on the death of William of St. Carileph, bishop of Durham, who planned and saw much of the present majestic church built, Walcher secured the see by means of a gift of £1,000 in the currency of those days. He relates that sanctuary in the church was forbidden to fugitives, that the bishop, who in virtue of his office was also abbot, served meat at the monastic table that was forbidden by rule, and that he

ordeyned wommen to serven hem with heer i-sprad behynde, that semede wowynge gigelottes in clothing, face, and semblant . . .

Yf a monke torned away his face he was i-cleped an ipocrite, and yf he were assentynge and accordynge with the marthe, then he was i-cleped a nyce man and a fool. But this is worthy to be greetliche i-preysed, for by his procurynge seint Cuthbert his body was doo oute of the grave and i-clothed in newe clothes, and kyng Oswald his heed was i-founde by twene his armes. . . .

Also this yere the see flood sprang up by Tempse [Thames] and drenshede meny townes ; the devel was seyn and spak with many men of the kynges malys and of his hasty deeth.

And the king died,

i-schote of oon Walter Tirel that was his owne meynel, that wolde schote to an hert ; and so the kyng deide, and fewe men wepte for sorwe. And so the kyng was i-leide on an horsbere and i-led to Wynchestre, and his blood dropped doun in the way as he was i-ledde. ; and he was i-buried with ynne the tour of the bisshopriche. That tour fal doun with ynne a yere after.

It is tempting to tell, in the quaint English of the translation of Trevisa, many stories of the past which our present history-books cannot include. That of the White Ship is especially worth recounting.

The sixte day tofore Decembre at Barefleet in Normandie up gooth the ankres and the kyng [Henry I] saillede graciously into Engelond. His sone William wolde seil after hym, and was i-drenched, and meny noble men nought fer from the londe. The kynges sone Richard, eorle of Chestre, bastard, was among hem, and Notha the contesse of Percy, and Richard, eorle of Chestre and his wyf, that was the kynges neese, and the arch-decon of Hereford, and othere in the nombre of an hondred and fifty : of hem alle escapede noe but oon cherle, a bocher, that swam al nyght uppon a broken mast, and come to the cleve in the morntide and tolde alle the geest how it was byfalle. Alle these wente be nyghte into a newe schip with dronken schipmen ; they fil anon uppon a rokke fer from the londe, and the schippe to cleef, and William the kynges sone was i-doo in a boot, in the whiche he myghte have be i-saved wel inow ; but whan he come to the cleef and herde his sister wepe and crye than he torned agen and took here into his boot ; thanne other men sterte into that boot and overladde it, and drenchede the boot and al that was therynne outake the forsaide cherle. But it was wonder that

grete tresour was i-founde fast by the cleves in the morowe, and
none of the dede bodyes were founde, but they were al eten of
the fisches of the see.

One historian then remarks that William had said
that if ever he became king he would make them " drawe
as oxen at the plowgh ", and that the earl of Chester
had threatened to destroy the monks of Chester, whose
house had been founded by his father.

Henry II and Becket

On the twelfth day before October, 1173, at about the
time of prime (one of the early " hour " offices), three
circles were seen in the sky, a sign of the strife between
the king and Becket.   In connexion with the martyrdom
of Becket, Higden quotes three sayings :

The yere of oure Lord enleven hondred and seventy Thomas
deide by a sword primat of Englische men.
Who deieth ? A bisshop. Why ? For the folk. How ?
With a swerd. Whane ? At mydwynter. At what place ? At
Goddis aughter [altar].
For Cristes spouse, in Cristes tyme, in Cristes temple, Cristes
trewe lyver deide.

These sayings reflect the popular horror at the murder
of Becket.   And the historians attributed the troubles
of the king which followed the murder and clouded the
last years of his reign to the judgment of God on him
for his evil acts.   On the first Sunday after Easter, in
the year following Becket's murder, after the king had
heard Mass he saw, standing by his horse,

a pale man with rounde tonsure, lene and long, barefoot, i-clothed
in a white kirtel,

who, addressing him in Dutch as " good olde kyng ",
told him that Christ, St. John the Baptist and St. Peter
had bidden him check the secular actions of his people
on Sundays and amend his own way of life, on pain of

dire penalties. As he took no heed, within a year three of his sons, assisted by the kings of France and Scotland and the earls of Chester and Lincoln, rose against him. Yet another ghostly visitant appeared to him in one of the knights of Lyndesey, who demanded of him seven reforms—to maintain the Church, to draw up righteous laws, to compensate those whom he had injured, to restore property that he had appropriated unjustly, to do right without reward, to pay the wages of his servants and to expel the Jews from his kingdom. The penalty for disobedience would be that he would die within four years.

It was in Henry II's reign that what was believed to be the body of king Arthur was found at Glastonbury,

> i-buried and i-naked in an holough stoone deep in the erthe, and so he was i-take up and translated worschipfulliche into the cherche and i-leyd honestliche in a tombe of marbil stoon.

Richard I

For the coronation of Richard I, many Jews came to London. The king gave orders that during the royal banquet in the palace of Westminster no Jew was to be admitted. Some Jews, having managed to get into the courtyard, made their way into the palace, and in a scuffle one of them was injured by an official. This was the sign for an attack on the Jews by the populace, who were under the impression that the attack had been ordered by the king. So, in the commentary, the king's reign

> was blenshed moche at its opening.

To raise money for the crusade on which Richard was bent,

> he resignede the castelles of Berwik and Rokesburgh to the kyng of Scotlond for ten thowsand pound. Also he begiled the olde

man the riche bisshop of Durham, and made hym begge his owne province for a greet somme of money. Therefore the kyng seide ofte in his game, I am a wonder crafty man, for I haue i-made a newe eorle of an olde bisshop . . . I wolde selle Londoun and I myghte fynde a chapman that myghte wel paye.

John

Early in the reign of John, a great thunderstorm took place in which the rain was so heavy and the hailstones so large—as large as eggs—that trees, vines and corn were destroyed, people were killed and houses were set on fire. To superstitious people, this was a judgment on the king for his evil ways. In the same year, Hugh of Avalon, the saintly and afterwards canonised bishop of Lincoln, died and was buried in his own cathedral. Also in the same year there were seen in the sky five moons, one each in the north, the south, the east and the west, and one " in the myddel of the heuenes ", the last compassing the other four six times in one hour, when the spectacle faded away.

The arrival in this country of the order of Dominican Friars, and a " scharp winter and a grisliche ", which " durede from yeres day to the Annunciation ", are chronicled, but not the signing of Magna Carta.

During this reign, the body of Becket was translated from its resting-place on the spot where the archbishop had been murdered to the space at the east end of Canterbury cathedral still known as " Becket's Crown ". The solemnity over, the archbishop, Stephen Langton, distributed hay and provender :

to alle men that wolde axe it, in the wey bitwene Londoun and Caunturbury. Also in the day of the translacioun he made wyne to renne in pipes continualliche in divers places of the citee. . . . On seynt Luc the Evaungelyst his day com a wynd out of the northside that brak doun hous, orchardes, and woodes, belhous and belfrayes. Also fury dragouns and evel spirites were y-seie fle aboute in the whirle wynd. At Oxenforde, in the counsail of bisshops, was oon y-take that hadde in his body woundes as oure Lord Christ hadde y-nayled to the cros. He seide that he was Iesus, bote by doom of holy cherche he was y-take to be y-punisched, and at Abberbury he was y-nayled to the cros.

Higden also records the translation of the bones of Edward the Confessor to the place where the shrine now is in the new abbey-church of Westminster built by Henry III.

Edward I

Shortly after the birth of the King's eldest son, the first Prince of Wales, at Carnarvon Castle, the heat of summer was so great on the borders of Wales that people died. At St. Botolph's, merchandise was burnt by " the develes children ", who set fire to it in many districts of the town (of Chester?). And attacks were made in verse on Llewellyn, the former ruler of Wales, who had been condemned at Shrewsbury to be drawn at the heels of horses and then hanged by the throat. One of the Latin verses, when translated by Higden, runs as follows :

> Here lithe the prince of erroures, theef and robber of men, traytour of Englische men ; a dymme brond and secte of evel dedes and doers ; god of Welsche men, a cruel duke, sleere of good men ; draftes of Trojanes, a false roote, cause of evel dedes.

A little later, there was " grete plenty of rayne in somer and in harvest ", the price of corn rose to 4s. a quarter, and, at the same time,

> this yere was grete deeth of men and beestes and greet fallynge of reyne in somer and hervest ; therof come grete derthe of corne, so that a quarter of whete was solde for xl s. A wryter that highte Iohn hadde a katte that was homeliche with hym. Aboute Pentecoste, at Oxenforde, this Iohn saide openliche that he was heire of Engelond. Therfore at Northamptoun tofore the kyng and lordes he was proved fals, and an-honged and to-drawe.

On the assumption that Higden continued his chronicle
beyond the year 1327, we should expect to find much of
interest in his last chapter, which covers the years from
1327 to 1348, the year when there began the most deadly
scourge that England ever had, the Black Death. One
who writes contemporary history is not able to judge
what events future historians will think it worth their
while to record, for it is only after the lapse of many
years that the comparative importance of past events can
be discerned. Let us see what Higden records. The
events are the king's coronation ; the removal of
Edward II to Berkeley Castle and his murder there ; the
birth of the Black Prince ; trouble with Scotland and the
surrender of Berwick-on-Tweed ; the homage of Edward
Balliol at Newcastle-on-Tyne ; the invasion of France,
the battles of Sluys and Crécy, the capture of Calais, and
the beginning of the Hundred Years War ; the doings
of Parliament ; and the beginning of the Black Death.
The compiler notices the death of two popes and the
accession of two others. Apart from the king's miraculous
deliverance from a storm at sea by the intervention of the
Virgin, there is nothing in this chapter which the most
convinced sceptic would object to. This last chapter of
Higden's own compilation without the use of any
authorities is one of the best in his book because it is one
of the most direct and straightforward. It will be convenient to group the quotations under headings.

Edward III

1. The Beginning of the Reign

Edward, his sone, the thridde Edward after the conquest, a
yong child aboute a fiftene yere olde, under warde yet levynge
his fadir, was i-crowned kyng at Westmynstre in a Candelmasse
day. In his begynnynge come forth gracious happes and fortune,
tho the erthe gave forth plenty, the eyer [air] temperure [tem-
perate], the see quyet and pees, and holy chirche fredom. The

thridde day of Averell [April] the olde kyng was i-brought out
of Kelyngworthe to the castel of Berkeley. There many men
conspired forto helpe at his delyuerance, but he dyde aboute the
feste of seynt Matheu the euangeliste ; of his levynge and of his
dedes is yit among the peple stryf, as was sometyme of Thomas of
Lancastre, whether he schulde be accounted among seyntes other
no. For nother prisonement ne persecutioun and greves proueth
a man a seynt, for evel doers suffren suche peynes ; neyther
offrynges ne likness of myracles proveth a man a seynt, but the
holynes of the lif rather accorde therto, for suche beeth indifferent
to gode and to yvel.

This refers to the attempt which was made to canonise
Edward II, whose death caused a profound shock. A
similar attempt a few years earlier to canonise Thomas,
earl of Lancaster, who was killed at Boroughbridge in
1322, ended in failure. It is interesting to have in this
paragraph the views of a medieval monk on the quali-
fications for canonisation. One indispensable qualifica-
tion was that the holiness of the candidate in this life
should have been so pronounced that miracles were
worked at his tomb after his death. The birth of the
Black Prince, even though he proved to be one of the
most romantic figures in the middle ages, is left without
comment.

2. Scotland

The invasion of Scotland by Edward Balliol threw the
king of Scotland into the arms of the king of England,
who came to his help and besieged Berwick-on-Tweed.

In the mene tyme the Scottes brent in Northumberland as
traytoures schulde, and seged the castle of Bamborough, therynne
lay the quene of Engelond, if they myghte in that wise breke the
sege of Berwyk. Thanne at the day that was i-sette the thrittenthe
day of Lammasse, anon at the fulle see the Scottes come aghenst
Englisshe men in thre batayles, alle on fote and ungert, in a place
faste beside Berwyk, that hatte Boothulle, besides Halyngdoun.
Englisshe men archers beet doun the Scottes, and horsmen

pursued hem and chased hem forto it was nyght ; so that there were dede of Scottes eyghte erles, a thowsand and three hondred horsmen, and of other men fyve and thritty thowsand. Whan this was i-seie Berwyk was i-yolde [yielded] up to the kyng of Engelond. And wonder it is to telle there were none dede on the Englische men side but a knyght and a squyer and twelve foot men. In the feste of Gervasius . . . , Edward Balliol, verray kyng of Scotland, dede homage for the reme of Scotland at the newe castel up Tyne, in presence of thre bisshops, of erles, of barons and of grete multitude of peeple, and sone therafter the Scottes weren rebel. Therefore in a cold wynter the kyng of Engelond went into Galeway and destroyde the contrey anon to the Scottische see, and reparailled the castle of Rokesburgh, and here he socoured hym and his men alle the wynter.

3. *The Black Prince*

Aboute seynt Gregories day in Lente kyng Edward in ful parlemente at Londoun made a ducherie of the erldom of Corne-wayle, and the erldom of Chestre also therto. Also he ordeyned fyve erles, oon to Derby, another to Northamptoun, the thridde to Huntingdoun, the fourthe to Salisbury and the fifte to Glowcestre.

4. *The Hundred Years War*

It must be remembered that for nearly three centuries, ever since duke William had seized the crown of England, English kings had been accustomed to regard themselves as rightful rulers of part of France. The reign of Henry II saw the English possessions in France at their highest point. The ostensible cause of the Hundred Years War, according to Higden, who relates it in good faith, was that

the kyng of Fraunce hadde wrongfulliche i-take in Gascoyne many londes and townes ; therfore the kyng of Engelond profred the kyng of Fraunce many faire profres and meke, for he wolde have his londes aghen, but al for nought ; than the kyng gadrede money in eche side and arrayed hym to passe the see, and aboute seynte Margarete hir day kyng Edward passed into Flaundres. . . .

Returning to England after he had decided to

medle the arms of France among his owne arms,

that is, to quarter the fleur-de-lys with the leopards of England, the king

made a parlement at Londoun and ordeyned for the nedes and charged Englische men with tribute of fifte deel of her hoodes and catel, and al men wole ; and the nynthe scheef everich glebe of Engelond he ordeyned for his owne iourneys, and made lordes of the next townes aboute answere hym of the profite that come therof. Also this yere was so grete skarste of money and plente of other thinges that men solde a quarter of whete at London for two schillynges, and a fat ox for an half mark.

The king sailed to Flanders with 200 ships, and near the coast he met the French navy off Sluys :

There was a strong bataile in the see ; suche a batayle was nevere i-seyn in the costes of Engelond ; there by Goddis help and favour Frenshe men and Normans were scharpliche i-schote, some i-slewe with strookes, some adraynt [drowned] by her owne good wille, and some i-take, and her schippes were i-take also, out-take fewe that flygh away as faste at they myghte.

By the influence of the pope a truce was agreed to by both sides, but before long Edward invaded France again and met the French army at " Cressy in Pycardie ", where

Kyng Edward gloriousliche overcome the kyng of Fraunce and slowth tweye kynges of Beem and of Majorik, the duke of Lothorynge, tweie bisshops, eighte erles, many noble lordes, two thowsand knyghtes and other men with oute nombre, and chased the peple that fligh awey on lyve.

Thereupon the king besieged Calais,

for Caleys was somtyme grete enemy to Englische men . . . Aboute seynt Bartholomeus feste Phelip kyng of Fraunce . . . flygh away pviviliche in the dawenynge, and left there his tentes and a greet deel of vitayles therynne. The men of Caleys seygh that, and yelded up that citee to kyng Edward.

On the way back to England, the king's ships ran into a great storm, so that he

made a wonderful compleynt, and seide, " My good lady seynt Marye, what is it, and what bodeth it, that in my wendynge in to Fraunse I wynde have and weder and al thing at my wille, and in my comynge aghen toward Engelond I have tempest and many hard happes."

And Higden adds :

This yere fil grete reyne from the feste of the Natyvyte of seynt Iohn, and dured forto mydwynter next theraſter, so that unnethe passid eny day but it reyned by day or by nyght.   That tyme fel grete deeth of men in all the world wyde, and began in londes out of the south est sides ; so that unnethe lefte half the peple onlyve, and in som hous of religioun of twenty laste but tweyne.

The battle of Halidon Hill, at which Queen Philippa defeated the Scots, who had invaded England while Edward was in France, is passed over without any mention of the name of the queen :

Englische men, and specialliche of diocese of York, seculers and reguouns [regulars or monks], beet doun the Scottes that were i-come by enticing of the kyng of Fraunce anon to Durham. There David le Bruce, kyng of Scotland, William Douglas and othere greet lordes were i-take, and the othere were dede and i-chasede.

5. *Parliament*

Higden makes two references to Parliament, the one at which the king made provision for the war in taxation, and the other in protest against the appointment of Italians to benefices in the Church of England.   Such frankness in a monk, who could have been silent about it, is refreshing :

Pope Benet [Benedict XII] deyde, and the archebisshop of Rothomage [Rouen] was pope after hym and was i-cleped the sixte Clement ; a man of grete clergie, but a grete wastour and, a spendour ; so that he gaf his cardinals dignytees of holy chirche that voydede [were vacant] in Engelond, and fondede to putte therfore othere titles in Engelond. Therefore the kyng of Engelond was wrooth, and the yere of oure Lord a thowsand thre hondred and foure and fourty the kyng fordyde provisiouns that no man after that tyme brynge suche provisouns uppon peyne of prisonement and lesynge of his heed.

This refers to the statute of Provisors.

At the end of his continuation of the chronicle, Trevisa printed the following note :

God be thonked of al his dedes. This translacioun is i-ended in a Thorsday, the eyghtenthe day of Averyl, the yere of oure Lord a thowsand thre hondred foure score and sevene, the tenthe yere of kyng Richard the secounde after the conquest of Engelond, the yere of my lordes age, sire Thomas, lord of Berkley, that made me make this translacioun, five and thrytty. DEO GRACIAS.

Caxton added this note to his printing of the work :

Therfore I, William Caxton, a symple persone, have endevoyred me to wryte fyrst over all the sayd book of Proloconycon and somewhat have chaunged the rude and old Englyssh, that is to wete, certayn wordes which in these dayes be neither voyd ne vnderstanden.

He says that he had been advised to issue Higden's work, but to print it apart from

his chapytres and his table . . . For I dar not presume to sette my booke ne ioyne hit to his for dyverse causes ; one is for as moche as I have not ne can get no bokes of auctoryte tretynge of suche cronykles except a lytel booke named Fasciculus Temporum, and another callyd Aureus de Universo, in which bookes I fynde ryght lytel mater syth the sayde tyme. And another cause is for as moche as my rude symplenesse and ignorant makyng ought not to be compared, set, ne ioyned to his boke. Thenne I schal by the grace of God set my werke after aparte, for to accomplysshe the yeres syth that he fynysshed his book vnto the yere of our Lord MCCCLX, and the fyrst yere of the regne of kyng Edward the fourthe which amounte to an honderd and thre yere.

Thus ends the history book compiled by Ranulph or Ralph Higden. How shall we assess it?

We cannot compare it with the work even of a historian of the sixteenth century, still less that of a more recent writer of history. Compared with these, a medieval historian laboured under many disadvantages. He had to work alone or almost alone, without the opportunity of discussing his study and his work with others. He was often a monk, and so had seldom travelled far beyond his chosen home. He was writing for a specialised set of readers, mainly men of his own kind. He lived in a sheltered and credulous world. There were no canons of historical criticism, and there was no specialisation, for history had not been divided into compartments such as political, social, economic, constitutional and military. Everything that seemed worth mentioning was put down; and the reader must admit that this freedom from restraint tended to result in a document which is almost childlike in simplicity and attractiveness. It is necessary to read only a few actual extracts, written as they are in the language of the time, which was suited to the expression of the ideas of the time, to be introduced into another world, the world of the medieval man with his credulity, his prejudice, his simplicity and his artlessness. The historian believed what he had read, and why should not his own readers be equally trusting? In a word, he was the product of his age. He was ourselves as we should have been had we tried to be historians in such a world. But it was a happier world than ours, and we cannot be transported into it without at any rate a desire to know more about it.

EPILOGUE

THUS ends this survey of some aspects of the life of the medieval man. We have seen the young at school—the boys learning Latin grammar in their copies of Donatus, so that they might be able to sing in cathedral choirs, some of them posing as bishops for a brief period during which they surely cannot have taken themselves in their new and short-lived dignity very seriously ; and other boys at Colet's school of St. Paul's receiving a groundwork of Latin which was classical in style even if ecclesiastical in content. Some of these boys proceeded to one or other of the ancient universities, there to mount, through the four floors of the tower of knowledge, right to the summit, where they might dwell with the Queen of all knowledge, Theology and the understanding of God. Some boys who were not able to go to school might make their preparation for life in the house of a nobleman, in which they might rise to one of the higher posts in the household. But, apart from the more or less formal preparation for after-life which was the lot of comparatively few boys, many fathers and mothers whose responsibility for their children did not lie lightly on their shoulders gave the best advice they could, which might contain much worldly wisdom, and, underlying it, a solid foundation of not only faith in God but also consideration for and courtesy towards others.

We have seen the medieval man growing up. He is now an adult, a man of his world. He finds himself in a world which he only partially understands. He has to earn his living by being a monk, a secular priest, or a member of one of the trade gilds which supplied the daily wants of the medieval man and his family ; and in his spare time he might be a member of the town or the city corporation, even a mayor or a sheriff or a bailiff, and also a player in one of the Corpus Christi plays. If he happened to be born " with a silver spoon in his mouth ", he would be a great lord, with a small army of servants whose duties have been described in this book. At the other end of the social scale stood the boy who, with no education as the term is usually understood, had no future but that of a menial in the house of the nobleman or the bishop. We know what his life would be like ; but, even though he got little except the crumbs which fell from the rich man's table, he saw and took part in many interesting things.

Other kinds of people have been introduced to the reader—the monk editing his description of the countries of the world and his history of his own country ; the cartographer, a secular canon, making his map for Hereford Cathedral ; the active little alchemist performing his experiments and claiming to have made an earth-shaking discovery, nothing less than the way to become possessed of perpetual youth ; the monastic physician, attending to royalty, the nobility, his own brethren, or the poor at his gate ; William of Killingholme, leech, visiting his lowlier patients ; the unknown leech who drew the rough sketch of the human body in the York medical book ; the palmist who sketched the human hand and the legends on it in the same book ; the scribes who copied the scores of remedies in the remainder of the book ; and, last but not least, because perhaps the most interesting of them all, Andrew Borde, ex-Carthusian monk, traveller, observer of men and things (and of human beards), and skilled physician—and in later life a little careless of his reputation.

All these people, of various kinds, have passed before us in rapid review. Every one of them was master of

his own circumstances—apparently at any rate. The
monks had given themselves to a life in which they had
found peace and security ; the cartographer, a secular
priest, was equally satisfied with life ; the alchemist and
the palmist were sure that they had discovered hidden
secrets of great moment to the human race. But all
these men, each of them one of a type, were face to
face with things mightier than they could cope with.
The psalmist was indeed right when he wrote that the
heavens declare the glory of God, but the sun, the moon
and the stars were full of mystery and had an unexplained
and unmeasured effect on human life. Dreams, too,
were things of strange origin and portent, and must be
as prophetic as they had been found by the two Josephs,
the son of Jacob and the spouse of the Virgin Mary.
There was no lack of men in any century from the
eighth to the fifteenth to interpret them ; and fearful at
times their interpretations might be. Luck seemed to
play a great part in human events. As far as possible,
ill-luck must be avoided by observing rules almost as
complicated as the injunctions of the Levitical law. But
nobody had power to avoid the birth of children on
certain days which were regarded as unfortunate and
unlucky for the children who might be born. So, over
and beyond what all these men regarded as certain and
sure, and part of God's will and plan for the human race,
was a realm beyond the reach of the human mind or
even of divine control. There evil reigned, and even
the devil himself. The medieval man was indeed near
to both heaven and hell. How could he escape the latter
and attain the former ? He could not dismiss them
from his mind, for he believed firmly in both. He lived
in the age of faith. In the city of York alone, which,
within the medieval walls, had a population of not more
than 15,000, there existed (1) a great cathedral church

with a staff of not fewer than 80 clergy, a number to
which 13 may be added for the clergy attached to an
adjoining chapel ; (2) the great Benedictine abbey of
St. Mary, presided over by a mitred abbot, and containing at the most about 60 monks ; (3) another large
Benedictine priory, the staff of which cannot have been
fewer than 30 ; (4) a Dominican friary with nearly 20
friars which, incidentally, had a library of more than
600 volumes ; (5) several smaller religious establishments
for women as well as men ; (6) a large hospital for the
sick ; and (7) quite 50 parish churches, an average of
one church for 240 to 300 people. As all these religious
foundations were, without difficulty, staffed, endowed
and maintained, and the clergy and others attached to
them, not fewer than 350 in number, supported and
maintained, it will be realised that in York more was
spent on the maintenance of the Christian faith than on
anything else, perhaps not excepting even " bread and
butter " and dwelling-houses. The Church, or rather
the separate religious foundations, was easily the largest
landlord in the city, and probably in the whole country.
Though many medieval churches in our historic cities
and a much larger proportion of the contemporary buildings of other kinds have disappeared, many churches
still survive because they were found useful in spite of
the change of ecclesiastical loyalty at the Reformation.
Even had whole medieval cities and towns survived
intact, the predominance of ecclesiastical buildings would
have excited as much comment as it does now.

In the extracts from the original books that are here
printed, the reader will have noticed frequent references
to religion. History, geography, maps, plays, scientific
works, medicine-books—all these and others—proceeded
from minds saturated with the Christian faith as the
medieval Church taught it. It is not easy for the man

of the twentieth century to find his way into the heart
of his medieval predecessor ; yet without an attempt to
do this he cannot hope to understand him. Owing to
the loss of quite as many medieval records as have
survived, it is not easy to arrive at exact figures except
for the period of the Reformation, when there was,
everywhere, a great " stocktaking ". There were at least
twenty-seven altars in York Minister that, for centuries
in most cases, had been set apart for holy things, each
having its chaplain, some having two chaplains, whose
chief work was to intercede for the souls of the departed
every day. In each parish church there was at least one
such chaplain, apart from the incumbent of the church.
The total number of these *capellani* (chaplains) or
personae (persons or parsons) was, for the whole city, 150.
The property set aside for their maintenance and the
maintenance of the chapels and the altars brought in an
annual income of more than £810. In the whole of the
county of York, the annual income from this source was
nearly £6,250. To arrive at the value of this income
in terms of modern currency, it is necessary to multiply
these sums by at least thirty—in the opinion of one
distinguished scholar, thirty-five to forty.

To arrive at the comparative value of these figures,
they must be placed not against the astronomical figures
of the cost of the war of 1939 to 1945, but against the
wages earned and the amounts paid in rents of houses.
A skilled craftsman would earn at this time no more than
5*s.* to 6*s.* a week ; and a reasonable house could be rented
for the same amount for half-a-year. It must be remembered also that the total population of this country of
England was probably not more than 1½ millions of
people.

No suggestion of compulsion or even of undue influence
is made to explain the prevalence of simple faith. It is

enough to give the figures alone. They reveal the pre-occupation of the medieval man with the problems of death and the hereafter, and such concern was not confined to one class. The king and the nobleman were as much concerned about their ultimate fate as the artisan and the peasant. To omit any reference to this in this book would have been, at the least, unfair and, at the most, inaccurate and prejudiced. So it was that Ralph Higden could not write history without implying, almost on every page, that he was a devout son of the Church ; that no medieval cartographer could draw a map without placing Jerusalem at the very centre of it and making the map circular ; that the leech was nearly always also a cleric, and was armed with his religious formulas to reinforce his physical remedies ; that the universe, while mysterious and vast, was at any rate finite, and that God ruled over it ; that the aim of all learning was a knowledge of God ; and that the alchemist guarded his secret because it had come to him from God. All this may seem to many to have been accompanied by ordinances as complicated as such ordinances alone could be. But at heart the medieval man believed that he possessed the pearl of great price. The modern man may in large part disagree with him ; but he cannot understand him unless he realises his religious faith. And he is compelled to admit that his distant relative was, in addition, an interesting, amusing and stimulating fellow.

INDEX